Ajeet Cour, a profound and powerful voice in Punjabi literature, is the author of twenty-two books including the novellas *Dhup Wala Shehar* and *Post Mortem*. Her novel, *Gauri*, has been made into a film while her story *Na Maaro* has been serialized for television. Her works have been translated into English, Hindi and several other languages.

In 1986, Ajeet Cour was awarded the Sahitya Akademi Award for her autobiography. In 2006, she was awarded the Padma Shri for her writing and her contributions in the field of social upliftment. She is the Founder President of the Indian Council for Poverty Alleviation, and has been President, Foundation of SAARC Writers and Literature.

In 1977, Ajeet Cour founded the Academy of Fine Arts and Literature, a non-commercial institution in New Delhi for the promotion of the arts, literature, theatre, music and dance.

Weaving Water

An Autobiography

AJEET COUR

Translated from the Punjabi by
MASOOMA ALI and MEENU MINOCHA

SPEAKING TIGER PUBLISHING PVT. LTD
4381/4, Ansari Road, Daryaganj
New Delhi 110002

Published in India by Speaking Tiger in paperback 2018

Copyright © Ajeet Cour 2018
Translation copyright © Ajeet Cour 2018

ISBN: 978-93-86702-51-7
eISBN: 978-93-86702-49-4

10 9 8 7 6 5 4 3 2 1

Part One of this edition was first published in Punjabi in 1997 as *Koora Kabara* and translated into English by Meenu Minocha; a version of Part Two was first published in Punjabi in 1983 as *Khanabadosh*, and translated into English by Masooma Ali. It was published as *Pebbles in Tin Drum* in 1998.

Cover painting and illustrations: Courtesy Arpana Caur

Typeset in Sabon Roman by SÜRYA, New Delhi
Printed at Thomson Press India Ltd.

All rights reserved.
No part of this publication may be reproduced,
transmitted, or stored in a retrieval system,
in any form or by any means, electronic,
mechanical, photocopying, recording
or otherwise, without the prior
permission of the publisher.

This book is sold subject to the condition that it shall not,
by way of trade or otherwise, be lent, resold,
hired out, or otherwise circulated, without the
publisher's prior consent, in any form of
binding or cover other than that in
which it is published.

Contents

Introduction	vii
Part One: Walking on the Razor's Edge	1
Part Two: The Ocean and the Seashell	239
Epilogue	358

Introduction

From the wreckage of agonizing devastation and turmoil, chasing the shadows of morbid, dark, bloodied memories, emerged standing and unbroken this fearless, intrepid woman with the courage and daring to carve out and define her destiny, as also to bequeath to her daughter, Arpana, the qualities that make her the remarkable, resilient, inspired person that she is.

Rummaging through the rubble, the debris of all that transpired, this narrative attempts to delineate the history and geography of this metamorphis; a history that besides being transcribed on paper, is deeply engraved on the body, the core of the heart, mind, emotions and senses; a geography that goes far beyond the physical boundaries of the play of a life in time and space, to exploring its interaction and limits in relation to death.

Pain and loneliness hold in them the ultimate truth of what life is. Regrettably, the essence of either of the two is not easily amenable to being shared with others. Every individual has to endure his or her own pain, and loneliness, in a way pertinent to him or her alone.

The only difference lies in how each one of us carried our cross while maneuvering the pathways of our mortal existence. Did we carry it in tears or with a smile, as it weighed heavy on sore shoulders proclaiming the inevitability of the end. Were we fervently eliciting the sympathy and pity of the throngs of spectators lining the route, or with the largesse and demeanor of royalty, handing out with abandon gifts of generosity and magnanimity.

But, having vehemently opined that pain and loneliness

are sentiments intensely personal, why then do I endeavour to chronicle and express the experience of them in my life?

In actuality I was perched like a mutilated falcon on the highest, leafless branch of an old, denuded tree humiliated, intensely ashamed by the wounds I bore, trying desperately to keep them under cover, traumatized by the terrifying quiet, the overwhelming emptiness, the muted solitude, when unbeknownst to me, my story found voice, my thoughts urged articulation.

Friends, I am not like Jesus the Messiah, who, even on the last leg of his journey, with one glance could alleviate suffering and bring about healing. I can neither bestow mercy nor proffer charity. Yet, I reckon a recounting of my life's happenings, such as I have done, may possibly be in some small way a redemptive miracle, a divine grace of creativity. Is it?

Now when I read what I have written it seems that with an unrelenting effort I have forcibly planted words, words that are like thorny cacti sown in a barren, endless desert; each plant holding ground surrounded by a plethora of blistering, scorching, dry sand, with no recourse to speech, in absolute silence.

Ajeet Cour
New Delhi, February 2018

PART ONE

Walking on the Razor's Edge

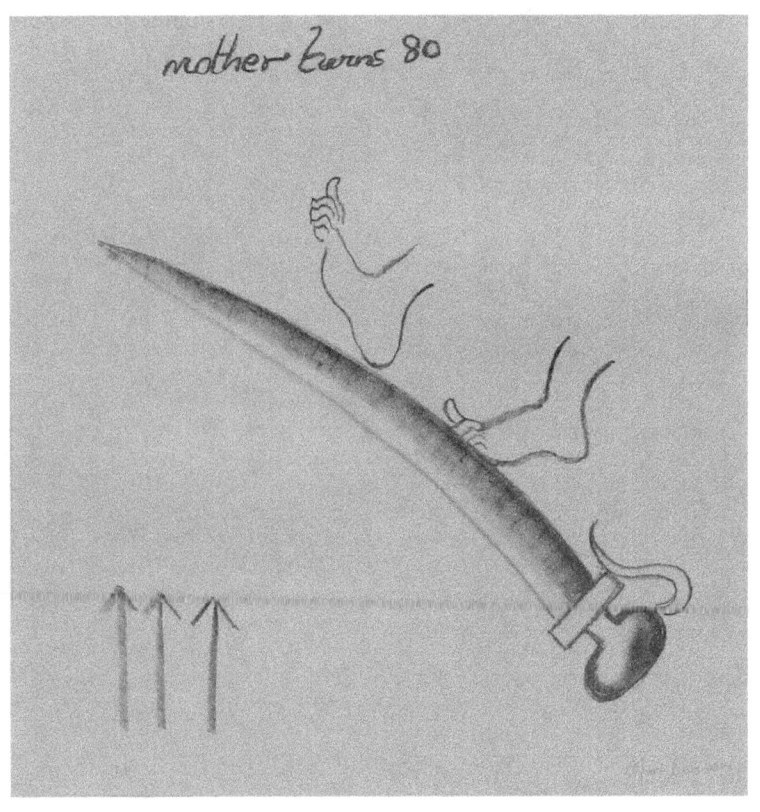

1

Fair-complexioned, full-figured, the midwife Sheela Dai was draped in a white saree. She was running agitatedly to and fro from my mother's room, carrying cauldrons of hot water into that room, then coming out hastily again.

In the midst of all this, she took time out to reassure me and carried me to the room in the corner of the courtyard. Making me sit there, she said soothingly, 'Sit here quietly. In a while I will come and show you something very special, and will tell you a story as well.'

It felt as if I had been sitting in that room for ages.

I was crying.

Crying and thinking that Sheela Dai must surely have forgotten that she had put me in this room.

Beeji, my mother, is not well. Her door has been locked from inside for the past two days. When the doctor comes, the door is opened for a few minutes, then is shut again. Sheela Dai remains confined in that room day and night, with my Beeji. I don't know what is happening in that room, what all these people are doing with Beeji in there.

A deep silence pervades the whole house, and a shivering dread.

༄

And Daarji, my father? How would he even think about me? Because he was the one taking the doctors back and forth. He would go into Beeji's room and come out looking worried. Deep in thought, he would go down to check his own patients, and within a short time come running back up again.

Baiji, that is, my grandmother, had been sitting in the kitchen ever since. After all, the people who were coming and going had to be served with buttermilk, lemon drinks, meals, and then there were those cauldrons of hot water...

Bhaiyaji, my paternal grandfather, as always, was sitting upstairs in the terrace room. In Babaji's room. Must be reading the scriptures. That was the only activity in which he found solace.

The servants were all talking in whispers. No loud voice had been heard for the past two days, and neither had anyone pounded clothes at the courtyard pump.

Everyone was busy, or sitting in corners in an intimidated manner. No one was going to recall that Sheela Dai had left me there, alone in that corner room.

Incidentally, the door to that room was not locked from outside. But the presence of an unnamed fear outside the door, paralysed the courage which I needed to open that door.

Time seemed to have come to a complete standstill!

Suddenly the door opened and a laughing Sheela Dai made her entrance. She picked me up in her arms, kissed my forehead, and said, 'Oh my, what a good child! Still sitting quietly. You are very fortunate, my child. You've been blessed with a baby brother.'

Then she carried me out of the room. Crossing the courtyard, she went towards Beeji's room. A smell of medicines, milk, cream and flowers, emanated from her. I held her tightly around her neck. All my fears and anxieties had disappeared.

There was a very faint light in Beeji's room. She was reclining tranquilly on the huge bed. Next to the bed there was a crib with a tiny pink baby wrapped in a white sheet, lying there like a pile of butter, shaking a pink fist in the air.

Sheela Dai put me down me near the crib and picking up the pink and white bundle, brought it near me. 'How lucky are you! Look, here's a brother for you. Especially come so that you can love him a lot and play with him. And of course, fasten a rakhi on his wrist. When he grows up, he'll take very good care of you, and send you to your husband's house.' So saying, she kissed the baby's face and swinging him in her arms affectionately, said, 'He is my Ghuggi.'

She looked towards my mother. Beeji was watching us with a gentle smile. Not us, her gaze seemed to be fixed on that pink bundle. I had never before seen the loveliness, the happiness, the contentment that was evident in her face at that moment.

A beaming Sheela Dai asked my mother, 'Yes, Memsahib, shall I name him Ghuggi? It's a good name, isn't it?'

Beeji just smiled but didn't say anything.

Sheela Dai took it as agreement and said enthusiastically, 'That's fine then, Memsahib, let's call him Ghuggi till the time a name is taken out for him from the scriptures. I'm naming him so lovingly, you must give some credit to my effort and call him so at least for a few days.'

Then bringing the bundle near my face she asked me, 'Like to kiss your brother?'

Timidly, I touched those pink cheeks with a finger, and immediately pulled my hand back.

She then very gently placed the pink bundle next to Beeji. 'This daughter of yours is very lucky, Memsahib. Very fortunate! It's her luck that has brought this boy into your household. Such a beautiful baby! Ghuggi...my Ghuggi!' She kept touching the baby's cheeks with her fingers and placing them laughingly on her lips.

Just then Daarji came into the room and she turned around to face him, 'I've given a name to your son—Ghuggi.'

Daarji started laughing. He looked at his wife with great affection. Then he took out a handful of notes from his pocket and pushed them into Sheela Dai's hands, 'Here, take these, our felicitations for you!'

Sheela Dai waved the notes over Ghuggi's head and kissing them, tied them in one corner of her saree.

Daarji said, 'Now don't disappear anywhere. Your Memsahib needs you for the next few days. You've to take very good care of her till she has her ritual bath after forty days.'

'I'm ready to serve her all my life, Doctor Sahib. You just have to order me to do so.'

And so my brother was born, in the year 1937, in our home in Lahore. I was three years old at the time.

A lot of activity seemed to be going on in the house. The mood was one of celebration.

My maternal grandmother, my Nani, also bestowed a lot of money on Sheela Dai. Bhaiyaji, too, waved a number of notes over Ghuggi's head and presented them not only to Sheela Dai, but also to Majha, the cleaning woman, to all the servants who worked in our house. Nani also donated the clothes Beeji had been wearing to Majha.

For many days all our relatives kept coming and going—my uncle, my mother's brother, my aunt, his wife, their children, my other aunts, my mother's sisters, and their children. Daarji's innumerable far and near relatives, among them his older and younger brothers, and his sisters. Daarji did not have any real brother or sister; only cousins, but he regarded them as his brothers and sisters. All came with congratulatory offerings, in the form of money, clothes and gifts for Beeji, and, waving money over Ghuggi's head, distributed it among the servants.

The neighbours also came to congratulate us. Not only our neighbours, but also my grandmother's Peer Makki area neighbours, my uncle's Kila Gujjar Singh area neighbours, Daarji's friends and patients…all came.

I didn't know many of the people who came to the house. It was only later that I got to know who they were.

In the kitchen, a sweet dish of milk and rice, full of dried fruit, almonds, pistachios and raisins, and sweet pancakes were being made. A sherbet of crushed and ground almonds was also prepared. Cakes, pastries and other sweetmeats were ordered from the market. This went on throughout the day.

From among all the hazy memories of childhood, one face shines out clearly even today, like the shimmer of bright sunlight on dazzling white snow, that of Bapuji, my Nanaji, my maternal grandfather. I still clearly recall the many boxes of sweetmeats and baskets of different types of fruits, especially maltas or sweet oranges, that he used to bring from Gujranwala, whenever he came to Lahore.

Towards the end of September, soon after Ghuggi's birth, he visited us again.

He brought bales of pure silk cloth with him. Miniature silken bedsheets, soft, springy, diminutive quilts and mattresses and light pillows. It is said that heavy, thick pillows make a baby's neck soft and delicate. The softer and thinner the pillow, the stronger is the baby's neck. He waved some guineas, with the impression of the Queen of England's head on them, over Ghuggi's head. He gave a fistful of them to Beeji, five to Sheela Dai, one to each of the servants and to Majha as well. He placed a fistful of them in my piggybank and said to me fondly, 'Go and keep this piggybank safely near your mother.'

That afternoon when Beeji showed the golden guineas under her pillow to Daarji, her face was glowing at her father's large-heartedness. Daarji was silent for a moment, and then said, 'He has given them to you, you take care of them. What is it to me?'

Beeji's radiant face turned ashen.

Bapuji was actually Beeji's maternal uncle. He had adopted her when she was barely forty days old. My grandmother had gone to her brother's house in Gujranwala for her delivery. Bapuji was a very powerful landowner—the owner of the nearby village of Ladhawala. Unfortunately, he had no child of his own. He had, however, never considered taking a second wife, as he was a godfearing, devout man.

When his sister, my grandmother, went to his house for her delivery, he said to her, 'Look sister, by the grace of God you have been blessed for the third time with a child. May both your sons have long lives! If this time also you have a son, you're welcome to take him back, but if you have a daughter, I beseech you to please give her to me.'

A daughter was born. And that daughter, that is my mother, was adopted by him after thousands of felicitations and a prayer ceremony at the local gurdwara.

I always believed him to be my real grandfather.

Bapuji never stayed at our place. He used to say, 'Even water shouldn't be drunk from a daughter's house.' But on this visit, he handed a wad of notes to Beeji and said, 'This time I'm going to stay for a few days with my grandchild. And as long as I am here, all the household expenses are to be from my account.'

His voice was a delightful mixture of softness and strength. It was like the sound of a gentle waterfall on one side, and tall, rugged mountains on the other—as if both were sitting together and hugging each other. In fact, the mountain seemed to be allowing the water to play in its lap, smiling benevolently.

He had a magnetic personality.

From among all the guests, he was the only one who actually paid attention to me after his initial tenderness for Ghuggi. He read the sadness hidden in my eyes and quickly picking me up, carried me out of the room. Then he sat and talked with me for a long time, reassuring me that I was still loved.

It was much later that I came to know that he could read the melancholy hidden in people's faces in the blink of an eye. No one needed to tell him what was bothering them. He had the capability of looking into the very soul of others and knew how to gently soothe away all their concerns.

A long time later—maybe when I was around seven years old—my Dadaji, that is, Bhaiyaji, taught me how to read the scriptures of the Guru Granth Sahib.

Bapuji, too, contributed to my formative years and taught me how to live life according to what was called 'the Sikhi way'. He used to say, 'The Sikhi way promotes a tradition of service and surrender. The path of self-sacrifice. If, with your sacrifice, someone's problem gets resolved or he finds happiness, then you should not hesitate. On this path, there is no need to make the body go through difficult meditative routines. This way is very simple and straightforward. It just needs us to love the Divine who has created us. We should regard Him as both our Mother and our Father. We can attain Him by walking on a path of love. We don't even need to reach the point of attainment, just walking a few steps along that path, brings Him running to meet us. We think only man is hungry for love. But actually He is also hungry for our love. God is alone—all alone.' Then he would gaze into the distance.

I used to feel, on the pretext of talking about God, he was actually talking about himself. He was also very alone. His wife, that is, Beeji's Mami, had passed away soon after Beeji's wedding, as if she had just been waiting to complete that task. Now Bapuji was completely alone.

Whenever he came to our house, he wouldn't stay. He

didn't like staying in anyone else's house either. Yet, whenever he came to Lahore, he did so with lots of presents and baskets of maltas. He would come in the morning and go back to Gujranwala by the evening—it was a two-hour journey by train from Lahore. By the time the baskets of fruit got finished, he would visit with more baskets.

He was the Santa Claus of my childhood. At that time I had no idea who Santa Claus was, but when today I look back and see the full white beard, pink face, pocketsful of gifts...some in his hands...and bigger gifts carried by his personal secretary and servants—my Bapuji was my very own Santa Claus!

His face would always be glowing with some inner light.

When he came at the time of Ghuggi's birth, his presence could be felt over the whole house. After the initial salutations and appreciation of the tiny new guest, he turned his attention towards me. Catching hold of my hand, he escorted me from Beeji's room to the round room, which was our living room. Sitting on the sofa there, he hugged me closely and started talking about, oh so many things.

Everyone called that room, the round room. I don't know why. It wasn't at all round! In today's parlance, however, I suppose it would be called the drawing room.

While talking, he caressed my head, stroking my tangled hair. Then my hair used to be very long and thick. As everyone in the house had been so preoccupied with Beeji, my hair hadn't been combed for many days, it was all entangled and wild. Bapuji quickly went and fetched Sheela Dai from Beeji's room. In a soft but authoritative voice he said to her, 'Please comb her hair. Just look at the poor thing, what a mess her hair is in!'

Sheela Dai looked at me and laughed. Then, taking a comb and some oil, she sat down and started oiling and combing my hair and at the same time kept up a lively chatter, aimed in the general direction of Bapuji, 'She's like the Goddess Lakshmi. Very fortunate. She's a lucky child, Bapuji. She has brought a brother in her wake. He is going to be the life and soul of this household. What can be said about daughters! They grace their father's house for a few days. A daughter is like a treasure entrusted to her parents for a loving upbringing, till the time she is handed over to complete strangers. Daughters are reared with love but one day go to set up someone else's home. They fly away like birds from their father's nest.'

Bapuji listened quietly to her. I have a dim memory of that occasion. A dark cloud seemed to settle on his face. Maybe the thought of his daughter—my mother—had come to his mind. At one time she had been the life and soul of his house. Now that courtyard was totally forlorn. It was not a tradition in our families to stay in the daughter's house and neither could she stay at her parents' home for long.

After Beeji's wedding, it was as if Bapuji's house had become home to a desert-like loneliness.

Once my hair had been combed, he led me by my finger and we went down the stairs. Daarji's clinic was on the ground floor, with a long wide verandah in front. The stairs opened onto this verandah. From there a few steps led down to the road. Bapuji waved a tonga to a halt, and climbing onto it, we first went to Dera Sahib Gurdwara and then to Anarkali Bazaar.

One of our relatives had his shop in that market—Banbasi Store. He was the son of a distant aunt or uncle of my mother. All that I remember about him is that his father was an official in the forest department. He had lived for many years in the bungalows provided by the department. He used to roam the jungles on horseback. That's why he started calling himself 'Banbasi'. And when his son decided to open a shop in Anarkali Bazaar, he named it Banbasi Store.

To this uncle of 'Banbasi Store', Bapuji said, 'I need some dresses for this girl. At least ten frocks. They should be ready by tomorrow evening, and even if I have to give double the amount, that won't be a problem. Call the tailor here itself.'

The uncle laughed, 'Take them all right now, Bapuji. Let me call everyone here. If you say, I will make a dozen tailors sit down in front of you without delay. They will get all Jeet's frocks ready while you wait. But first tell me, dear child, what will you eat? Will you have an ice cream or a kulfi?'

He sent for ice creams, not just for me but for everyone. For the salesmen working in the shop, for the tailor with his henna-dyed beard! Bapuji paid for them all.

'I'm treating everyone for my daughter's frocks and also to celebrate the birth of her brother,' said Bapuji.

All my melancholy evaporated. I started chirping like a bird. But maybe it was the effect of Daarji–Beeji's strict discipline that I neither spoke or laughed loudly, nor jumped about much. I was happy just basking in Bapuji's warmth and tenderness.

I was allowed to choose the cloth and colours for my frocks. The Banbasi uncle spread out rolls of cloth in front of us. Whichever roll I pointed to, the cloth was measured and cut and placed aside.

༄

And what of my own birth?

Isn't it ironical that man remains totally ignorant about the two most significant events of his own life, his birth and his death? The first takes place due to negligence and the second leads to the disappearance of its protagonist from the world. Dust into dust and air into air. You can go on searching eternally but you won't find those who have blended into the earth and air.

Poets are free to make the elements—the earth, the air and the sky—as romantic as they like but I assure you that these elements are not only deaf and dumb, they are also blind.

I was told about the first major incident of my life by my mother and grandmother long after it had taken place. Showing me a large, spacious bed they had said, 'You were born on this bed.'

The bed was placed in a spacious, airy room in my grandmother's house in Peer Makki Gali in Lahore. A wide bed made of strong wood, it was supported by thick, round, carved legs which reminded me of the silver-encircled ankles of Haryanvi women working along with their men in the fields. At times, the legs of the bed also looked like the arms of an Amazonian African pub owner who had donned chunky Mexican bracelets from her wrists to her elbows.

The bed was placed against a wall to the right of the room. A few feet above the bed, there was a narrow projection in the wall which my Nani referred to as an angeethi.

'Why do you call it an angeethi?' I would ask her, 'an angeethi is where you light a fire.'

Nani would turn to my mother and say, 'This child is so inquisitive, Jaswant Kaur. Do you think she is going to become a lawyer when she grows up?'

ଓ

One of the doors in that room in my grandmother's house opened onto a wide, inner corridor. At the end of the verandah was the kitchen. During summer, my Nani would place her angeethi on the threshold of the kitchen and cook there. She would cool herself by waving a palm-leaf fan with a colourful handle as she cooked. In winter she moved inside the kitchen.

The third door of that room opened into an inner room. However, this door was almost always closed and a big padlock dangled firmly from the bolt. It was usually opened on the night before my aunts and their children who came from Delhi and Gujranwala to spend their two-month-long summer vacations were to return home. My mother, with her two children, was also given permission to stay the night at my Nani's house on that occasion.

That inner room was full of magic. The walls whispered with charms and spells and secret rituals.

In that room were many steel trunks with big, heavy locks on them. They reminded me of wide-bottomed, old sorceresses wearing dim and dusty robes and squatting on the floor.

My acquaintance with the world of magic and make-believe did not come about through Hans Anderson. Nor had the stories of Gulliver, Sindbad and Alif Laila contributed to it. My mother hadn't even heard of these books and Daarji thought such books corrupted young minds. It was through that room that I was introduced to the world of magic spells.

My mother used to feel thoroughly ashamed at the impatience with which I would wait for the night when the magic chamber would be unlocked. I would keep asking Nani, 'When will my aunts go back?' I also pestered my cousins by repeatedly asking them, 'When are you leaving?'

And at last when that night came, I would be so excited that I couldn't eat. My cousins were told to go to bed before the door of the room was opened. It was explained to them that children had nothing to do with that room.

As quietly as I could, I would hide behind the door. Soon the lids of the trunks would be lifted and my mother and aunts would bend their heads over the treasures inside. And when Nani took out lengths of gorgeous fabrics like gold-embroidered silk, satin, velvet, plush and brocade and spread them on the carpet, I would be drawn irresistibly towards them. Like a snake driven by the music of the 'been' I would glide from behind the door and settle down by those fabulous piles.

The colours of all those fabrics looked strangely moist and they melted in the dim light of a low-powered bulb. The smooth silks shimmered as if they were breathing and the Benarasi sarees and dupattas looked as if they were woven with the colourful rays of the sun. Every fold of those silk fabrics seemed to hide something inside them—something living, breathing and with wings, like a fairy.

Hiding amidst the trunks, I would reach out to touch and feel those gorgeous silks. And when my presence was noticed Nani would say irritably, 'Jaswant Kaur, I say, this daughter of yours...' I would sense that my mother was embarrassed because of me and I wanted to walk away. But where were my feet? They seemed to be missing and my body seemed to have been tied up by all those silken skeins.

I still remember a lovely, yellow silk fabric. Its memories still come visiting me softly. It was really smooth, like a soft dough prepared with refined flour and butter. It was a shimmering satin fabric. Nani gave it to one of my aunts to make a quilt. I was really angry with Nani for that. I felt like sulking and never speaking to anyone for that injustice. Why couldn't I have a frock made with that fabric? Or maybe a long robe like the Sufis wore in which I would feel lighter than the clouds.

2

All the decisions in our house were taken by Daarji, so the decision to not send me to school must also have been his. According to him, decent, well-mannered girls turned into spoilt brats if they went to school. They became rebellious and out of hand.

So a Master was hired to come to the house for my education.

He used to come every morning to teach me. Sometimes he would teach English, and sometimes maths. In those days, maybe, knowledge of only these two subjects was considered to be relevant for girls.

Maths I could never learn, and the type of English he taught, even if I could have learnt it, would have been a poor mixture, the type that middle-class women usually speak.

The whole day Beeji would either be getting herself massaged or then cuddling her young nawab, Ghuggi, or Jasbir as he had been officially named. (I had been given the name of Ajeet Cour, but everyone called me Jeet.) She had had the child after a lot of ardent supplications to the Divine (that's what she used to say to my aunts and other relatives) and so she doted on him. She used to place him on his stomach, on her knees, and would lovingly massage him with mustard oil. At that time she would forget all her own aches and pains, even the ones that were ever present in her knees and legs.

On Ghuggi's, that is Jasbir's, birth a lady was employed to take care of the child. Such a lady, who nowadays is called an ayah, was called Maai in those days. Ghuggi's ayah was only thirty years old but still she was called Maai.

Whenever she bathed Ghuggi in the tub, Beeji would sit by them and watch with eager, wistful eyes, delighting in his gurgling laughter. Then she would take him onto her lap and tenderly wipe and powder him. The whole room would be filled with the aroma of his powder. She would laughingly wipe his dribbling chin with the corner of her soft, white, lacy veil.

Then, hiding him beneath that veil, she would feed him at her breast. There was a glow on her face at these times. Ghuggi would kick out strenuously and soon his little legs would be free of their protective covering. His closed fists and tiny arms would move energetically like oars. I found his tiny, soft pink fists very endearing. I felt a doting affection towards him.

The whole house was filled with Ghuggi's presence. I was nowhere.

༄

I was totally alone.

Even at the tender age of four, I was leading the life of a recluse. Every morning, all the neighbourhood children of my age would head for school, dressed in neat and clean uniforms, wearing shining shoes, with a school bag hanging from their shoulders, laughing and dancing all the way. I used to watch them forlornly, standing on the balcony of our house. Our house had a long, big balcony which overlooked the street with all its hustle and bustle—its busy-ness, comings and goings, the pedestrians, the horse carriages and buggies, the confusion of cars and cycles—amongst all this cacophony, the balcony was like an island, still and unchanged for aeons.

And I was imprisoned on this island. Like an antiquated portrait from a bygone era, hanging on the stained, peeling walls of an ancient dilapidated haveli.

At that time, comparisons didn't occur to my mind. In fact, nothing occurred to my mind. Not even this thought, that if all other children could go to school, why couldn't I?

Then, whatever was, had to be accepted. Whether it was good or bad, just or unjust, appropriate or inappropriate, full of love or resentment, equality or inequality, all of it was beyond my understanding. My intellect had not matured to the extent that I could think of all these things.

It was just the age of becoming aware. Like a sponge absorbing and learning about life from all the events happening around me.

And in that budding awareness was hidden the prickle of sadness. A wave of despondency emerging from the well of my heart. An inexplicable melancholy. That which couldn't be put into words.

It was as if my body and mind were shrouded in dark clouds which refused to move either forwards or backwards, didn't even come down as a deluge all over me. I couldn't touch and feel them with my finger. Couldn't push them away with my hands. You can fight with something tangible, what can you do with something as ethereal as clouds?

Even earlier, Beeji had never contributed much in the running of the house. Now after the birth of Ghuggi, her legs had unexpectedly given way completely and she couldn't even walk. Sheela Dai would come every day to ask after her. She had even sent a young nurse to look after Beeji, who would give her a bath or sponge her, powder her body, help her change her clothes, comb her hair.

And sometimes when she was feeling even more ill, the nurse would bathe Ghuggi as well, change his clothes and after wrapping him in a sheet, would place him in Beeji's lap, so that she could feed him, hiding him under her veil.

Observing all this, I used to wonder how she could love the child so deeply, the child who had given her so much pain that she had become incapable of even walking? How could she actually hold him to her bosom, hide him under her veil and feed him? And the moment she took him into her arms, how could her face glow with so much happiness and love instead of sadness?

She had never taken me onto her lap like that or held me with such a radiant look.

Today when I look back and recall that thought, it seems nonsensical, because naturally I had forgotten the times when she must have fed me at her breast, cuddled me, just as I can't remember being in her womb for nine months. Every child has a birthright to that mothering and experience even though it doesn't remain in their conscious memory. How difficult it is to be a mother, I got to know this only later. In spite of it all I loved Jasbir a lot.

I would wander aimlessly from room to room the whole day, once my lessons were done. As dusk approached, I would go to the terrace and sit on an old charpoy, and gaze dreamily at the setting sun, at the line of crows flying back to their nests—how happily they seemed to be beating their wings, spreading them out, then folding them, leaving an imprint of their existence on the vastness of the ocean-like blue heavens, crooning, jabbering, smearing the blue skies with the black streaks of their flight, flying quickly towards the haven of their nests. Towards their own sanctuaries.

Their homes must definitely be more beautiful than our homes. Their children must be there, in their homes, waiting for them. Surely the birds must love their children a lot. These were the thoughts that came to me.

3

There was a girl in the house next door—Rohini—with whom I was allowed to play a little. The low platform, a sort of open portico, in front of her house joined the one in front of my house. We used to stroll from one end of that platform to the other.

We could ride a three-wheeled cycle from the end of our open portico to the very end of Rohini's, from one end of the world to the other.

Both our lives were restricted to this platform. That was our playground and that was the paradise of our childhood.

We would have just begun talking when some servant, from either her house or mine, would come with the message that we were being called inside. Then she would be confined to her house and I to mine, interred in our similar tomb-like existences.

From within, our houses were huge. Overpowering, like old mansions usually are. And the moment we entered our houses, we became tongue-tied. All our playfulness got left outside. The environment inside was such, curbed by the walls of those houses. A very strange, constrained environment.

Every morning, dressed in a beautiful frock, Rohini would go to school in her grandfather's two-horse carriage. She had a book of pictures and a big notebook of thick pages in which she used to make drawings of trees, houses, birds and animals.

Rohini's house was a palatial mansion with beautiful white marble flooring. Pots of palms, servants, horse-carriages! Despite there being everything in it, that house was still full of a deep sadness, a sadness which was like a heavy pall of smoke permeating every nook and corner of the house.

Rohini had been hardly one and half years old when

her father passed away. I had heard Beeji and Daarji talking about it many times.

Everyone addressed Rohini's grandfather as Rai Sahib. Daarji always said that he had not become Rai Sahib due to his own efforts. 'He has become so by buttering up the British officials.' Daarji was totally against the British government. That's why he maintained only a formal politeness with Rai Sahib. After all, they were neighbours.

Rai Sahib had sent his only son abroad to study law. He himself was a chartered accountant. Before he left the country, Rai Sahib performed his son's wedding. The new daughter-in-law was really doll-like. Very beautiful, delicate. The son went abroad soon afterwards and left his wife behind to look after his parents. By that time Rohini had been conceived.

When Rohini was born, her father was not present. He did come back, but suddenly, one day, he just quietly expired.

Rohini didn't have any memories of her father. And nobody would talk to her about him. Maybe she regarded her grandfather as her father, who, like Daarji, would sit in the lower portion of the house, and from there he practised his chartered accountancy.

She had a grandmother also who was almost always sitting in the prayer room, from where came the continuous sound of soft chanting which sounded more as if someone was whimpering in deep pain. Otherwise she would keep lying in her room, facing the wall.

In the big kitchen of Rohini's house, her mother would sit the whole day on a big, low, wooden stool. Wearing a plain white cotton saree, she would either be cutting or chopping something, frying or sautéing all the time. The servants were there just to grind the condiments and chutneys.

One of her tasks was to cut the areca nuts for her in-laws' betel leaves. The nutcracker would work like magic in her hands. Within minutes, the hard, round areca nut would be reduced to a pile of fine symmetrical pieces.

Rohini's mother herself never ate betel leaves. Maybe widowed ladies were not permitted to eat them.

She worked silently, with a closed expression, as if she was scared and apprehensive of even drawing breath in such an opulent household. Rohini's grandmother always spoke angrily to her, saying God knows what. Sometimes even when she was sitting in her own room, she would hurl loud tirades at her; and in the kitchen, Rohini's mother would hide her face in her knees and cry softly. Only the movement of her dark hair rolled into a bun on her fair neck, quivering like the flickering of a candle flame, would show that she was crying.

Rohini would put her arms around her neck and try to soothe her, 'No Amma, no Amma, no,' and then would start crying herself. As soon as the sound of her howls reached her grandfather's ears in his office below, he would come furiously upstairs and would loudly scold his daughter-in-law, 'Bahu, I will not tolerate this crying in my house. You're not even considering this tiny child! See you have made the poor thing also cry.'

Then talking comfortingly to Rohini, he would take her downstairs and quickly send a servant to buy ice cream or chocolates for her.

Now when I think back, I feel that Rohini's grandparents made every effort to keep her away from her mother. She always slept with her grandmother, whose bed was huge with a soft, warm quilt.

No one knew when Rohini's mother went to her room to sleep. And she was always up before the others in the morning. She used to wake the servants, make them fetch the milk, churn the curd, make tea for the grandparents…

After all these morning chores were over, Rohini's

grandmother would lovingly awaken Rohini. Once she was awake, getting her ready for school was her mother's task.

It was unclear why they tried to keep Rohini away from her mother. Maybe it was because they hated her. Maybe they blamed her for bringing tragedy into their lives. They had put in a lot of effort in bringing up their only son and then had sent him abroad to study law. Now after his wedding, after his wife had come into his life, their young son had departed from life in the full glow of his youth, leaving them alone.

After their son's death, they had grown attached to their granddaughter. Their son's only progeny. The only scion of such an esteemed family. They wanted to protect her from even the shadow of their accursed daughter-in-law.

Actually the three of them, Rohini's grandparents and her mother, all were deeply wounded. And all three were struggling to hide their pain from each other.

My earliest memories are full of only Rohini's friendship. Let alone the neighbourhood, Daarji wouldn't let me go anywhere at all. He must have thought that girls shouldn't be allowed to roam about or play with just anyone. Otherwise they became wayward. He tried to control not only my thoughts, my conversations, my movements, my playfulness... but even the turmoils taking place within my body and mind. It was not even 'trying to control', for when you lock a cage and pocket the key, where is the scope for even trying then? You're completely controlled.

All other avenues of communication were closed for me. Just walking along my open portico and reaching Rohini's, this was the only avenue open for me.

And this was because Daarji knew that Rohini's grandfather also trimmed and whittled her with an equally disciplined strictness.

After all, her grandfather had been educated abroad. He

was a chartered accountant. He used to check the accounts of many government departments. If there was even the minutest misappropriation of funds, he would get to know of it.

In a similar manner, he was not allowing a single mistake to be made in Rohini's upbringing.

Those who live abroad usually tend to be a little more broadminded. The way of looking at things does undergo a change, living over there. If her father had been alive, Rohini would definitely have had a little more leeway in things. Rai Sahib must have thought, 'Once we are gone, she will be left all alone. If she is not hewed and disciplined now, she maybe unable to adjust in the house she goes to, and a big problem could be created.'

But Rohini was of a carefree nature. She was happy and glowing all the time. She would order her mother around in the same manner that she ordered the servants. In her eyes, the position of her mother was no better than that of a servant. In such a palatial house, she was the most inferior and pitiable person, even more so than the servants.

I still clearly recall Rohini's gay chatter tearing through the smoke-like, suffocating melancholy of that house. Even today, my thoughts are full of the image of her mother's white marble-like body turning yellow in a white cotton saree. The whole day she would be sitting on a low stool in the kitchen, as if trying to escape the notice of all the members of the house.

Her despondency went and settled in that very dark corner of my heart where my own despair and loneliness lay coiled up.

4

Every morning the Master came to give credence to my education. He would carry on in his efforts to teach me maths and English. I used to feel very angry with him. If he refused to come, then Daarji would have to send me to school. I did not want to learn anything from him.

After many days of teaching, when he failed to make me learn even the two times table, he finally lost his patience, and going to a huge tub placed over a big drain in the middle of the courtyard, pushed it aside and threatened, 'If you don't learn the table quickly, I will stick my head inside this drain and give up my life.'

I was really scared. Oh no! What if he really put an end to his life! I immediately learnt the table.

And soon all the tables till ten were learnt. I even learnt a little of addition-subtraction. I read the first level of the English reader, the 'Nelson Reader'. It took me a whole year to learn all that.

And then an incident happened that changed everything.

I couldn't learn any more tables after ten. I was the most irritated by the thirteen times table. One day, the Master had made me sit on his lap and was trying to coax me to learn it. At that very moment Daarji happened to come from somewhere. A sharp glance...and then it was as if an earthquake had shaken the floor and the walls, or a volcano had erupted.

Catching me by my arm, he pulled me off the Master's lap and threw me aside and started beating him. Shocked and bewildered, the poor Master could do nothing but keep on pleading his innocence, asking for forgiveness...I don't know what he kept blubbering. There was a shivering whimper in his voice.

Daarji beat the Master mercilessly and then furiously shoved him down the stairs. That was the end of my studies.

I was very happy, but also sad, because I couldn't understand why Daarji had beaten the Master so much. His quaking, tearful, pleading voice still sometimes resounds in my ears.

After that, Daarji, I think, consulted with Rai Sahib and then got me admitted to Sacred Heart School. Rohini was not in that school—I don't know to which school she went.

Our house was situated on a crowded street called Chamberlain Road. Patients came and went through the large dingy rooms lit by electric bulbs even during the day to Daarji's clinic on the ground floor.

From Chamberlain Road, past the Delhiwala Sweetshop, across the road and through the Bharat Building, was the shortest way to the school. There was a maid who would take me from my home to the school and then bring me back again.

Stretching from the school gate right up to the school building, were huge, rolling green lawns, beautified with trees and flowers. A red stone gravel driveway, flanked by these lawns, led to the school building. There were also magnificent, white-trunked eucalyptus trees on either side of this driveway.

Touching any plant or tree on the school premises was forbidden. But I used to pick up the fallen leaves of the eucalyptus trees from the ground, crush them in my palms, breathe in their tangy scent, and would feel as if I had been drenched with all the intoxicating aromas of the universe.

There were nuns in this school, dressed in black gowns with a cross on a chain around their necks and a pure white wimple on their heads. They looked so beautiful that let alone thirteen, if someone asked me to learn the tables of twenty-three or thirty-three, I would have willingly done so.

But in that school they did not stress on learning tables. Along with English and geography, a hundred and one other things were taught. Lovingly. Effortlessly. With no form of force or compulsion.

This year and a half of my childhood was the most peaceful time of my life. Though, when I look back, I feel as if childhood never really came into my life. That was only a phase of my infancy, after that I grew up immediately.

Not just that, reflecting back, I feel forced to ponder whether youth also ever come into my life. Maybe it never did, or if it did, everyone made an effort to suppress and sacrifice it completely.

By the time I became aware of this, youth had already passed me by.

Doesn't it sound strange to hear about a lifetime from where both childhood and youth have gone missing!

I had just been admitted to school when Daarji decided to shift to a new house, on the other side of the road, almost opposite our old house. It was the house next door to Dr Raghubir Singh, in fact, it also belonged to Doctor Sahib. He had built a huge mansion with a marble portico for himself and next to that, a smaller house. Maybe he had built it with the purpose of renting it out. But what he told Daarji was, 'You're like my younger brother. It would be wonderful if you came and lived next door to me. We will live like brothers.'

But the doors between our houses, were never opened, neither from his side nor from ours.

New house. A new environment. My loneliness increased even more in this house as Rohini was left across the road, and in between us was this relentless flowing river of cycles, cars, phaetans—a sort of royal buggy drawn by two horses—many other horse-carriages and tongas.

Initially, Rohini and I would stand on our respective balconies and try to talk to each other in sign language. But within a few days, once everything had been organized in the house, the kitchen had started functioning, the purpose of all twenty rooms on five floors decided, the doors opening to the outside world were curtained with bamboo chiks. And Daarji had announced in the style of the Mughal kings that no one was to lift the chiks to peek outside.

There was only one close friend of mine in my life and she too was now so far away. Across a flowing river of vehicles and pedestrians.

5

I was unable to make even a single friend at school. Why I couldn't do so, was a mystery to me at that time. But when I look back now, I'm able to understand a little as to why it was so.

Maybe one reason was that my clothes were inferior to theirs. Everyone in our house wore khadi. Not because Daarji didn't have the money to buy good stuff. But more due to the fact that both he and Beeji believed that girls shouldn't be well dressed, otherwise they became immoral and sinful. I used to wear poplin and khadi frocks which were stitched either by my aunts or by Beeji. My undergarments were also stitched at home. (I wore salwar suits made of the same khadi and poplin material even while doing my Master's).

There could be another reason for this lack of friends. Other girls used to bring sandwiches, cakes and chocolates in colourful lunchboxes. I used to get a small parantha, which I would eat quietly, hiding in a corner, away from prying eyes. Getting a sandwich for lunch was out of the question, because bread had never been allowed into our house. According to Daarji there was nothing more filthy than bread, as dirty servants kneaded the dough for it with their bare feet.

Keeping to myself, I would quickly swallow the contents of my tiffin during lunchtime and then surreptitiously collect the fallen eucalyptus leaves and rub them on my palms, inhaling the pungent smell deeply. It was like a solace to me as I watched beautiful, butterfly-like girls all around me, laughing and talking, chirping gaily. Sometimes, whenever I saw some girl looking at me and whispering something into her friend's ear and then laughing, I would feel as if my whole being had been ruptured like a balloon, and would cringe within myself.

Thus confined and restricted by Daarji's rules, immersed in loneliness, going down some dark stairs within my own mind, I completed eight and a half years of my life.

In these eight years, my most beloved, happiest memories were of those times that we spent in the hills.

The first time that Daarji took us to the hills, I must have been around five years old. The year was 1939, and the Second World War had started.

Even after that, every year till 1945, we would go to the hills. That first time we had gone to Dharamshala, but after that every year we went to Kashmir. Jasbir was just a toddler—cute and innocent like a toy. He was chubby and had a rosy complexion. However, he used to lose his appetite and turn anaemic in the summer months. As it was he hardly ate anything except sweetened yoghurt and potatoes but in the summer he would go off even that. So for the sake of his pampered only son, Daarji used to lock up his clinic and take us to Kashmir. We generally stayed in Pahalgam. On a gentle grassy slope to the right of the road, there was a stretch of flat ground surrounded by low hills where our tents were pitched. In those days, you had to arrange for the tents from Srinagar. We had one large tent which served as a sitting-room cum bedroom. Two smaller tents served as kitchen and bathroom respectively.

On a slope right behind our tents was a dense forest encircled by a narrow pathway which looked like the rope wound around the waists of the hill women.

Traversing that pathway unfolded a new mystery at every turn. Like the bioscope in a green box which showed moving pictures of the Red Fort or the Qutab Minar or the Taj Mahal, the views from the pathway never lost their charm. After walking some distance you came to a place where the pathway began to descend ever so gently. It was here that you heard the sound of flowing water, a rumbling sound like the sound you hear when you place a large seashell against your ear.

As you moved ahead, the sound grew louder. Suddenly, after a turn you could see the river right in front of you. Swift-flowing, sparkling white water!

∽

The mountains were strangely intoxicating. My friendship was with the fir and pine trees, lolling so comfortably on the slopes. My friendship was with the moon and stars which seemed to be very close from up there. As if they were trying to build nests in the branches of the pine trees. It was my cherished wish that I could climb the branch of a tree and pluck the moon like an orange from up there and suck it. Hide a fistful of stars beneath my pillow. My friendship was with the moonlight sliding off the needle-like leaves of the fir trees, into the crystal waters of the river Lidder. My friendship was with those unseen cheetahs and hyenas, who sometimes hovered around our tents in the dead of night, and whenever they did so, the servants would light bonfires to chase them away. Yet, despite their being chased away, the whole night I could smell the wild scent of their bodies. My friendship was with those blades of grass shivering in the night-long cold outside, yet supporting diamond-like shining, snowy dewdrops in the morning. All the rainbow hues of the sun would shimmer momentarily in those snowy diamonds and then quietly melt away. That droplet of water, which drew breath not only from the light of the moon, but also from the sun, and from the greenery of the verdant grass. My friendship was with the swimming, running clouds on the mountains, which sometimes paused to shed their load of water and sometimes just quickly flew by in a flurry. Ever so often, these very clouds would be spread out down below in the valleys and at other times, would slide off the mountain peaks. My friendship was with the mountain rains, which caused a cascade-like surge within me. The mountains turn me into a small child even today. I am ever ready to drown in a gushing mountain waterfall, or a fast-flowing river or a cascade. Even today I can gather a fistful of stars during a dark mountain night and tie them up in the corner of my veil.

At the time of Partition in 1947, we were in Shimla. We had gone there for two months, so that we would be away from the horror unfolding day and night in Lahore, away from the murderous riots. We planned to return once things had quietened down. What we didn't know was that we were not destined to see either Lahore or our house ever again.

༄

This was the same time around which our neighbour's delicate, beautiful daughter, Muan, happened to pass on from this world without any commotion.

It is so strange that the life in one's own house appears to be as uneventful as still waters. Other people's lives seem to be full of action where all kinds of exciting incidents occur. For example Jhaiji, the lady of the house opposite ours, massaged milk cream into her round, fair face. She talked and laughed a lot with her five children. She also screamed at them sometimes. When her eldest son got married his twinkle-toed bride came to enliven the house all the more.

Life in that house seemed to be an interminable movie show viewed through the iron bars of the windows.

Beeji used to scold me, 'You should not peep into other people's houses like this.' Daarji would lament, 'We have never let her play with the street urchins. She has received the best care and protection at home and still she has no manners.'

Thinking of all that today, I am reminded of writer Saadat Hasan Manto's habit of peeping from behind the jute curtains.

Muan was the youngest daughter of the family living in that house. She looked extremely pale, thin and depressed. Her eyes had the desolation of the drifting, yellow autumn leaves in them. They said Muan had tuberculosis.

Muan's plates and glasses were kept separate from others. Nobody sat on her cot. During winter she would lie in the sun on the terrace all day. At night she slept in a separate room on the first floor. It was the kind of room where we stored onions and potatoes in our house.

Whenever I woke up in the middle of the night I would wonder about Muan, that she must be lying alone and scared in her room. She must definitely be crying. Thinking of her, I would find it hard to go back to sleep.

Our two families were next-door neighbours for at least six years. Our houses had a common wall in between. But the first and last time that I went to that house was on the day Muan died. From across the iron bars of her window, her sister had said, sobbing, to my mother, 'Masiji, Muan has passed away.'

That was my first encounter with death. I had not seen death. I had just heard its name. I sat in my room and cried for a long time.

I was seized with a strange, demented kind of melancholy. I couldn't understand my pain. I was restless and angry that life was going on as usual. Day and night, food being cooked in the kitchen, Daarji's patients, sleeping and waking up, bathing, eating, going to school. Nothing had changed.

I thought everything must have come to a standstill in the house opposite. But on the fifth day, I caught a glimpse of Jhaiji rubbing milk cream on her face. After a few more days Muan's brothers were seen flying kites on the roof and her sister-in-law was laughing as usual as she moved in and out of the house, her bangles clinking.

One day I approached my father with trepidation and asked, 'Daarji, why didn't you give medicines to Muan?'

'Children should not talk about such things. Go and read your books,' he answered sternly.

I went out of the room but Daarji and Beeji started talking about Muan. Snatches of their conversation floated up to my room.

'Dr Raghubir Singh told me they had taken Muan to him for treatment last year.'

'The disease couldn't have advanced much at that time.'

'No, it couldn't have. It is curable if detected early. There are drugs...'

'Why didn't they get her treated, then?'

'There is only one cure—injections. And they are very expensive.'

'But imagine...a young girl...'

'They probably did not want to spend so much money. It is a long-drawn-out treatment.'

'They would not mind spending money if one of their sons was ill. But for a girl...'

'They would have had to spend thousands of rupees on her treatment and she could have survived. But would it be easy to marry her off after that?'

'They would have had to spend a lot of money if at all she married.'

'They must have considered all that before deciding not to get her treated.'

'Waheguru!' My mother sighed deeply.

It has been years but Muan's eyes and her pale, yellow face covered with the mist of hopeless melancholy are still alive in my mind.

After all these years, I'm still haunted by the pros and cons and the expenses Muan's parents must have calculated before passing a death sentence on their flesh and blood.

6

Amrita Pritam's father, Giani Kartar Singh Hitkariji, once came to our house.

He had come to Lahore from Gujranwala as his daughter Amrit Kaur, who later became famous as the writer and poet Amrita Pritam, had got married to Sardar Jagat Singh Kwatra's son, Pritam Singh, in Lahore. Hitkariji knew my grandfather Bapu Ishar Singhji in Gujranwala very well. My grandfather was the president of the Gujranwala Gurdwara Managing

Committee. Hitkariji was also one of the adminstrators of the committee. He was very learned and was also a poet; Bapuji really appreciated such people.

Hitkariji said, 'I will teach Jeet Punjabi. Bapu Ishar Singhji's granddaughter is studying in a Christian school, and so must be learning English and I don't know what else. She has to know Punjabi also.'

Almost immediately, I was removed from Sacred Heart School and put into Hitkariji's care. He got hold of the books of the Budhimani (Punjabi Intermediate) course and started teaching me.

He was always hugging a book covered with red rexine—a type of thick plastic sheet. On this red cover, in golden letters, were written the words 'Amrit Lehran' and the author's name, Amrit Kaur. Amrita Pritam's first book. This book was also included in the Budhimani course in those days.

I felt a rush of jealous longing. I also yearned to write poetry. Then I too, would have a beautifully bound book with golden inscriptions to my name. Maybe Daarji would also hug it to his chest.

At the tender age of eight and half years, I was reading *Heer Ranjha* by Waris Shah, Peelu's *Mirza-Sahiban*, Hashim Shah's *Sassi Punnu* and many other such love stories. I did not understand these stories at all. My task was to learn the word-meanings by heart and also all that Hitkariji made me write, explaining the nuances in their excellent poetry.

The seeds of these stories, however, were definitely planted in the fertile soil of my mind, and kept me tied for years to the dreams and hopes of finding such a love in my life.

It was this love that I tried to find in my adult years, first with Baldev and later on with my husband.

The desire to be loved by your husband! Isn't that the limit of stupidity? How can marriage and love be connected? It took me thirteen years to understand this simple fact.

The most difficult thing to master was the grammar of the Gurbani verses. With every vowel, the meaning of the word changed. In the Gurbani, even those vowels which seemed to be of no use, suddenly gained meaning.

But so many books…so many verses of the Gurbani…so many love stories…poems…novels…Sometimes it felt as if there was a loud churning inside my head, as though I would be totally crushed by the weight of these words.

The whole day would slip by in the company of Baba Budh Singh, Puran Singh, Waris, Hashim and Peelu. This tough routine only intensified the expectant wait for the evenings, when my grandfather would take Jasbir and me to Lawrence Gardens or Shimla Hill or the zoo, for an outing.

Hitkariji was very happy. Daarji was also happy that his young daughter would be qualified to sit for the university exams. Beeji seemed happy too—though I had seen her happy on very few occasions, except when she used to have Jasbir sitting in her lap. And later when he started going to school, she would be happy plying him with food when he returned. Otherwise she would remain serious like any other respectable housewife.

Jasbir didn't like either vegetables or cereals. No non-vegetarian dishes were made in our household. It was only at times when some distant relative or neighbour from Bhera had come to visit—either due to some court case, or because someone needed to be taken to hospital, or to set up a match for their children—that mahaprasad was prepared at home for them. This is how mutton was referred to in those days.

Beeji had a separate stove and utensils to cook mahaprasad. Whether they were used once or ten times, after being used they were again put back in a basket and stored in the loft.

Small potatoes were also added to the mahaprasad and

Jasbir and I loved to eat these. Slowly Jasbir started liking potatoes a lot, cooked in a variety of ways, including with curd and sugar

As I was saying, it was evident that Beeji was happy, because now I did not sit alone on the terrace all the time. I didn't even insist on flying kites during the month of Basant. Neither did I peep through the chiks to talk in sign language with Rohini across the road, nor go to school, where there was every possible chance of going astray. There was also no chance of any untoward action on the part of the Master, as the old white-bearded Hitkariji was teaching me and he was deeply respected by the whole family. Then, the whole day I was under Beeji's scrutinizing eye.

Whenever Bapuji came from Gujranwala, with his baskets of maltas, he would be pleased that his granddaughter was reading such heavy tomes...and was even understanding the meaning of the Gurbani verses.

I was just a little over nine years old when I gave the Budhimani examinations. Hitkariji would fuss over me, then carry me to the examination hall and seat me at my desk every day.

Many a times I felt that I wanted to avenge myself on Hitkariji. It was because of him that I had to leave such a good school, which I had loved, and submit to his teaching me at home, all those tomes which made my head spin!

I wanted to avenge myself on Daarji also, by failing the exams. Every day, I saw all the neighbourhood children going happily to school. Jasbir would also go jumping to school. A servant would carry his bag and escort him every morning, and then bring him back in the afternoons. After coming back from school he would have his food and then, picking up his bat, hockey stick or racquet, he would go off to play with friends. He would come and go as he pleased. And then there was me whose whole education had become a joke. Just to make a show of it and let people know that the girl was studying, a Master would come home to teach. What was I doing but just sitting at home the whole day and studying thick tomes. What sort of education was this! So I decided to fail to show Daarji that though I was merely a girl, still...

I was still wavering about not clearing the exams to retaliate against Daarji and Hitkariji when I was declared passed, much to my chagrin.

'A nine-year old clears the university exams'—this news, along with a horrible-looking photograph of mine, appeared in the *Tribune*, *Milap*, *Pratap* and other newspapers.

When the newspaper people asked for my photograph, Beeji refused to have my picture taken in a frock.

Till then, I had never had a photograph taken. No one had ever clicked one. Neither was it a routine in our house—clicking pictures.

So quickly, a satin kameez with small motifs and a satin salwar, were stitched by the darzi. And a Benarasi veil to cover my head and shoulders. It was the first time I had worn a salwar-kameez, and the salwar felt so loose, I was sure it would fall down.

The heavy veil refused to stay put on the satin suit. It kept slipping away. I was looking very tense in the photograph. On one hand, there was the fear of the salwar falling down. On the other, hanging onto the constantly slipping veil. The head should not be bared, it should be covered. Worries and more worries. The picture on the front page of the newspapers looked as though someone had stuffed me into a bag of satin and made me sit there.

When I cleared the university level examination, the

question was raised by the Punjab University Senate as to how such a young child been allowed to sit for the examination? This way the university would be treated like a grocery shop! So the committee decided that henceforth no child below fourteen years of age would ever be allowed to sit for any university examination.

Now this record of being the youngest to clear the university exams could never be broken as no one of that age would be allowed to take the exams. This distinction was, as the saying goes, like a pigeon coming under a blind man's foot—meaning, it happened just by chance!

7

Even before the exams I had started writing short poems to please Hitkariji. When I would hesitantly present them to him, the loving pride in his eyes would shine through the thick glasses of his spectacles. He would very seriously go through them and correct them. He used to say, 'Those who think their compositions to be the ultimate truth, and are not ready to correct or add to them, cannot be great writers. Urdu poets used to get their verses revised and amended by their mentors for years before finalizing them.'

Now I surreptitiously began sending these same poems to magazines like *Panj Dariya* and *Fateh*. I only wrote my name, Ajeet, not my address. One reason was that I was scared of Daarji and Beeji's reaction. What if they got angry?

Daarji's voice was always echoing in my ears, 'Girls of respectable families don't write poetry. From today everything must stop—your going onto the roof, gazing at the sky...'

And along with that, Beeji's voice acquiescing to everything, for she always agreed to all that Daarji said.

Daarji might say, 'The world will disintegrate tonight,' and Beeji would definitely add, 'Why won't it disintegrate? It should disintegrate. After all there are no religious convictions anywhere nowadays.' Now she would say, 'I told you not to put her in that convent school with white Christians. If you wanted to send her to school, what was wrong with the Khalsa School? I told you so many times, this girl goes onto the terrace the moment it starts getting dark. Sitting alone there, she must be writing her poetry. Stop all her education. Stop her from going onto the roof. Earlier you used to send her for a walk with Bhaiyaji and Ghuggi. You had to stop that as well, no? Why do girls need to go out anywhere? Go for a walk or not, they will keep growing like a wild creeper.' And so on and on...

The second reason was that the editor of *Panj Dariya*, Mohan Singhji, and the editor of *Fateh*, Laabh Singh Narangji, were both Daarji's patients. All of Daarji's patients were his friends. I have never been able to understand the charm and geniality that Daarji must have shown to his patients, that they all became his close friends. These two were also his friends. I didn't want them to know that these were Dr Makkhan Singh Bajaj's daughter's poems, so that they felt beholden for his sake, to publish them.

I wanted to have an unbiased opinion about my poems. I wanted to see how high I could rise without any support. How far I could go.

Some of my poems got published, some didn't.

To see your name in print in some magazine at the tender age of nine or ten years, gives you an indescribable exhilaration and intoxication. Pride as well. Earned all by your own self.

∽

Budhimani was complete, now what should be done with me? So I was admitted into the Khalsa School. Hitkariji had also started teaching Punjabi in that school. Maybe he was the one who made me the president of the school's literary society.

The classes of the Khalsa School were held in small barrack-like rooms, the college was in a bigger building. The president of the college literary society was Prabhjot Kaur. Her younger sister, Surjeet, was also in the same college. Both the sisters wrote poetry. Even at that time, Surjeet was as quiet and shy as she is today while Prabhjot is as sharp and brilliant as she was then. That's why Prabhjot always remained more in the headlines. She was not only beautiful but also a poet. Why wouldn't she be in the news?

One annual function of the school has always been a valuable part of my memories, the one in which a very beautiful, fair girl had played the sitar. That was Amrit Kaur. Hitkariji's daughter. Today's well-known Amrita Pritam, who greatly influenced my childhood, as my ideal heroine. And one very delicate-looking, slim, duskily beautiful girl had sung some Punjabi songs. This was Surinder Kaur.

ॐ

The school and college had a common library. From this library I got my first Punjabi book, a book which was not compulsory reading as part of the Budhimani course, nor was it to be read under any pressure, meaning I read it of my own free will, and that was Kartar Singh Duggal's *Saver Saar*. And that was the first time I thought, 'Oh, why can't I write such stories!'

Other than Punjabi books, there were also English and Urdu books in the library. Till now no one at home had given me permission to study Urdu, because Daarji was of the opinion that Urdu shouldn't be taught to girls. Urdu poetry was full of stories of love and lovers. All useless things.

But I had covertly learnt enough Urdu to be able to read. Jasbir was being made to learn Urdu and had to practise the letters by writing them on a wooden board coated with China clay, using a bamboo stylo dipped in an ink made from plant resins. He had to inscribe them by saying them out aloud as well, and that gave me a chance to learn along with him, unknown to him.

One day, I got an Urdu book by Saadat Hasan Manto out of the library. I hid it among my school books. When everybody had gone to sleep at night, that's when I read it.

It was maybe the fourth or fifth Urdu book—that too by Manto, which, after reading till late at night, I placed under my pillow and went off to sleep. The next morning I forgot to take it out from under the pillow and hide it. The moment I came out of the bathroom, all hell broke loose. 'What is this?'—Daarji threw the book in front of me, reminiscent of the way a murderer is shown a blood-covered knife and asked, 'What is this?'

I was shivering with fright. It was as if my legs were giving way. I could feel quivers all over—the floor, walls, roof—everything was shaking as if an earthquake had struck. The book was torn to bits in front of my eyes and Daarji's royal decree was issued, 'From today, you're not going to school.'

Then there was only one punishment for all transgressions, 'No more going to school'. As if school was a chocolate, which could be snatched away.

For Jasbir school was neither a concession nor a chocolate. He could do whatever he liked, say whatever he liked to anyone, be as naughty as he liked, no one ever threatened to remove him from school. Sending me to school was a special indulgence for me, a real concession on their part.

It was also essential to send Jasbir to school because he had to grow up to be a doctor like Daarji, bring fame to the family name. I, according to Beeji, was someone else's property. I had to go to a different, strange family. After all, I was not going to become a district collector or a barrister, so what did I need an education for? I would have to look after the household and kitchen work. That is what I needed to learn.

Along with that I had to practise guidelines befitting a girl, for my betterment—how to speak softly, how to be able to talk pleasantly, how to keep my eyes lowered, not to lift the bamboo chiks to peek outside, not run in a hoydenish way down the stairs...so on and on...

8

Childhood had never come into my life, maybe that's why I also grew up quickly, physically.

I must have been about ten or ten and half, when one day, my lower garment—a salwar—which was rust in colour, became bloodstained. I just couldn't recall when and where I had fallen. Where, when and how had I hurt myself so badly that the blood was flowing non-stop down my legs.

Feeling really scared, I told Beeji. She hit her hand on her forehead as though I had committed a grave crime and said, 'Good Lord, so soon?' That was all that she had to say. That too, in a voice filled with despair!

Those words are still engraved in my heart, even today. The action of her hand hitting her head and those words.

The first thing Beeji did was to take out a bundle of thick cotton cloth and stitch it into a bandage-like strip, cut a little deeper at the corners. There were thinner strings attached to either edge. The order given forth was that from today onwards, whenever the bleeding started, I was to wear it between my legs, inside my salwar, and tie the strings around my waist to keep it in place.

Wearing it made me feel as if I was a prisoner bound by these strips of cotton swathes instead of manacles.

I wore these cotton swathes up to my MA classes. It was only then that one day, a friend of mine took me to Karol Bagh. She was the one who bought my first bra for me. She said to me, 'Stupid! Idiot! Your mother stitched your bras for you and you wore them! Enough is enough now. Even the boys who study with us laugh at you. You try this now. If the fitting is good, we'll come back to buy more.'

All that happened much later. At this time, we were still in Lahore. I was studying in Khalsa School. As stated earlier, after every transgression, I was withdrawn from school. And after being kept at home for a few days, when Daarji felt I had been suitably punished, I would be sent back again.

Beeji would often fall ill. Whenever she was more seriously ill than usual, my going to school would stop. When Jasbir fell ill, then also my going to school would stop. In fact I, too, had begun to feel that if someone was ill in the house or if some guest was expected to come, I shouldn't go to school.

I remember once, Jasbir came down with chickenpox. He had very high fever. I was the one who stayed with him and nursed him. With folded hands, I would pray to the Almighty, 'Dear Babaji, please heal my brother. Give all his troubles to me.'

Everyone would tell me, 'You have only one brother.' And I would forget all his atrocities towards me and continue to love him. Secondly, it was totally clear in my mind that

Jasbir's value and importance in the family was much more than mine. He should get well. I didn't matter.

Otherwise also the wish to die had come many times to my mind. When I was scolded unnecessarily; needlessly beaten or withdrawn from school, then. And every month when I would be soaked in blood, then also...

And God heard my prayers. Jasbir recovered and I was taken captive by the chickenpox. High fever. I was not conscious for days on end.

The day I regained consciousness, it was evening. The first thing I asked the maid working in our house was, 'Where is Jasbir?' and her answer was, 'Must have gone to play hockey.'

9

In the summer of 1945, we had gone to Pahalgam as usual. There Daarji contracted 'hill diarrhoea'. On returning to Lahore, Daarji was completely bedridden. No medicine had any effect on him. Daarji's own lifesaving homeopathic medicines, Dr Raghubir Singh's allopathic medicines, the treatment of the big doctors of Meyo Hospital, ayurvedic, unani...none had any effect whatsoever.

As must be evident by now, my going to school had, of course, been stopped. I was made responsible for the kitchen and had to take care of everything there. The servants were there, but it was the norm in our household that all the cooking was done by Beeji. Now, I too, had to learn how to make the various dishes.

Beeji kept crying day and night. Many relatives and neighbours came daily to visit the patient. She would serve lemonade or buttermilk to them, share all her worries with them and then start crying again. The rest of the time, she sat at Daarji's bedside.

Dr Raghubir Singh had arranged a nurse for Daarji as he had to be given a bedpan, sponged and given his medicines on time. In fact, two nurses—one came in the morning and one in the evening. They also had to give glucose to Daarji. He had become very weak so there was a bottle of glucose continuously hanging upside down on a tall stand next to Daarji's bed. The glucose needle was perpetually stuck in his arm.

Many of his patients would come and start crying. Many were the entreaties made to the Divine for his good health.

For three long months he battled with death before getting back on the path of recovery.

He was still very weak so he could not go to his clinic. Then Beeji, too, fell ill and took to her bed.

One of Beeji's kidneys was full of stones and didn't function at all. There was also a stone in her gall bladder and whenever it got stuck in the opening of the bile duct, her liver would stop functioning and the accumulated bile would become poisonous. Her lips would turn blue and she would contract high fever.

Normally, with the help of the medicines Daarji gave her, she would recover in ten or twelve days. The stone would slip back into the gall bladder from the bile duct, and the poison created in the bile would slowly dissolve. But this time, due to Daarji's long illness she had become so weak that the medicines were having no effect on her. Daarji was hesitant about giving her any strong medicine. What if her body, in its weakened state, couldn't withstand a strong medicine?

During this time, one of our two servants, who helped in the kitchen, ran away. So a large portion of the housework fell on my shoulders. The whole day I sat in front of the stove cooking vegetables and making chapattis. The family itself was very small. But all day long, relatives would keep coming and going to ask after Beeji, and they all had to be served lemonade and buttermilk. I spent the day going back and forth from Beeji's room to serve the visitors, and the kitchen.

At about this time, for about five or six days, I had not felt like eating anything at all. The smell of the vegetables being cooked or even of the lentils, would make me feel sick and nauseated. I would quietly go to the bathroom, throw up and then get back to the kitchen. This continued for sometime and soon only a sort of yellowish bitter water was all that came out.

It must have been the seventh day, when I felt like having a savoury dish of potatoes and spicy nuggets made of dried ground lentils. Due to Beeji's illness only light dishes like split green gram lentils, and a variety of gourds like bottle, green ridge, ash, round, were being cooked in the house. I wanted to eat something spicy and I loved to eat the dish made of potatoes and nuggets.

So I decided to make it for myself and soon the dish was ready. I placed one piece of potato and a chunk of the nuggets in my bowl and broke a portion of the chapatti. Wrapping half a piece of nugget in the chapatti, I placed it in my mouth. And it felt as if it had bloated in my mouth, almost choking me.

Just then Daarji came into the kitchen. 'What dish have you made?' he asked. The morsel in my mouth could neither be swallowed nor could I spit it out in front of Daarji.

Daarji was usually loving towards both his children. But his own and Beeji's long illness had disturbed him so much that he had become short-tempered and irritable. He just needed an excuse to get angry.

His eye fell on the bowl of vegetables. 'Potato and spicy nuggets?' he exclaimed angrily.

I have no recollection of what happened after that.

∽

When I regained consciousness, I was lying on the bed in the terrace room. A fat maid was sitting on the floor a little away from my bed. I had never seen her before.

The moment I opened my eyes, she quickly came near me and looked at me, with an anxious and amazed expression. Then she started calling out to everyone in a loud voice—'Come quickly, come quickly, the child has opened her eyes...'

And the next moment I found myself the focus of Daarji's and Beeji's sad, tearful eyes.

For the first time in my memory, Beeji caressed my head tenderly. Her tightly compressed lips were quivering with emotion. Her face had become red with the effort of trying to control her tears.

Then, Bapuji came upstairs, chanting the name of the Lord, 'Wahe Guru, Wahe Guru'. He, too, caressed me lovingly, 'Tati waao na lagayee gur paarbrahma saranayee... Wahe Guru! Satnam Shri Wahe Guru! Dhan Shri Guru Nanak, the true King! Dhan Mehranwale Datiyaa! You've sent the child back to us. Parmeshwar ditta banna, dukh rog da dera bhanna.'

Bhaiyaji also came and sat at the foot of the bed and gently stroking my legs, started crying loudly. 'Great Divine! Great Divine! Great my Lord! Great Protector of both worlds!' he kept repeating. He used to talk in a similar fashion with God in the Guru Granth Sahib room—sometimes sullenly, sometimes pleadingly and sometimes as friends.

He used to address God as Yaara. But today he was not calling Him that.

My grandmother was rubbing the soles of my feet. For the first time I saw the always petulant, stone-like grandmother melt with emotion.

These were the best and most soothing moments of my life.

All were showering me with their deepest love. In that moment, I was the queen of the whole world!

If, on becoming ill, you receive so much love, then my dearest God, my sweetest Babaji, let me ever remain ill! A ball of happiness bounced in my stomach and got lodged in my throat. I wanted to simultaneously laugh and cry with joy.

Slowly, as I became fully conscious, I realized that I was so weak that I couldn't even turn on my side on my own. The same fat maid had to help me turn and would also gently massage my back. My back felt as stiff as a wooden plank. My legs and arms looked like the withered branches of a dead tree. When lying on my side, if I drew my legs up, my knees would knock together and waves of pain would shoot up and down my legs.

Then one day I saw that while the maid was combing my hair, she was repeatedly removing bunches of hair from the comb, rolling them and placing them under the bed.

I lifted my hand and touched my hair, 'Oh no, where is my hair?'

My beautiful wavy hair that came down to my knees!

'Show me all the hair that you have been rolling and throwing away,' I asked the maid in a quavering voice.

She placed a fistful of the hair in front of me. Then she said, 'Daily at least this much falls. But there is no need to fear now. Thank God your life was saved. Let the hair be. It will grow back again.'

'Life was saved? What had happened to me?'

'How do I know, my child! The doctors only know that. You ask your Daarji about it.'

The taste in my mouth had become so bad that I wanted to eat something tangy to relieve it. But I was only given sago, watery lentils, watery porridge and milk. I had begun to hate all these things.

One day, my fat maid was holding a few paranthas in her hand and having them along with buttermilk. She hit an onion with her fist, removed its covering, spread pieces of onion on the parantha, sprinkled some salt and red chilli powder on it, and started eating it.

'Please give me a morsel along with the onion,' I pleaded with her.

'My child, you can make me do anything you like, but I can't give you this...' she replied.

'Just one bite...' I implored again.

At that moment, one piece of that parantha along with the chilli and onion seemed to be the most deliciously royal food on earth. I had never pined for any kind of food. Never before then, and never after.

I tried to recollect the time when I had fallen ill. But then it had been summer. Now the winter had set in. The afternoon sun coming into the room was very enjoyable. Keeping my head in the shade, I loved the feel of the warm sunlight on the rest of my body. Wherever I wanted to be, the maid would pull my cot there.

I asked her, 'What's the date today?'

She told me.

'And month?'

'Now child, how do I know anything about these English months? I am just an illiterate villager,' she said, looking the other way.

I looked at the calendar on the wall, it showed the month of July.

I couldn't understand it—in the month of July we usually cooled the rooms downstairs, and sat there with the fans on. I don't know if there were coolers or air-conditioners then, but we didn't have them in our house. Rohini's house also didn't have them. There were none in my Nani's house either, even though my Nanaji had held a senior post in the railway department for many years. Beeji used to tell us, whenever he travelled, four bogies were usually booked for him. One was where he sat and slept. One was his office where his secretary and steno sat. One carriage was for the servants and one was a kitchen. Indeed, he had executed his job in a royal manner. Though Daarji always tried to humiliate Beeji by saying, 'He spent his whole life licking the shoes of the Britishers.' Even then, many of his British friends came to visit him at his house in the Peer Makki lane. We kids would look at them with wonder, and feel proud of our grandfather.

If this was the month of July then why was it not hot? Why was my bed up in the terrace room where we only slept in the beginning of winter? Or else, it was used only during the rainy season, as all the cots and beddings used for sleeping on the open roof were placed in this room. But where was the rain now?

After a few days I came to know that I had been virtually unconscious for four months. The day that Daarji had kicked the bowl of potato nuggets, the day the morsel had got stuck in my throat, that day I was running a temperature of 104 degrees. It was a serious attack of typhoid. As I had not been eating at all for the past week or so, I had become very weak. And no medicine had any effect on my typhoid for a long time.

The moment the typhoid abated, pneumonia set in. During the time I had had very high fever, an old nurse had been placing cold compresses on my forehead. What she had overlooked was that the cold water from the compresses used to trickle down my neck to soak my chest and back, and this had made me vulnerable to pneumonia.

However, once the pneumonia had been brought under control, my lungs became filled with water. Or maybe it was my brain that was full of water. I don't recall now correctly what I had been told then.

Then one day the doctors also gave up and told Daarji, 'Stop all her medications. At least let her breathe her last breath comfortably. Let's not give her any more distress. Let her go in peace now.'

At about that time, one of Daarji's doctor friends, Dr Muhammad Yusuf, requested him, 'Let me try one last time. By inserting a needle into her spine, I will try to draw the water from her brain. What's the harm in making one last effort?'

Daarji agreed. And Dr Muhammad Yusuf was able to drain the water out of my brain.

The maid told me, 'Child, such a thick needle. Thicker and longer than a needle used for stitching quilts. The doctor took out a basinful of water.'

In this way I was literally saved from certain death.

If I had died how would I have known how cruel life actually is! How would I have known that life was another name for walking barefoot on thorny paths without even a murmur or a groan! How would I have known how it felt when a being, whom you loved from the very depths of your heart, whom you had created from your own flesh and blood, who was attached to your very being even after the cutting of the umbilical cord, sinks into the arms of death in front of your eyes, and still you are forced to remain alive! How do the days and nights pass then!

And if I had died, how would I have known the euphoria of stars literally falling into my lap when my other daughter achieved worldwide acclaim and renown! What pride is felt in oneself when you realize what an exceptional, alluring lotus you have helped to grow from the quagmire of life.

If I had died, how would I have known the secrets of friendship and enmity, love and hate, life and death, laughter and tears, comforts and hardships! If I had died, then how could all these good or bad stories that I have written, reach you, the reader!

Who would have stood up to the forcefulness of life, its depredations, shoddiness, self-centeredness, political manipulations and tyranny! The quest and effort that had been written into my destiny, who would have gone through those tribulations!

Now that I had come to know the whole truth, then the old calendar, whose month hadn't been changed for so long to mislead me, was updated to display the current month.

Though I had not been to school for a long time, the months had continued to roll by and the classes, too, had moved accordingly. So by this calculation, there were barely four months left for my tenth class exams as I had been admitted towards the end of the eighth class in the Khalsa School. Daarji and Beeji used to say that there was no need to think about the exams. Just 'read your scriptures'. But I kept studying my books while lying in bed, and in the month of March or April 1947, I gave my tenth class exams.

After that we went to Shimla in May.

10

Before we left for Shimla, arson and rioting had started in nearby Rawalpindi. There was a strange terror in the air, like a pall of heavy smoke.

My heart felt as if it was quivering like a wounded bird

in my ribcage. I knew that everyone's hearts shivered in the same manner. Though elders would ever remain elders. They knew how to hide and silence the clamour of the wounded birds within themselves and continued going about their daily routines. However, there was something which was boiling like lava within them. It was as if they were all sitting atop a volcano that could erupt at any moment.

We all tried to believe that these were just times like when an epidemic of cholera or plague had struck. It would attack a few people, kill some, and then pass on like all epidemics.

The whole day would be full of frightening rumours, news, heartrending horror stories, and the night would turn all the terror into reality. All that was whispered during the day, was enacted during the night. All the stories that were told in the camps set up for the people who had been uprooted from Pothohar, as Rawalpindi and all the areas around it was known, took on real hues. Thousands of stories of thousands of people. Of murders, of flowing blood, of fires, of savage insanity, of women jumping into wells to kill themselves to protect their honour, of murders of innocent children, of burning houses and fields. Of those half-dead people, who had crossed a sea of terror, leaving behind the bodies of their loved ones. Without either burning or burying them, leaving them just like that on the naked earth, under the open blue sky, bodies of those very people around whom they had built their whole life. What could be more horrifying than that?

Only those who had seen wealthy landlords being forced to eat in communal kitchens, could understand the anguish their souls must have been going through. Mere words couldn't portray the torment they were being made to face.

And the agony of those parents, whose daughters were snatched forcibly from them by hooligans. Those daughters, whom they had protected even from the very winds, snatched from their arms, as if by eagles and vultures, as they watched helplessly.

And still they had survived. This was all they had to say, 'Oh, why did we survive, when…'

But to remain alive, to continue living just by being alive, can this be experienced at only one level? Aren't there thousands of layers of living? Is there only one kind of awareness after escaping death?

When I ponder over this even today, I find it beyond my comprehension, for it's an unfathomable mystery to me how a person who has gone through innumerable horrific deaths can still manage to stay alive, and for what!

Yet, even at that time, I could feel that those who were alive were living with a heavy burden of guilt. It was as if, even in a new environment, they were carrying their own corpses in the open graves of their hearts—despoiled, clawed, like torn bundles from which tattered rags were hanging out.

The whole day in our house, tailors would sit and stitch clothes and quilts for them. Daarji had daily meetings with the prominent dignitaries of the city. Even today I can recall the helpless moist eyes of Giani Gurmukh Singh Musafir, who later became the chief minister of Punjab, once freedom was gained by our country.

Daarji would go daily to the camps that had been set up. If anyone referred to the camps as 'refugee camps' he would become very angry. They were people who had taken a beating and had been robbed, they were not refugees. They had left behind the mortal remains of their own dear ones, they were not refugees. This is what Daarji used to say.

My love for Daarji grew a lot in those days.

He would take clothes and medicines for those people. He would even bring the very ill back to our home or get them admitted into Mayo Hospital where Dr Raghubir Singh was in a position of authority.

Whenever Beeji went to the camp, I would also tag along.

∾

Cases of arson and rioting now started in Lahore too. All the things that we had heard from those evicted, homeless people, those tales of terror, which were just talk to us till then, and could only be imagined, all those horrible things had started happening in Lahore as well. Similar incidents were beginning to become a reality right in front of our eyes, and step by step were coming closer to us.

The whole night all of us, people from all the houses of Lahore, would either stand guard on the roads, in small groups, or would climb onto rooftops and try to guess which locality the blaze visible in the distance, was soaring from on this side, and from which on the other side.

'Shahji, that is Shahalmi from where the blaze is rising.'

'Sardar Sahib, a phone call has just come from Ravi Road that looting and pillaging is going on within the Bhaati Darwaza. People are also being murdered.'

Just then a surge of slogans would come from the direction of Gawal Mandi, 'Nara-e-Takbeer...Allah-hu-Akbar!'

Everyone quaked with fear. We children would cower like wet chickens.

Then all of a sudden supportive slogans could be heard from the Gandhi Lane behind our house, answering calls from all directions, 'Jo Bole So Nihal, Sat Sri Akaal'...'Har Har Mahadev.'

And throughout the night, this flood of exhortations rising like a whirlwind from all sides would continue.

Daarji–Beeji would keep telling Jasbir and me to go downstairs and sleep. But on nights such as those, where does sleep just disappear, I don't know.

All night long there were blazing infernos all around. Sometimes from here, sometimes from there, suddenly flames would arise, leap towards the sky, as if they were in a conspiracy to burn the very firmament.

The sky would get burnt, all the stars would burn up like fireflies, and their charred remains would be wafted by the wind onto our roofs. This is what I imagined at that time.

Then that night came, the night we saw from our rooftop, a man running frenziedly on the road, screaming, followed by a bloodthirsty crowd, ready to pounce on him and finish him off. And then, the sudden gleam of a knife in that darkness. A devastating scream. The man fell down on the ground. We could hear his shrieks of pain for some time. Then everything was quiet.

A quietness worse than a nightmarish silence.

Everyone watching from their rooftops seemed to have turned into statues of ice.

Then Daarji spoke in a tone I had never heard before, 'We will leave in the morning.'

'Leave? Where to?' That was the question that hung in the silence around us.

∞

Morning had to come. It came.

We saw a heap of intestines lying next to the dead man on the road, before the body was removed.

Beeji was making stuffed paranthas and placing them in a hot box.

Daarji said, 'We'll take only one trunk, just pack a couple of sets of clothes for us all. Take off your bangles and give them to Baiji. We will take only enough for the journey, these paranthas, one trunk, one earthen pot of water. And nothing else. We have to take the children out of here, that's all. People are being killed on the way for their belongings. So that's why nothing is to be taken with us. We just have to reach Shimla somehow.'

My aunt, my mother's sister, was in Shimla. She had already been informed on the phone.

So that's how we left Lahore and went to Shimla.

Everyone was desperately trying to console themselves, 'This is madness. It's like a wind of insanity. It will stop within a few days. Then we will come back. Back to our homes.'

In time I started getting used to living in Shimla. I became acquainted with a few bushes, made friends with some pathways and shared my secrets with some trees.

I also made friends with a girl in the neighbourhood. Her name was Savinder. The basis of our friendship was our shared passion for long walks and the resistance to that by our respective families. They did not consider it proper that girls of our age should go for walks alone.

Savinder's parents argued that she had been betrothed from her infancy to the school-going son of her mother's best friend. It would bring dishonour to her family if she was seen roaming around like a stray animal. My parents had the argument that I was growing up and I should learn something worthwhile instead of going for walks otherwise it would be difficult to find a match for me.

Somehow or the other we managed to extract permission from our parents to allow us to go for walks together, if we could not go alone. But apart from that we had nothing in common. She talked incessantly of her latest clothes, matching dupattas, fancy footwear and jewellery. She also prattled about her husband-to-be and in-laws. I was not in the least interested in her future family and my parents were not in a position to buy me new clothes and matching footwear every day. In those days I used to dress in simple, light-coloured salwar-kameez suits with wide muslin dupattas and purely functional footwear. As a special concession after much entreaty, I was given a pair of canvas shoes to wear for my walks.

Many years later, when my identity was subsumed in Baldev, I suddenly discovered that Baldev was the same school-going boy to whom Savinder was betrothed in her infancy.

I was very young at that time but my conscience and an understanding of the moral code were well-developed. I told Baldev, 'I am not going to meet you from now on. You belong to Savinder.' He had answered, 'I broke that engagement a long time back. It was nothing but a girlish game between two friends and I refused to be their pawn!'

Even then I can't help thinking at times that the reason behind my homeless, nomadic existence was that I had, inadvertently, caused the shattering of Savinder's dreams.

11

My tenth class exam papers must also have got burnt to ash in those raging infernos around Lahore. Those whose answer sheets had turned to ash, how could their results be declared? So when the results were announced, RLO, Result Later On, was written in front of thousands of roll numbers.

But no result was declared later on. The country had been divided into two parts.

If the papers had not got burnt, it goes without saying that I would have failed, because I had not answered even a single maths question correctly. I just couldn't master algebra and geometry. I had just made a few triangles, squares and circles on the blank paper. After all, it was necessary to spend three hours in the exam hall!

After the results came out, Beeji said to Daarji, 'Get her involved somewhere. She keeps roaming the whole day with that Savinder. Isn't there any stitchcraft school here in Shimla?'

Daarji didn't find any stitchcraft school, but from the in-charge of the Court Road Gurdwara, he brought some books of the Giani syllabus, that is, of graduation in Punjabi. 'You have already cleared the Budhimani exams. As you're free nowadays, you might as well study these books and clear the Giani level also. I don't know when things will get better and we will be able to go back to Lahore.'

So I started studying the books he got for me.

We were still in Shimla when the country was divided into two parts and Lahore became a part of Pakistan.

It was as though a catastrophe had struck. Daarji's hair turned grey overnight. On the morning of August 16, he announced, 'I'm going to Lahore.'

Beeji started crying. 'How can I allow you to go into the jaws of death?'

But Daarji was determined. 'My poor old parents are still there, sitting in the face of sure death. It's essential to rescue them from there.'

Beeji then said, 'My old parents are also there. If they are destined to live they will somehow manage to come here. Otherwise like those people who saw their entire families being murdered in front of their eyes, we will also find the strength to face our grief. Think of those whose young daughters were taken away by rioters. Be thankful to the Lord that you're sitting safely here with your family. What was to happen, has happened. Whatever is to happen, cannot be avoided.'

It was the first time I had heard Beeji so confidently verbalize a decision in such a resolute voice. That, too, in front of Daarji!

In the neighbouring houses, in my Nani's house, my aunt's house, in all houses, no woman could utter a single syllable against any mandate issued by the man of the house. If any woman dared to challenge and defy his authority, the man would ignore her, considering her to be dimwitted and stupid.

So it was inevitable that Beeji's advice had no effect on Daarji. The same night, he took the train for Lahore. Beeji kept crying, though her tears were of no use. Both Jasbir and I also sobbed the whole night. We all felt that he would never come back.

With Daarji's departure, the realization that a separate country, Pakistan, had been created, hit us hard, and along with it the realization that overnight we had become poor.

I stayed with Beeji the whole day—cutting vegetables, kneading the dough, making chapattis, washing the clothes, chopping wood into small pieces so that the clay oven would heat up quickly, sometimes breaking the coal into small bits to light the oven. I would mix the residual coal filings with cow dung and mud, make small round balls from the mixture, and place them on the roof to dry. These balls could also be used like coal, to save the cost of buying it; for all the time we were very much aware of the fact that Pakistan had been created, we had become homeless, and suddenly also poor. If we put a few balls on the embers at night and placed a degchi with either some pulses or gram on it, it would get cooked by morning, on its own.

Now Savinder and I no longer thought of going for walks. Nor to the gurdwara. We used to just keep sitting at our respective gates. In silence.

12

It took Daarji twelve days to reach Amritsar. Sometimes the train was stopped on the way and terrified, screaming, entreating families were made to get off and were murdered. Sometimes the train would run out of fuel and come to a halt in desolate areas. In this way, travelling at times on foot, sometimes on a bus or a train, he somehow managed to reach Amritsar.

But from there, there seemed to be no way forward. The army refused to allow him to go any further. All the trains that were coming from across the border, were full of bloodied corpses. Even the trains allotted to the military to evacuate any of the displaced people they could find, were not ready to take Daarji with them. To take a Sikh from this side to that was a sure invitation to disaster. No one was ready to take such a risk for another.

Then Daarji came across an old friend, Sardar Ujjal Singh, Sardar Khushwant Singh's uncle. He had been given the responsibility of taking Muslim refugees from India to the camps in Pakistan safely and bringing back Hindu refugees from there to the camps here. He tried desperately to make Daarji understand the risks involved, but when Daarji remained adamant and unconvinced, he finally said, 'If you're bent on going into the jaws of death, then let's go, I will also accompany you. You're not going to go there alone.'

This is what friendship was, in those days.

In this way Daarji crossed the Wagah border in Sardar

Ujjal Singh's official jeep and reached Lahore. Sardarji's driver was also a Sikh and so were his two bodyguards. Sardar Sahib would often laugh on the journey to Lahore, 'Folks, "Panj Pyare" are going to get martyred.'

They reached the refugee camp in Lahore. The camps were overflowing with people. To find one person from among them all was like looking for a needle in a haystack. But somehow Daarji managed to meet up with Baiji and Bhaiyaji, my grandparents.

Bhaiyaji was a broken man, and the first thing he said to Daarji was, 'Son, we had to abandon the house you made with so much effort.'

Daarji responded calmly, 'No matter about the house, we'll make another. At least you're safe and sound.'

Now he had to look for my maternal grandparents. He went in the same jeep to the Peer Makki area where they lived. Nanaji's friend, Haji Sahib, had a shop at the corner of that lane. He told Daarji that just a month ago, when my uncle had been posted to Delhi, he had shifted his parents to his Kila Gujjar Singh house before leaving. He must have thought it was a safer place than the Peer Makki area.

'If they had been here, we would have kept them close to our hearts,' Haji Sahib said, 'I thought many times about going there to check on them...but you know how the situation is...That area is full of Hindus and Sikhs.'

But this fact was no longer true. By now there was no neighbourhood of Hindus and Sikhs. But then people of all races and religions had always lived in the Kila Gujjar Singh area. In fact, the horses of the Karbala used to be tied up right opposite my uncle's house. That itself was an assurance of security.

Needless to say that in the current turbulent times, all lies had become truths and all truths had been negated. Every honest person was in mortal fear, whether he was a Muslim from Amritsar or a Hindu or a Sikh from Lahore. Death, dishevelled and screaming, was dancing all around to the sinister beats of a dumroo, the small hand drum.

Both Daarji and Sardar Ujjal Singhji reached Kila Gujjar Singh along with the others who were escorting them. The moment they entered the lane, they saw a charged-up crowd surrounding my uncle's house and yelling, 'Let's break down the door! Drag the old couple out! Are they still alive? Or are they already dead? Come on, let's break the door and find out.'

Just then the jeep came to a halt near them. When they saw the latest arrivals, the mob became even more aroused, 'Five of them…together! Five goats…sacrifice them!'

Somehow Daarji gathered his courage and facing them, said, 'Sure go ahead. But this gentleman here is a minister of Punjab. If you kill him, then the governments of both countries will not let you off. Okay, let's do one thing, you spare them and I'll come to you. You can do whatever you like with me.'

The horde of mobsters discussed it among themselves. Maybe they too had got tired of the daily murderous bloodbaths. Maybe they just wanted to take over my uncle's house. For they then said, 'Okay, get the door opened quickly. If they are alive, take them away.'

When Nanaji heard Daarji's voice, he opened the door with shaking hands. Both Nanaji and Naniji were almost half dead. Sardar Ujjal Singh's bodyguards had to pick them up and carry them to the jeep. Then all of them returned to the camp. There Ujjal Singhji arranged one more jeep. He also got hold of four military gunmen to escort the two jeeps. In this way Daarji brought all four destitute old people safely back to Amritsar.

Back in Amritsar, they tried to locate my maternal uncle's wife and family in the refugee camps there. Naniji had told them that my uncle had left for Delhi the previous month. He had received a government mandate to reach Delhi immediately to take charge in the food ministry. My uncle was actually a railway employee. But in those days, the supply of grains would get exhausted, sometimes in one place, sometimes in another. So the government had decided that the charge of managing the scarcity should be given to high-ranking officials of the railways, so that they could be responsible for transporting the grain wherever needed, from wherever it was available. Before leaving for Delhi, my uncle had brought his parents to live in his own home.

But after August 15, when the city of Lahore was burning, and there was chaos all around, the military started evacuating people from some of the neighbourhoods, taking them to refugee camps, under their protection. When people started leaving from the Kila Gujjar Singh area, my aunt also decided to take her children and go along with them. But my Nanaji refused to go, saying, 'Kartar Singh has made us responsible for his house. He had made us responsible for you as well, but now I think you will be safer in the camp. We will stay here. We are sitting in our own home, why should we be scared? The whole situation will simmer down within two or three days.'

But now, my aunt and her children couldn't be found anywhere, neither in the Lahore camp nor in the one in Amritsar. Daarji couldn't find any place to stay in Amritsar. So he went to Jalandhar. Along with him came my Dada–Dadi and Nana–Nani.

Everyone was also worried about Bapuji. No one knew whether he was still in Gujranwala or had crossed over. My Nani kept asking all the travellers at the station, who came from there, 'Oh child, was there anybody in your carriage from Gujranwala?'

Bapuji was my Nani's only brother. As I have related, he had adopted my mother and had brought her up as his own daughter. In that respect he was actually my elder Nanaji, and Beeji's real father, my younger Nanaji.

Finally we got to know from the passengers coming from Gujranwala that Bapuji had started a communal kitchen at the railway station. He was serving food and water to the tired, terrified people travelling on the trains. He had fearlessly set up his own camp on the platform and was doing his best to provide whatever solace he could, in those times of terror and strife. If anyone tried to warn him by saying, 'Bapuji, someone is bound to stab you here itself. Enough of serving others. Come with us and sit in the train,' his response was, 'God will help me complete the number of breaths he has given me. If the number finishes, then no one can save me anywhere. You don't worry about me. May God protect you. May you reach there safely with your family.'

13

One of Daarji's old patients was the commissioner in Jalandhar. He was able to allot a mansion-like house on Grand Trunk Road to us.

It was a huge corner house, opening onto G.T. Road on one side, and onto another road on the other side. I think maybe that road led directly to the Hira Gate. It had belonged to a Muslim family. Such properties were called 'Evacuee Property' (property of those people who had abandoned their houses and left). A family property, whose owners had gone to a strange land, a new country, to save their lives. The new country that had been created by their political leaders ostensibly for them. Perhaps they had gone to live in that country willingly or had been forcibly uprooted and sent to live there.

Despite having been given their own country, everyone was wandering around like lost strangers in an unknown land. From wherever they passed, they left behind flowing rivers of blood and torn and tattered pieces of their own lives...

My grandparents from both my mother's and my father's side, were trying desperately to recover from the trauma they had gone through. Daarji was still getting the house cleaned and set up, when they got the news from the Jalandhar camp that my aunt and her children had been found. They were thinking of going to my uncle in Delhi. But in those days, as all communication channels had been affected, there was no way to send letters anywhere. Besides, nobody knew my uncle's address or phone number.

Daarji said, 'This is such a big house. You folks can also come and live here. The old people will gain support from your presence. I will find out about Bhai Sahib and let him know that you're with us.'

Daarji returned to Shimla and took us back with him to Jalandhar.

One of my maternal aunts and uncle had been in Delhi for sometime now. We found out about my Mamaji by calling up this uncle in Delhi. From them we got to know that he was, in fact, staying with them. No government residence had been allotted to him as yet. Uncle elaborated further and told us, 'You know Bhai Sahib's nature. He reaches office at seven in the morning and comes back only at about eleven in the night. Working non-stop the whole day...It's only if he takes some time off that he will be able to arrange a house for himself. But yes, he has been really worried about his children and his parents. It's good they've all reached Jalandhar safely. Thank the Lord for that! Whenever they want to come to Delhi, they're welcome to do so. I have a government house allotted to me in Lodhi Colony. We will manage to live there very comfortably. I would even say that you too come here along with them. All your patients from Lahore have reached Delhi and are settled here. After Lahore, where else could they settle other than in Delhi? What's there in Jalandhar?'

After being uprooted from Lahore, it was as if we were being tossed about like straws in a storm. There was, of course, no need to consult with Beeji. How would women know anything about such tangled matters?

Daarji announced his decree, 'I cannot even think of staying anywhere outside of Punjab.'

∽

I gave my Giani exams in Jalandhar. I don't know how I passed them.

Daarji now decided that the girl would study medicine. So I was admitted into pre-medical classes, despite all my protests. I had no wish to become a doctor. In fact, Jasbir was still in school when he had decided that he would become a doctor. My uncle's middle son also wanted to be a doctor. Only I had no such inclination.

In truth, right from childhood, it was as if I had been tied to a rope and was led by Daarji in whichever direction he wanted, and I was so used to this that I was totally confused about what I really wanted to do.

I felt that in actual fact I didn't want to do anything. I only wanted to gaze at the changing colours of the sky. Wanted to dissolve and flow with the waters of mountain rivers and streams. Wanted to become a boulder on a mountain peak, which would become one with the snow that covered it and a boulder once again when the thaw set in.

I desired to become a bird so that when dusk fell, I could fly in the open sky, flapping my wings like oars, and return to my nest.

I craved to become a tree which could shed its old leaves and yet always grow new ones. Evergreen trees...which whether anyone watered them or not, looked after or not, could survive with the support of sunlight and rain, spreading out their arms towards the vast sky, like the holy mountain hermits. Whose other branches would bend down towards the heart of the earth. Birds and crows would nest on them, give birth to young ones, and putting them in the care of the trees, roam the whole day for food and fly back only at dusk to enjoy the warmth of their nests. If anyone has the temerity to chop up such a benign tree for fuel, may he burn like that very wood, blazing, giving off sparks and slowly turning to ashes.

I had been going to the pre-medical classes for only a few days when we were to be shown the dissection of a frog in our anatomy class. In the laboratory, the professor of anatomy first made the frog unconscious. Then he placed it on its back on a small wooden plank. Its greenish-white-brown stomach was quivering with every breath. The professor straightened one of its legs and anchored it with a pin to secure it firmly on the plank.

That was it, the moment the pin pierced the frog's leg, I fell down in a deep faint.

I don't know who brought me home, how long I was unconscious. When I regained consciousness, I had very high fever. That fever showed no sign of abating for two whole months!

∽

In those days I was reading only Urdu books which I had found locked up in a dark room of that house. Ceiling-high cupboards full of alluring books!

When the owners had to leave the house and run, looters must have stolen everything from there. Because when we came, there was nothing left in the house other than a hand pump. Even bedsteads and cots had been stolen. Utensils, beddings, clothes, fans, jewellery, money…everything.

Such a big house must have been really luxuriously furnished along with all the associated trappings of wealth, valuables, ornaments, adornments, things to bedeck oneself with. I could imagine how the whole family—maybe many brothers had lived there with their families—must have lived happily together, laughing and talking. The aroma of delicious dishes must have wafted out from the kitchen. The type of aromas that used to come from Haji Sahib's kitchen in Lahore. How the feast must have been spread out and all the family members must have sat down together to eat it.

Poetry must also have been read in this house, along with the Quran Sharif. Namaaz would definitely have been performed here.

But when they departed from here or were evicted, the looters who had cleaned out the house, must not have considered the books worth stealing.

Beeji would sigh and say, 'Our house in Lahore must also be in the same condition.'

Bhabiji would say, 'Dear Lord, may these people also have reached the other side safely. If they haven't already, may they do so. The way You protected us, Divine Lord, please protect them as well. I don't know where the owners of such a huge mansion must be drifting aimlessly.'

One of the rooms in this house was locked. It was really strange how this lock had been left intact. It was a big and strong lock. One of its arms extended down to the floor and was anchored there. In their haste, the looters may have been unable to open this lock. Or maybe someone had put in that lock afterwards as he wanted to take over the house. Who knows! Anyway, none of us touched that lock.

There were many windows in one of the rooms upstairs. Lots of windows. Such a huge room. Yellow-coloured walls and innumerable windows. The outside of the house was also painted yellow. Maybe that's why people called it the 'yellow mansion with many windows'.

We stayed on the ground floor. There was a pump in the courtyard. The pipes and taps put in by the municipality had been taken away by the plunderers. Daarji didn't try to get any new connections.

There was a Muslim refugee camp in Jalandhar from where the people were slowly being sent to Pakistan. And there was also a camp for the Hindus coming from across the border. There were also rumours of cholera spreading in the city, the inevitable outcome of any such concentration of human beings.

Opening onto the courtyard was a long verandah, where twenty-five cots could easily be spread out. In the beginning this verandah was our home. In the corner of this verandah was our kitchen, for which, slowly and gradually, our maid was getting some essentials from the market at Hira Gate—saucepans and frying pans, ladles and spoons, a griddle and a high-edged flat platter, earthen waterpots and buckets, tongs and rolling-pin and so on. In that same verandah, our cots would be spread for us to sleep at night. The two trunks in which all our clothes were stored, were also kept in the verandah.

On the other side of the verandah was a long line of rooms. A neighbour had told Beeji that the people of the house had been murdered in these very rooms. We didn't know if that was true or not. Maybe the neighbour had spun that tale to scare us into vacating the house. Whatever the truth, we never did go towards those rooms. It seemed as if, even today, the souls of those people who had lived in this house, were still wandering about the rooms. We could hear the sound of their sighs. At night, it seemed as if someone was scratching at the doors with their nails. Softly knocking at them.

On the side that opened onto G.T. Road, Daarji had opened his clinic. My maternal grandparents, my aunt and her children, were also living with us. Food for everyone was cooked in that verandah adjoining the courtyard with the pump nearby.

That room full of books was my sacred refuge. Especially during the days that I was ill, those books were my friends, my confidantes. They were the ones to soothe me to sleep at night. And shake me awake in the morning.

Among those books, there were some worn, handwritten as well as printed books about holistic remedies. Maybe one of the older members of the family was a doctor or hakim like Daarji. When I visualized him, I could feel that his eyes were big and authoritative, again like Daarji. He must have had a full, fair face, might have been older than Daarji, with a majestic forehead, white beard, finely trimmed moustache. Holding a patient's wrist, he must also have closed his eyes, like Daarji used to do. And more than half the treatments were done within a few seconds by checking the momentum of the flow of blood in the arteries.

Whoever was the owner of the house, whether a doctor, a vaid or a hakim, was also fond of reading literature. Or maybe his brother or son was the one fond of books. Because along with the curative books, there were many storybooks, books of poetry and also innumerable novels.

The two months that I was down with fever, it was these books that I was reading.

Now you tell me, wasn't this studying? All the mysteries of life's intricate relationships were being revealed to me, layer by layer. Can only algebra and geometry's farfetched and mindboggling formulas be classified as an education? And that in which a live frog is placed on its back, pierced with pins, anchored onto a wooden plank, and its stomach slashed to force unwilling students to understand, that when it was alive, then why was it so!

14

Summer was once again at the doorstep. The whole city was in the grip of cholera.

About that time, one day, Ranbeerji, owner of the newspaper *Milap*, came to meet Daarji and said to him, 'Everybody in Delhi is feeling miserable without you. What are you doing here? Come on, come to Delhi. All your patients from Lahore are in Delhi now.' Without giving him a chance, he himself started gathering the things in Daarji's clinic and placing them in his vehicle. He also packed Daarji's personal belongings. He then made Daarji promise that after leaving us in Shimla, he would come to Delhi.

And so, we went back to Shimla.

After reaching Delhi, Daarji got involved in getting a place allotted to him for his clinic and also in picking up the scattered threads of his life.

He couldn't find a place to live though. The chief editor of the *Tribune* newspaper was not only one of Daarji's old patients but also one of his best friends and ready to help him in any way he could. Consequently, though Daarji would roam here and there the whole day, at night he could go and sleep in the *Tribune* office.

In Shimla, Daarji had bought me the books for the BA English course and told me to study them and prepare for the BA exams. It used to be called 'English only'. Refugees had been given the permission to give the exams in two parts. First only English, then later the other two subjects.

After a few months, Daarji managed to get a couple of rooms on rent in a distant cousin's house. This house was next to a water-drain in Dev Nagar, near West Patel Nagar. (Today that drain has been filled up and reclaimed with houses built over it.)

∞

Now that he had found a place to live, Daarji brought us to Delhi. I was then admitted to a college, which looked more like a dilapidated roadside eatery rather than a college, and which belonged to Harcharan Singh, a famous Punjabi playwright. The college was in Karol Bagh on Hardhiyan Singh Road, across from the gurdwara.

Isn't it surprising? That all these shortcuts—studying at home and sitting for peculiar examinations, a college more like a roadside eatery—were there only for me!

Pakistan had been created in everyone's life. Why didn't my brother's education suffer like mine? Why were only my studies superfluous?

Because he was the son. He had to uphold the prestige of the family lineage. He had to give a concrete shape to our parents' dreams. Daarji had to fulfil his own vision of making him a doctor like himself.

And I was just a girl. Right from birth, I was being chiselled and sculpted to prepare me to go to my husband's house.

❦

Darshan Singh was our college manager. A slim, smart young man, always wearing black glasses. He looked as if he was all the time in deep thought.

One day he asked me, 'Do you know anything about Communism?'

No, I didn't know anything. So with great feeling and dedication he started educating me about Communism.

His brother-in-law had a shop just outside the gurdwara, opposite the college. He used to sell books on Gurbani, booklets, combs and karrhas, the steel bangles of the Sikhs. He also used to keep some of Darshan Singh's personal books on Communism in his shop, taking a great risk, as the Communist party was banned at that time and so were their books. He also had books on Communist philosophy by Marx and Engels. I read each and every book he had, one by one. I began to feel that human misery could be eradicated only through Communism.

After this, Darshan Singh introduced me to many other comrades.

The comrades held their meetings in half-hidden terrace rooms or in some isolated corner of the gurdwara.

Once we had just emerged to go to one such meeting when we met Beeji coming from the other direction. You can imagine the storm that swept through our home!

During our Lahore days, facing innumerable odds, Daarji used to hold meetings of renowned Congress workers in the afternoons, in the ante-room of his clinic, where there was a long cushioned table on which he used to examine his patients. Eminent people like Giani Gurmukh Singh Musafir, Sardar Amar Singh of the newspaper *Sher-e-Punjab*, the proprietor and editor of the newspaper *Milap*, Mahashaji, often came to these meetings.

Now Daarji no longer trusted the political scenario. He held the people who played with politics like a game of chess, responsible for the gruesome Partition.

However, I was given permission to work with my fellow Communists, who were members of either the student federation or were working with the trade unions. But the condition was that these meetings were to be held only at our place and nowhere else.

Many a time, posters for the meetings of the trade unions had to be printed, which couldn't be done in any press outside. With great dedication, I made the symbol of the hammer and sickle with red ink on big placards, and wrote messages on them with black ink. The posters would be pasted on the walls around town by the comrades in the darkness of the night.

15

In those days I was madly in love with Baldev, but he regarded me only as an immature child.

Baldev was our English professor. He gave me a lot of books to read from his personal collection. He even gifted me a book. The plays of Ibsen. I treasure it to this day.

Baldev's love added a new dimension to my life. It seemed as if the moon and the stars, the clouds and the wind, the rising and the setting sun, the waxing and waning moon, the Milky Way flowing across the sky, the chirping birds on the trees, the grass growing on cliffs, all had a new meaning, which had been created especially for me.

My heart would start beating loudly the moment I saw Baldev. So loudly that I felt scared that someone would hear it beating. A mysterious jal-tarang seemed to be forever echoing within me. Playing softly, humming musically.

My days melted into one another, every moment full of emotion, as if there was a waterfall within my very being.

The nights were exceedingly cold yet tender. Bathed in the radiance of the moon and the sheen of the stars. Nothing seemed better than watching the movement of the stars and weaving a bouquet of fantasies. I evaded sleep. I felt that this charming cavalcade would disappear over the horizon if I slept.

And, indeed, where did sleep come to me!

The first story that I wrote, was also to make Baldev aware that even if I was much younger than him, the intensity of my feelings was at par with those of his age.

I read that story at some inter-college function. Professor Ram Singhji, the editor of the magazine, *Naviyan Keemtan*, was present at the function, and asked me to give him the story. Soon after, he published it in his magazine.

Imagine, if I had not written that story and Professor Ram Singhji had not published it, then today I would have been making chapattis in a clay oven. And I can't say for sure even today if writing stories is better than making chapattis!

ॐ

After completing my BA in English, I started studying for the other two elective subjects, economics and political science. Baldev had started preparing for the IAS (Indian

Administrative Service). Instead of meeting in college, we would cycle to the Ridge to meet.

I needed an excuse to go towards the Ridge area, so I took admission in a stitching course at the Singer Sewing Machine Centre, which was in Connaught Place. To go to Connaught Place from the Karol Bagh college, one had to cross the Ridge area. Maybe there was another route, but I knew of only this one. On either side of that road were ancient mounds of rocks, rain-washed and sun-baked, on which we would sit and talk, feeling as though the whole world had been encapsulated and bestowed at our feet.

Naturally, people at home would have got to know about it sooner or later. And so they did. A storm came, clouds thundered, lightning flashed. Finally, Daarji himself met Baldev. And very surprisingly, became his admirer.

Baldev was, after all, very good-looking. On top of that he was preparing for the IAS examinations. Daarji was ready to bless our alliance. But on the condition that till the wedding, Baldev wouldn't meet me. I would have to sit quietly at home and prepare for my BA exams, and he for his IAS.

So my going to college came to a stop. I tried to disregard the suffocation of the present with dreams of tomorrow's pleasant rainfall.

I think that was the first time, and maybe the last, when I put all my effort into my studies. After all, Baldev was appearing for the IAS, so how could I fail my exams?

〜

During those days I wrote a number of stories. Many of them were published in magazines like *Naviyan Keemtan, Lok Sahitya, Preet Larhi*.

The first fan letter that I got was from Nanak Singhji. I felt as if I was floating on air. What a great personality he must be, who, despite being a renowned writer himself, took out time to encourage a new and unknown storyteller, one who, due to shyness and hesitation, had never sent her work to any well-known author for advice.

Incidentally, what I thought of Nanak Singhji then holds good even today, that he was in no way less than Munshi Premchand. It was the unthinking Punjabis who didn't value this novelist, this father of the new-age novel. If he had been a Hindi or an Urdu writer, the critics would have had a tough time comparing the value of these two eminent writers. Where Munshi Premchand based his stories in a rural background, Nanak Singhji depicted the travails of a middle-class urban lifestyle in his books. Each writer is one up on the other in portraying the difficulties of life, its rebuffs and rewards, its magnificence and ugliness. Each is better than the other in unveiling the human mind, layer by layer.

After this first letter, I got a number of letters praising my stories, from people like Balraj Sahni, Sardar Gurbaksh Singh and his son, Navtej Singh, Mohan Singh and Kulwant Singh Virk. I began to feel that I had actually become a writer!

The one letter that didn't come was from the person from whose library I had borrowed the first Punjabi book I read, that is, Kartar Singh Duggal Sahib. Today when he praises any story of mine, I feel like asking him, but stop myself from doing so, 'Where were you when I was eagerly waiting for a few words of appreciation from you!' Now it doesn't matter, for he has even dedicated one of his books to me, and I am very proud of it.

But the situation in my house was still the same. I had to write and post my stories secretively. When they were published, I had to hide that newspaper or magazine.

One day I was quietly reading a book when suddenly

a huge shadow fell on it. I looked up. Daarji was standing there. He was holding a Punjabi magazine in his hand. His eyes were blazing, and his cheeks were red with anger. He seemed incapable of finding the words needed to scold me. If whipping had still been practised, as was done in royal palaces in the time of kings, to teach arrogant servants a lesson by whipping them to the bone, then he wouldn't have needed to think twice.

He thrust the magazine towards me and asked, 'What is this?'

I was silent.

'What is this nonsense you have written? Considering yourself a great story-writer! What brazenness! Did we bring you into this world so that you could show us such a day? What have we done to deserve this disgrace?'

I was silent.

He was unable to decide what more to say to me and how to say it. So in a thundering voice he summoned Beeji, 'Jaswant Kaur!'

Beeji was right there, hiding behind the door.

First, both of them must have torn the story apart. Then both must have beaten their heads and lamented, God knows how much more this girl is going to trouble us. What is written in our destiny! 'Ask her, what she has written in this story, how did she know all this? And tomorrow, when everyone asks us the same question, how will we answer them? It's our image that will take a beating. Tell her this, I am warning her, if after today she ever dares to write a story, what will be the consequences! And if she wants to write, she has to first show it to me. I will read it first and then decide if it's worth being read by others or not. Now listen to me carefully. Tell her all this. Otherwise no more studies. I will lock her up in a room. This is the only punishment for such an insolent girl…' Daarji, standing one foot away from me, brandished the rolled-up magazine like a sword, ordering me through Beeji who stood in the doorway with tears in her eyes.

I wept without saying a word. Beeji glared at me as if to say, 'Heard all that?'

She said to Daarji, 'I have always said, what is the need of educating girls? We also learnt Punjabi from Gianiji at home. We are not dead because of that. We're still alive. And that Prakash, whom Bhaiyaji allowed to study up to tenth class, what comfort was she able to give? Did she become a Collector? Her husband went off with another woman…and she quietly took the poison given to her by her husband. What did she manage to do by becoming educated? She couldn't even make a statement to the police. Left a lifelong, relentless grief for those who gave birth to her. All your studies will remain completely unusable. Even an illiterate is regarded as efficient and competent if she settles into her new family. If she can't adapt herself, even the most educated ones remain sitting in their own homes. You just make her give up her studies.'

Normally Beeji rarely spoke at such length. But now it seemed she had got a good opportunity to do so. If a culprit is receiving a lashing, all the passersby pause to watch the show. This was my mother! Even though she had never taken me lovingly onto her lap, at least she had carried me in her womb for nine months. She had a right over me. With great difficulty she had got this opportunity to show a discerning wisdom. How could she let it go?

Daarji asked, 'When are the exams?'

'Next month,' I managed to say in a quaking voice. Daarji said to Beeji, 'Till her exams she will stay at home. She will not go anywhere outside at all. Kaka will take her with him for the papers and bring her back as well.'

Kaka, that is Jasbir, studied in DAV school then in the ninth or tenth class.

He was being appointed my bodyguard.

16

I passed the exams in both the elective subjects and got my BA degree. That was the end of my studies.

Daarji wrote to Baldev, 'We want the wedding to take place as soon as possible.'

He had been selected for the IPS (Indian Police Service) instead of the IAS, and was in Mount Abu for training. Baldev's response was, 'I had told you earlier as well that I will first marry off my sister. But if this is your wish then you can get the ceremonies done as soon as I finish my training.'

And he wrote to me, sending the letter to me through a friend, 'If you also want the wedding to take place so quickly then so be it,' as if the onus of it all was completely on my shoulders.

I saw red. 'If you also want,' what did that mean? My self-respect was really hurt.

Like Mansoor, I could have willingly accepted the stones thrown at me by the people and happily gone to the gallows. But just a flower tossed towards me by Baldev had left me blood-spattered.

I made an announcement, 'I will not marry Baldev.' I knew what effect that dramatic statement would have on Beeji and Daarji, but nothing would make me change my mind.

～

Life has a strange way of playing out. I was no princess but like the princesses of folk tales, I used to send messages to Baldev through a friend, a girl whom I knew.

It was a period of emergency and letters coming through the mail were bound to be censored. The days of the carrier pigeons had long been over.

Reproachfully, my friend had conveyed my decision to Baldev. He had reacted sagely, explaining the philosophy of love to her. He said that love was akin to worship. It was pure as driven snow and it was not affected by the states of being married or unmarried. Whether you live together or not, your devotion remains the same, etcetera, etcetera.

To cut a long story short, my marriage was arranged with someone else. My friend conveyed the news to Baldev. He was still under training for the IPS at Mount Abu.

I got married and went to Karnal. I'll tell you that story a little later.

After five or six days Jasbir came to Karnal and brought me back to Delhi as was the convention. I had been in Delhi for about ten days. My husband was scheduled to come and take me back in a few days. But my parents didn't know that I had been threatened by my husband that as the daughter-in-law of his house, I was found to be deficient in the usual domestic skills such as cooking. I was advised to learn cooking, especially non-vegetarian dishes. He would come and take me back only when I had mastered this art. Otherwise I could stay at home with my parents.

Duly chastised, I had set about learning the so-called domestic skills, particularly cooking, when my friend, the one who used to carry my letters to Baldev, gave me a letter from him.

'If I understood before your marriage what I have come to realize now, I would not be faced with such terrible suffering. I cannot bear it. Whenever I think that I can no longer hold your hand and talk to you sitting in the sun, a violent storm begins to rage in my mind. This storm is so overpowering that my frail body cannot contain it. For the first time in my life, I am dying to hold you in my arms. For the first time I have learnt that spiritual proximity is meaningless without physical closeness. I think the accident of your marriage was necessary to destroy the misconceptions with which I have been living for the last three years. I have come down from Mount Abu to take you back with me. I shall wait for you at the railway station tomorrow night. If you do not come by the midnight of November 2, I'll place my pistol on my temple and…not because of any resentment or anger against you but only because I can bear this suffering no longer.'

That letter came to me on October 17. I still remember that misty day.

I rushed to Baldev's house with the friend who had brought the letter. I should not say Baldev's house because I waited at the other end of the street where his house was situated. My friend went and fetched him.

I felt as if I was being rocked by an earthquake. The ground under my feet seemed to have converted into a crumbling wooden plank adrift on stormy waters.

But the biggest miracle was my self-control. I don't know how I managed to prevent myself from falling into Baldev's arms.

So, I stood courageously watching Baldev walk towards me with his familiar rhythmic gait.

I have no recollection of when my friend left, when Baldev hired a taxi and which route the taxi took. I was aware of just one thing—that he was close to me and he was holding my hand in a tight grip.

I don't know how and why he took me to Roshanara Garden. We had never been there before. Maybe he wanted to avoid the familiar rocks and trees so he took me to an unfamiliar place.

At the far corner of the garden was the gardener's house. The gardener greeted him with affectionate familiarity and placed a string cot under a large tree thick with foliage. He asked us to be seated and fetched an earthen pitcher full of water. He poured cold water from the pitcher in an earthen bowl and offered it first to me and then to Baldev.

We spent several hours there sitting in complete silence. A silence that was much more eloquent than the conversations we had had for three years.

We had discovered a third dimension during that silent conversation, even a fourth dimension if such a thing exists.

Dusk fell and it was evening. The gardener returned and started lighting his hearth. Like hearing the distant cry of a bird, we were reminded of the time.

We stood up in silence. In silence we came out of the garden and got into a taxi. He asked the taxi driver to stop near my house, pressed my hand and said softly, 'On November 2. New Delhi railway station.'

Today when I look back I am filled with wonder. How firm were our beliefs at that time! For example, the faith in God and the confidence in our willpower. It seemed that the intensity of love and the purity of our hearts were enough to protect us from any eventuality.

Baldev had said that he would wait for me till twelve o'clock on November 2 and if I did not reach there, he would place his pistol...Oh God, how I trembled to think of that. By then, I would be back in Karnal. However, somewhere in my mind there was the firm belief that I would stretch out my arm from Karnal and hold his hand and that critical moment would pass.

Do not ask me how I spent those fifteen days. It was like being on the bank of a river of fire through which I had to swim in order to reach the other side.

On November 2 at midnight I felt as if my soul was being nailed to a crucifix. The nails were not driven through my hands and feet. They were driven through my heart and my forehead.

It seems strange now because I have left behind unburied the carcasses of so many beliefs. But while my convictions were still alive, I had felt that at midnight on November 2 I was standing close to Baldev and I had placed his hand on my eyes. His hand could not have pressed the trigger, besides it couldn't have ignored the responsibility of brushing off my tears.

∾

Years later, I went to look for the road Baldev and I used to travel only to find that it had disappeared. Like a child lost at a fair, I searched hard and for a long time, but that old road seemed to have been sacrificed to a maze of new streets. Not only that road, but all those lovely trees, rocks that looked like squatting sheep, the sun quivering through the swaying blades of grass, and the ancient ruins—all were gone.

That is what I call a massacre! Genocide!

The new roads went a different way. The rocks that had been blasted to lay the new roads still showed their wounds which were red like newly spouted blood.

I could see a few bushes still standing terrorized but they were not the ones I was familiar with.

Even if we search for and find our old haunts after a long passage of time, we discover that we can't identify with them in the way we did before. In my case, I couldn't even locate those places.

∾

More years went by. The crystal clear waters of time were muddied by a stream of dirt and trash.

My convictions and beliefs started falling off like yellow autumn leaves leaving all the branches of the trees bare like helpless, outstretched arms.

And then, I don't know how, but like a turtle-dove returning from alien lands, my elder daughter Arpana, who was just Dolly at that time, alighted on a bare branch. I used to be filled with compassion for that tiny creature when I looked at all those bare branches around her.

Arpana was very ill one day. Her father, who was a doctor, had laughed and said, 'She is not likely to survive now.' He lifted a white, thread-like object with a matchstick from her stool and commented 'See, this is a part of her intestines which are disintegrating.'

Saying this he had left for his clinic to treat and cure other patients while I sat stunned and scared, holding Arpana in my arms. I had gone weak in my legs and arms and could not even call out for help.

Suddenly there was a knock on the door. I saw a tall and beautiful girl wearing a red choora standing at the door. 'I am Baldev's wife,' she said gently. Through the fog surrounding my mind at that moment, her features looked soft and lovely. There was a tender expression on her face. However, because of the numbness that had settled on me due to Arpana's illness, I can't recollect exactly how she looked. I wouldn't be able to recognize her if I saw her now.

Later, whenever I tried to recall her face I would see just her hair and Baldev's face bent over her face.

'Baldev has told me everything,' she spoke again, 'We have come to meet you.'

'We?' I asked, surprised.

'Yes, I have left Baldev waiting at the turn of the road,' she said.

You cannot see the 'moment of decision' but we have all

felt it challenging us sometime or the other. I said, 'Please give him my good wishes. That is all.' She stepped forward and held me tightly in her arms.

Even the most generous and broad-minded woman considers the 'other woman' in her husband's life a dead weight on her chest. Her embrace had the feel of gratitude at being freed from that dead weight.

She removed a gold ring from her finger and slipped it on mine. 'My name is Satwant. From now on we are sisters.'

Considering my state of mind at that moment I shouldn't have heard anything, but obviously I did for I remember each word she spoke.

A long time passed after that incident. I never met her again. Neither her nor her husband. But I did catch a glimpse of Baldev on one occasion.

I was teaching in a school at Daryaganj in those days. A good movie was showing at Golcha. One day the school was closed unexpectedly early and I decided to go and see that movie.

Before the feature film they showed a newsreel, which included the coverage of the Tansen Festival being held in Gwalior. One shot showed Ustad Bismillah Khan playing the shehnai. Suddenly the camera moved towards the audience and I saw, with a thrill of recognition, Baldev sitting in the front row! In a moment, the camera moved in another direction. Baldev was lost to me once again.

The next day I went to Golcha again. I bought a ticket and went inside. I had decided to watch the newsreel and then leave. But it was a different newsreel that day.

∾

Still more years passed and then my autobiography started being serialized in *Nagmani*. After reading about Baldev, a woman came to Amrita Pritam and said, 'I am Baldev's sister-in-law. He is now in Delhi. Here are his house and office addresses and this is his telephone number.'

I did not write those addresses and that telephone number in a diary. I wrote them down in my heart. But I never called him up. Somehow, I felt safe now. Delhi was no longer an alien place. Baldev resided somewhere close by.

17

Let me reel back my story to the time when I made my pronouncement, 'I will not marry Baldev.' Daarji lost no time and immediately started asking all his friends and relatives to quickly find a match for me. A couple, who were his patients, told him about a potential match. The wife used to write poety, and the husband, novels. He had self-published his first book at his own cost. They told Daarji, 'We know a very good young man. He's a scholar. It's a good family. He used to bring out his own newspaper.' The man's name was Dr Gopal Singh Dardi. Daarji said, 'That seems good enough. Please arrange a meeting, let's meet him.'

Daarji's friends came over within a couple of days with the prospective groom and his family. After tea and snacks, Daarji left the two of us alone.

I was shivering. There was no question of looking at him. Not just him, I could not look anyone in the face in those days. I was scared, that others would see Baldev in my eyes.

He said, 'I have read a number of your stories. Writing such profound stories at such a young age is something really great.'

I became a little confident.

He asked again, 'Have you heard about the place Honolulu? I have been thinking, that we should go to Honolulu for our honeymoon.'

Honolulu? Where was that? It must be some place outside India. Honolulu.

The boy's family liked me and gave their approval for the match to Daarji before leaving.

The very next day the writer couple arrived at our place again. 'Today is Tuesday, please hold the engagement ceremony on Saturday,' they said, smiles writ large on their faces.

Daarji exclaimed, 'So soon?'

They said, 'The boy has to go to America for a month. When he returns, the wedding can take place then. His family and yours will have a whole month to prepare for it.'

Daarji agreed without further argument. Why wouldn't he agree, he was getting rid of a troublesome problem, me!

Daarji was not able to find out much about the boy and his family. From the boy's sister, who happened to be one of his old patients, Daarji got to know that the boy used to publish a newspaper. However, according to his friends (the writer couple), this was temporarily shut down, but would start again after the wedding. It was a weekly paper, that too, in English. That is, the esteemed English language. Daarji had also read that newspaper a number of times. This was more than enough information.

'Bringing out an English newspaper is no mean task. Not everyone can do it,' he told Beeji proudly.

There were hardly three days for the engagement, and these passed quickly in preparations. Daarji did everything on his own as Beeji was again unwell.

All the relatives were informed on the telephone to come on Saturday. It was to be a simple ceremony. The boy's family had said so, and Daarji said the same to all.

There was a lot of activity in our house on Saturday. We were still living in Dev Nagar. Where nowadays stands the Prehlad market, that area was an open space then. There was a row of houses just a little away from the road. Our bungalow was in the row of houses directly opposite to it.

As much activity as there was in the house, that much weary sadness was present in my heart. Not even sadness; it was a sort of disinterested apathy. Like just before the storm, there is a stillness in the air. Like the way the high-flying kites pause before a heavy downpour, testing the strength of the coming storm with their outspread wings. The way the wind-carved lines on the sands in hot deserts await with bated breath, the touch of the gouging wind.

But I was not waiting for anyone.

A little while later, the sound of a band could be heard coming from the end of our lane. As soon as he heard it, Daarji, in great agitation, hurriedly went out. Beeji was still not well, and was lying on the bed in the inner room. A number of our relatives and their children also followed Daarji out into the lane.

Daarji became a little troubled when he saw the cavalcade bearing down onto his house. He had not made any special preparations to welcome the prospective in-laws' family arriving in such a grand way. He had only prepared for a small, simple ceremony.

Anyway, they had arrived now and had to be welcomed. Tea and snacks were served. The groom and his family were seated in the drawing room, and Daarji and my relatives struck up a polite conversation with them.

The boy's sister took me to Beeji's room where she was lying down, with all the ladies of my family sitting beside her. Despite not being well, Beeji's face was glowing.

The boy's sister, that is my sister-in-law-to-be, opened a few boxes. In the first, there was a very heavy saree. The second contained a jewellery set. There was a makeup box as well. She laughed and said, 'The ring is in my brother's pocket. He will put it on your finger soon enough.'

Then she asked me, 'Will you be able to wear the saree yourself or should I help you?'

I kept quiet. I had never worn a saree. Neither did I possess a petticoat or a blouse. She went on to say, 'In the hurry, we forgot to take your measurements, and so didn't get a blouse stitched. What should we do now?'

Beeji had a loose shirt-type blouse of an old saree. Made of 'china boski', it was full-sleeved with pleated cuffs. That blouse and Beeji's petticoat—and somehow the saree was wound around me.

I kept feeling that any time the saree would slip down and I would stand exposed before all.

My sister-in-law-to-be laughed openly at that and then gathering the saree pleats, pinned them together with a big safety-pin. She pinned the shoulder pleats firmly to my blouse with another safety-pin. And made me wear the jewellery set.

In the outer room, her brother placed the ring on my finger.

ॐ

During this whole pageantry, my youngest uncle, that is my youngest aunt, Avinash's husband, seemed to be very tense and gloomy. He didn't smile or laugh, neither did he give me his blessings like the others. He didn't even bless the boy. He kept wandering in and out of the rooms in a lost way.

Eventually everyone left. Night had fallen. Uncle was still sitting there as if buried in the chair, immersed in deep thoughts.

Daarji asked him, 'What happened, Bhai Sahib, are you not feeling well?'

Uncle literally burst out, 'Go to hell, Bhai Sahib! I live in this city, couldn't you call to consult with me? I agree you're older, very wise, but at least you should discuss and take the opinion of your relatives. Let me tell you one thing, no one is so wise that he doesn't need anyone's advice.'

Daarji laughingly responded, 'Oh, you've taken offence! But what could I do? There was so little time. They gave their acceptance on Tuesday. There were just three days...'

'Why? Was the girl running away somewhere? Or becoming an old maid? As it is she had to complete her BA in a shortcut way due to the Partition. But she is hardly sixteen. Girls at this age are still playing with dolls. What was all the haste about? They said, the engagement will be on Saturday and you agreed. You should have sought counsel. Found out about his family and home. Had we all died? You could have asked us.'

Daarji looked at him worriedly and said, 'It seems you know something particular about them, that's why...'

Uncle looked at me in a way as if he didn't want to share anything in front of me. He stood up and said, 'Let's go to Behenji's room.'

The lines on Daarji's face deepened with anxiety. This was the first time that I had seen such distress on his face. Looking at his face, I felt a surge of pity for him.

For the first time in my life I became aware of the fact that I had always created problems for Daarji and Beeji. In that moment I decided in my mind that come what may, I would not give them any more trouble. After my marriage, however much my in-laws troubled me, beat me up, I would not let my parents be aware of it.

And I didn't go back on this decision for a long time.

The other marriage that took place a year and a half later, I kept roasting like corn in a furnace in it for thirteen years, yet never uttered a word of complaint in front of my parents.

Uncle told Daarji that he knew this family well. He played bridge daily at the club with the boy's brother. The boy was not twenty-eight years old but forty. He had brought a large amount of money from abroad in the name of his newspaper, which he had exhausted, maybe dissipated it in buying properties and other things. He now wanted to get married to maintain a dignified image in society.

Forty years! Daarji was horrified. He himself was barely fifty years. No, no it wasn't possible, how could he have been so badly mistaken! He had been made a fool of! The first time in his life.

Uncle said, 'I can show you his correct date of birth. The person from whom they have got their insurance done, is also my bridge partner. I can call him up right now and ask him. Tomorrow is Sunday. He will get his file from the office on Monday and show it to you.'

The file was examined on Monday. Uncle was proved right. He was just a few months short of forty.

There and then, Daarji called up the writer couple, 'I have some urgent work with you. I need to discuss something important about the marriage. Please come right now.'

They came happily. Uncle and Daarji took them into a room and closed the door. For a long time Daarji's and Uncle's loud and angry voices could be heard admonishing the writer couple, who were instrumental in setting up the match. There was not even a whimper heard from them.

The door opened. Daarji came out. From Beeji's room, he took the box with the saree, also the one with the jewellery set, and the ring, and went back into the room. He put all the things into their hands and said, 'Take all their stuff. Give me a receipt for all this. And also write that you people have fooled me. And that this match is at an end. Put all of this down in writing.'

Whatever Daarji said, they wrote it down. And so this chapter of my marriage was closed right there.

We got to know the inside story later on. The novel that the husband had written and published at his own expense, had not sold a single copy. His house was full of those books. The person I had got engaged to, had a good influence on the board of Punjab University. Maybe he was a member of the board or what, I don't recall clearly now. The deal was, if the couple got him married to a good girl, then he would refer the book for the university syllabus.

Whatever had to happen to me, happened! God knows what happened to his novel!

18

Now again, the same problem. What was to be done with me? In my mind I used to say, slice me up like a turnip and put me in the sun to dry, you'll get dried wedges!

It was as if I was hanging in mid-air. Not only to Beeji–Daarji, to myself, too, I felt like a superfluous burden. I would either be doing the household chores or reading books. Beeji would get angry whenever she saw me reading and insist, 'Stop reading these worthless books, recite the scriptures.'

And so, to make me focused on prayer-reading, she gave me the responsibility of reading the Sukhmani Sahib every morning, the Rehaas Sahib in the evening, and a recitation of Kirtan Sohila at night before going to sleep. I pleaded with Beeji and Daarji to allow me to do my Master's, but to no avail. I had neither the right words nor the daring courage to talk to a father like Shahenshah Alamgir. I could only make him aware of my anger and discontent by not having my meals, wearing dirty clothes, lying around the whole day, or periodically disappearing onto the terrace. But these childish rebellions had no effect on anyone.

Daarji was busy looking for another match for me, Jasbir in his studies and Beeji in her various illnesses.

When she was not ill, she would be busy around the house. Even though I was the one doing the maximum work in the house, I still felt completely unnecessary.

It was at about this time that Principal Niranjan Singhji came to our house. Daarji had given him his newly constructed house in Patel Nagar to live in, for he had once been his teacher and now had nowhere to live.

I brought a lemon drink for him and he asked me, 'What are you doing nowadays, child? Are you studying?'

Daarji said, 'No, she has finished her studies.'

The principal looked at me carefully from behind his glasses and asked, 'Till where have you studied?'

Daarji said, 'She has completed her graduation. Now we are looking for a match for her. If you know of any good boy...'

He intervened, cutting Daarji off mid-sentence, 'What's her age?'

'She is sixteen now.' Daarji was feeling like a criminal. He became a little distraught. It was not easy to accept a transgression in front of a teacher. 'Actually her mother remains ill a lot. She says she would like to have henna applied to her hands before she goes. How would I manage on my own later on?' Daarji tried to excuse himself.

'Apply henna? Do you want to apply ash to her hands? Is this any age to marry her off?' Niranjan Singhji reproached Daarji gently. Then he asked me, 'Why child, why don't you join post-graduation?'

I was quiet. I looked sideways at Daarji. In front of his teacher, he was in a fix.

The principal repeated again, 'Why child, don't you want to do MA? If you wish to, then come to Camp College tomorrow. You will get admission, but half the session is already over. Will you be able to catch up?'

Daarji sat stiffly in his chair, and fidgeted with discomfort. Hesitatingly, he said, 'But…Camp College is co-education, isn't it?'

'So?' the principal demanded, looking straight at Daarji. In his look, in his tone, there was a mild rebuke.

Daarji was silent.

'I am the principal of that college, am I not? Can anything go wrong there? I am really surprised, Doctor, that despite being so intelligent…' He stopped meaningfully, refusing to say anything more.

Maybe the spoken words wouldn't have been as effective as that which was left unsaid.

'Yes, as you say, Sir…' Daarji capitulated.

I felt such an affection towards Principal Niranjan Singh in that moment, that I wanted to throw my arms around his neck and hug him. I felt like kissing his feet. But I could only say, 'Would you like some more lemonade?' My voice was quivering with happiness.

Niranjan Singhji smiled, sensing my emotions. 'Next time I will come and have food prepared by you. But today I will take your leave.'

I couldn't sleep that night, I was so happy.

Actually, if you ask me, I was not very fond of studies. Neither did I want to hang the medal of an MA degree around my neck. I was just delighted with the fact that now, for at least a year and a half, the chapter of marriage would be closed. Who knows, maybe in the interim, Baldev may burst forth from somewhere like a spring shower. Maybe he would realize his mistake. The second thing was, now I could spend some time outside the house every day, breathe freely in the open air. And the third thing was that I really wanted to do my Master's in English literature, so that I could read lots of novels, stories and plays in the language. Then nobody would be able to question why I was wasting my time reading useless books!

ॐ

Classes at Camp College used to be held in the evenings.

Punjab University had set up this college in Delhi for those students who had had to drop their studies in between on being uprooted from the new Punjab across the borders and now had been forced to settle here in Delhi. During the day, they had to work to earn a living. But if they wanted to continue with their studies, they could come to this college after their office timings, at five o'clock.

Like there were camps for the refugees, in the same way Camp College had been set up for their studies, on what was then known as Reading Road, from where you take the turning to Gole Market, just before Birla Temple. In the morning, the same premises functioned as a school, and as a college in the evening.

The very next evening at five, Daarji reached the college along with me even though this was his clinic timing. Daarji was very particular about timings.

In all the eighty-two years of his life, anyone could synchronize their watches with his reaching and leaving the clinic, he was so precise.

So he was in a hurry to drop me at the college and get back to his clinic.

Reaching the office he asked, 'Where does Sardar Laabh

Singh sit?' Principal Niranjan Singh replied, 'I will explain to Laabh Singh. The first year is already half gone. But he will have received my orders. You go and get your daughter admitted tomorrow. He's in charge of the office. He will also inform you about the fees, which you can then deposit.'

Laabh Singh welcomed Daarji with great respect. He offered us water and tea. He must have understood that Daarji was a special friend of the principal, since he had given such specific orders for the daughter.

As I said, Daarji was in a hurry. 'Please give me the form quickly, I'll fill it up. And tell me the fees also, I'll deposit that as well.'

Laabh Singhji placed the form in front of Daarji. Daarji filled in my name, his own name and the address. The next column was for the subject. He looked at me and asked, 'In what subject do you want to do your Master's?'

I said, 'English literature.'

My heart was pounding wildly as if I had suddenly been given the moon to play with as a ball.

After filling up the form and depositing the fees, Daarji asked Laabh Singhji, 'What are the timings of the class?'

He told us, 'Usually it is the third or fourth period. Once a week, it's the second, and once, the fifth.'

'When does the third period start?'

'The college starts at five-thirty. Each period is of forty-five minutes. So the third period starts at seven o'clock. And the fourth ends at eight-thirty.'

Daarji faced me and said, 'Then you can't do post-graduation in English. Out of the question! How will you come back alone so late? Do you want to do it in any other subject?'

All my enthusiasm vanished. In a half-dead voice I said, 'Political science.'

He asked for its period timings. There, too, the situation was similar. Third and fourth.

So political science was also consigned to the waste basket like a useless bit of paper.

Now only one more subject was left, which I had studied for my BA. And which I hated desperately. That was—economics.

Daarji himself asked Laabh Singhji now, 'And what is the position of economics?'

'That is in the first two periods. First and second.'

Daarji gave me a decisive look and announced, 'If you want to do it in economics, I'll get you admitted, otherwise let's go home.'

He was getting late for his clinic and I knew he was in a hurry. Now I had no option other than to hold onto a straw to stop myself from drowning. I nodded my head to give my consent, 'All right. Economics.'

Another form was filled up once again. Dreaming of English literature, I got admitted into economics. If not chapattis, then roasted gram. If not roasted gram, at least a sip of water.

Then and there I decided in my heart that I would come to college, read a lot of English-Punjabi-Urdu books, would make a few friends, gossip with them. Even if I didn't make any friends, I would sit in a corner of the lawn, under a tree, and write stories. And after one and half years, would fail with flying colours!

At least for the next one and a half years, the sacrificial goat's neck would be safe from the knife of marriage. For at least one and half years I would be able to spend some part of the day away from the oppressiveness of my home.

But I didn't fail. I had not read any economics book. I had not even filled up files with written notes like the other students. I had not put in any effort at all. Whatever the professor lectured every day, that, like debris, got stuck in some corners, some ruts, of my brain. That is what made everything go wrong. I passed with a third division!

19

Just about then, one of Daarji's old patients from Lahore, called up from Karnal to say, 'Last year you had asked me to look out for a match for your daughter, and I had told you about the sons of a doctor friend of mine. One son was studying in a medical college in Amritsar and though he was still in college, had already decided to marry a classmate, once they had finished their studies. But the second, who ran a poultry farm, could be considered as a match. At that time, you refused saying that poultry farming was not a worthwhile job. If it had been the son who was studying to be a doctor, then you could still have considered it. Now, that boy has completed his medical studies and has started practising as well, and his father is looking for a match for him. Have you fixed up your daughter's match yet?'

Daarji trusted this friend of his totally. Once, his son had been bitten by a mad dog in Lahore and Daarji had been able to save the child's life. Since then this friend regarded him as God.

Daarji told him, 'No, I haven't fixed it up yet.'

He said, 'That's fine then. Those people will reach Delhi today. They will come by the three o'clock train. Please go and receive them at the station.'

Daarji quickly reached home. We had shifted to the Patel Nagar house just ten or fifteen days earlier. My Naniji had come to this house for the first time. She had brought a salver of almonds as blessings for shifting into the new house. Beeji, as usual, was unwell. Naniji was sitting and talking to her.

Daarji said, 'Give me my lunch quickly. After that, I have to go to the station. Some people are coming to see Jeet. Pray that all goes well and the match happens.'

Nobody gave importance to the fact that the boy, who till last year was so much involved with another girl that not only his family members, but even his father's friends knew about her and that he planned to marry her. How had he suddenly consented to get married to a girl of his father's choice? What had happened to the other girl? Where had she gone? What happened to that love story?

About three-thirty in the afternoon, Daarji returned home, bringing them with him. The doctor-boy, his doctor-father, and his sister.

The guests were served tea and snacks. After that, the father and son duo stood outside on the verandah and had a long whispered conversation. His father then came back into the house and laughingly hugged Daarji and said, 'Congratulations, Bhai Sahib! We like the girl.'

Then he asked, 'You must have a special room for Guru Granth Sahib in your house?'

Daarji told him, 'Yes, the Darbar Sahib's room is over there.'

He said, 'Okay, let's go and finalize this alliance with His blessings.'

When he entered the room, he knelt down in front of the Darbar Sahib, and touched his head to the floor, then he rose to his feet and prayed, 'Oh true Lord, please place your reverential hand on this couple's head.'

After coming out, he said, 'Please place a rupee in the boy's hand, as your blessings. Only a rupee is enough.'

It was as if he was the stage director. In this show of puppets, all the strings were in his hands. Daarji went into Beeji's room and said, 'They have accepted the match. They are asking us to perform a small approval ceremony for the confirmation.'

Beeji exclaimed, 'Do a ceremony right now? Why? Why are they in so much of a hurry? You please tell them that we'll come to Karnal to talk to them, and we will decide the date also then.'

Daarji objected, 'Impediments should not be placed in the path of auspicious happenings.'

Naniji placed one hundred and one rupees on the salver of almonds she had brought. Daarji placed a wad of notes on it and presented the same salver to the boy.

My father-in-law (as he had now become) said, 'Let's decide the date of the wedding also. Today is Wednesday. I think within fifteen days is fine. Or the weekend after that.'

Daarji said, 'How can the preparations be made in such a short time? My wife doesn't keep well.'

He said, 'What do you need to prepare so much for! It's not as if you need to buy horses or elephants! Or sit with the goldsmiths to get the jewellery patterned and engraved. Everything is available ready-made in the market. You don't worry at all. Please just give us your daughter. You can get her married off in only her wedding dress.'

Daarji was on top of the world! What marvellous people they were! No mention of dowry, no greed at all.

A weekend almost a month later was decided upon as the wedding day. The wedding procession would reach on Saturday. The ceremony would take place on Sunday morning, followed by lunch and then we would depart for Karnal.

There was no question of asking me anything. Even if

I was asked, what could I have said? I had not even seen anyone's face carefully. I had just sat next to them and nervously sipped my tea. If I had met any of them on the road, I wouldn't have recognized them.

Since the beginning it had been drummed into our heads that a girl's eyes should always be kept lowered. It was unthinkable for anyone to go against an age-old mandate.

Nothing happens if you get a Master's degree.

The only difference it makes is that parents are able to proudly tell others that their daughter is an MA pass, meaning that she comes of a better breed of mules! All the stone-pebbles of your family, sacks of flour, tins of oil, the future grandsons and granddaughters (no no...discard the granddaughters! Coming of a good breed, she has to bear only grandsons!), all your relatives, your friends and acquaintances...she will take care of all of them.

She is very tolerant. We have reared her like a cow. She has all the qualities that should be present in the daughter-in-law of a respectable household, she has been fed with a pulverized version of those qualities since her birth. Eyes down, low voice, how to talk, how to sit and stand...we have taught her everything. You won't get a chance to complain.

MA is apart from all this. That is of no value. She will do the cooking, why won't she do that? She'll take care of the whole house. The cleaning, washing clothes...ironing. She knows everything. She has even done a stitching and embroidery course, from the Singer Sewing Machine School. All her dowry sheets, pillow covers, napkins, she has embroidered each one of them herself.

She can play the harmonium. She used to learn devotional songs from a teacher in Lahore, and after coming to Delhi even learnt how to play the sitar.

She reads the scriptures also very well. She was hardly six or seven years old, when her grandfather set her to read the Guru Granth Sahib. She knows Sukhmani Sahib, Japuji Sahib, Rehraas Sahib and Kirtan Sohila by heart. She will recite it for you day and night.

Don't worry about her MA at all. Nowadays you have to educate the girls. But it doesn't make any difference.

And a month later, the wedding took place. I got married and came to Karnal. That is, I was untethered from the Delhi hook and was taken to Karnal by my new owners, to be tethered there!

That was the time when I used to think that whatever was happening with me, that sort of tragedy couldn't happen to anyone else.

Maybe every person who passes through such a situation feels the same.

But then, if I had been born in China, in some village of olden times, in some tribe, or even in some distinguished family living in a city, then at the age of two or three, the soft toes of my feet would have been folded downwards. They would have been bandaged and bound up in wooden shoes. Not for just a day or so, nor for a month either, for years and years, so that I wouldn't remain capable of running away when I grew up. (Though I was always made to understand that having small feet was a sign of beauty. The smaller the feet, the more beautiful the woman.)

I would have waddled slowly like a duck, from one room to the other.

I would have cleaned the house, done all the kitchen work, walking with short, duck-like steps. With every step, I would have felt a twinge of pain. Of those twinges, some would have been for the present, but many would have been for those years when my feet had been tightly bandaged and stuffed screaming into the wooden shoes.

At every word, my back would have to bend over double. I would have had to keep bowing in front of all, my husband and his guests, my in-laws and family.

And to maintain his status, and show off his manliness, my husband would have kept five, ten, fifty concubines. And I wouldn't have had permission to say a word about it.

Perhaps, even in India, if I had been born in some backward village of Rajasthan, my mother would have been forced, threatened or even beaten up to give me poison. She may even have been forced to rub poison on her nipples and on the pretext of feeding me, exterminate me.

If in some way I escaped that sort of death, then at the age of playing with dolls, I would have been married off.

It could also be possible that before I even knew the meaning of marriage or before I could actually go to my husband's house, my husband would pass away. My parents and my in-laws would then take a decision together, that is the menfolk of both households! And as a result, I would be anointed with turmeric, dressed in wedding finery, beautifully made-up, given some herbs to become unconscious and then supported to sit on the burning pyre of my husband. I would have been burnt alive.

Sometimes I think, if I had been born in some Middle East country, I would have been circumcized at an early age so that for my whole life, I would have been unable to experience the pleasures of sex. I would have been raped all my life, and given birth to babies one after the other to propagate my husband's family. I would never have been allowed to understand what were the physical needs of my body nor feel the satisfaction that comes when those needs are fulfilled. Depriving a woman of such a satisfaction was considered the way to keep her virtue intact. A virtuous and chaste woman should have no knowledge about sex. Even though her husband slept with her every night.

All the sensations in my body would have been murdered, torn and thrown afar and that, too, at an age when I would have had no understanding of what was being done to me.

My body would have been made just a utility item, a vessel. And I would not only have been unaware of one of the foremost pleasures of human life, but also be deprived of it.

Sometimes I think, if I had taken birth in a country where it was unacceptable to be seen alone with a man, then I would have been labelled as a woman of loose character and burdened with guilt. As a punishment I would have been whipped or stoned to death. Whipping is an age-old custom and is done with a sturdy leather whip. When it lashes the back, it literally tears off a strip of flesh. If the whip is moistened, the welts are deeper.

To kill a woman in this manner, was considered to be an act of virtue, if that woman had broken the rules of society. And every man was ready to earn this virtue.

Sometimes I think, if I had taken birth in the house of a temple Devdasi, then serving all the 'Lords' of the village would have been a moral obligation for me. I would have been taught that if I spread myself out like a welcoming flower-bed to satiate the desires of the menfolk of the village, then that would make the deity and goddess, whose temple was in the village, very happy.

And the daughters born to me would also have suffered the same fate.

Sometimes I think, if I had been born in some village in southern India, amongst simple-minded rural folk who had faith in Yellamma Devi, to a mother who had borne only daughters, then my father, uncles and grandfather would have been devising ways to get rid of me.

If, in that village, a gang seeking girls for a brothel happened to come, and somehow managed to involve some person of the village, then for a small amount, and the temptation of having a stomach full of food for a few days, a loving hand would have caressed my head, with the purpose of anointing gum on a strand of my hair.

After a few days, my mother would have been shocked to see that gummed-up strand while combing my hair. For a gummed-up strand of hair is the sign of Yellamma Devi. Yellamma had called this child. Had asked them for her.

In this country, a storm or even an earthquake can be ignored, but not gods and goddesses.

So I would have been bathed, got ready, made up with vellum powder, and taken to Yellamma Devi's temple and left there. From where, once I reached maturity, I would have been taken to some brothel in the city.

Or, if I had taken birth in some village, in a working-class family, in any village or tribe of any part of Hindustan or Pakistan, then the landowners whose land my father tilled, any of them, could have at any time abducted me, and thrown me away after despoiling me.

Not a single soul in the whole village would have uttered a whimper, for the owners of the village had a right over every girl, every girl-child, every maturing girl, every matured girl. This belief had been encouraged and inculcated in everyone for ages.

Through the umbilical cord joining the mother and child, age-old convictions, trust and distrust, fear and terror, criteria for respect–disrespect, for happiness–sadness, and ways of living life in a half-dead fashion get transferred to the psyche of the unborn child. In the mother's womb itself.

On the birth of the child, the cord gets cut, but the transferred bundle of beliefs remain grounded in her, lifelong.

That's why the whole village was of the conviction that their masters had the first claim on a girl's virginity.

It was even possible that after the wedding, on the first night itself, my husband might take me himself to his master's doorstep, and leave me there, humbly folding his hands, even prostrating before him.

But all this I can think today. At that time I could only feel that there was no one more unfortunate than me.

20

The wedding was over. I was taken to Karnal.

By car from Patel Nagar to the railway station. By train from the railway station to Karnal. Again by car from the railway station in Karnal. Roads. And then after the roads, a network of dimly lit bylanes. The car stopped outside a wide doorway and was immediately surrounded by women. They were humming something in low voices. I don't know what they were singing.

I was helped out of the car and taken inside the house. No one welcomed me with the ritual of pouring oil on the doorstep, nor any of the other rituals connected to a new bride entering her new house.

I didn't realize it then. It didn't come into my mind at all. Later on when a lot of nonsensical debris had gathered around me, all the old incidents would come back to me. My mind would segregate and dissect every small occurrence that had happened.

After this dissection, I would understand some things and some, not at all.

The moment I crossed the threshold, the first thing that hit me was a strong, unpleasant odour. Just inside the main door, on the left side, was the privy-room, like the one in Lahore, without a flush system. But in Lahore, the privy was on the roof, that too in the far corner, so that the smell wouldn't be wafted around the house. But here the stench was all over the house.

A little further, the reek of cow dung and the odour of animals. Even though the buffalo and its calf were not inside the house but tied up outside in the lane. I got to know about the buffalo only the next morning; at that time, I could only experience the unidentified, nauseating smell coming from the cow dung and the other animal stenches.

Then a long courtyard. And after the courtyard, a verandah. There was a cot placed near a post in the verandah, and I was made to sit on it. There was an eerie silence in the house.

Today I can look back and see myself at that time. A pink bundle sitting wrapped up on the cot. In the late evening of the 5th of October, in a closed courtyard, surrounded by the women of the neighbourhood and the family, sweating profusely in a pink suit, wrapped in a pink veil.

Even today when I recall that moment, I feel the pinch of the zari embroidery on my suit. The kaleeras hanging from the bangles on my wrists had started to pinch, as much as the calculating looks of the women touching and feeling my jewellery. Even today when I recall that, I get drenched in sweat.

And the words of the women surrounding me...'Oh, she's more beautiful than the other.'

The other? Who?

Dinner had been laid out on the table. Everyone was eating, there was chicken, or maybe mutton.

I found it difficult to eat even half a chapatti. When my husband had eaten his fill, he got up from the table. When I saw him standing up, I, too, stood up.

Nobody noticed, or paid attention to the fact that I had got up without eating much.

After dinner, my sister-in-law took me to a room on the terrace on the roof. There were two cots outside that room on the open roof. She made me sit on one of those cots. While going, she informed me, 'Your trunks are in the room behind. If you want to change your clothes, do so.'

I was in the habit of taking a bath at night. But on the roof there was not even enough water to splash my eyes with, let alone have a bath!

I went inside and opened my trunk. Nightie? Should I wear a nightie? No. Maybe I should remain in these clothes only. Let 'him' come, then I will ask him...I looked around me. There was a pile of wheat in one corner. In another, onions. Against the wall, huge trunks of quilts, with smaller trunks on top. A mountain-like pile of dirty, discoloured trunks. On the other side of the room was a pile of dirty cotton, the kind taken out from old quilts and mattresses. Winter would start the next month. Maybe the old cotton was lying there to be carded and refilled into new quilts before the onset of winter.

The roof and the corners of the room were crisscrossed with spidery lines, as can often be seen in old houses. Lines of white ants. The air in the room was stale, and it was full of spider-webs. And in the centre of the room, were placed one trunk and a small suitcase, a part of the numerous trunks I had brought as dowry.

Suddenly, I heard the sound of his footsteps climbing the staircase. I came out and sat on the cot, shivering.

The moment he came up, he asked, 'What's the matter? You haven't yet taken off these useless things?' He pointed towards the kaleeras on my wrist.

This was the first dialogue—'You haven't yet taken off these useless things?'

I stood up nervously. I went back into the room and started to open the trunk. He opened a small cupboard on the wall and said, 'Keep them here.'

I could not unbind the kaleeras. My hands were shaking too much. I removed all the red bangles that I was wearing along with the gold ones as the kaleeras were tied onto them. I kept them in the cupboard along with all the jewellery I was wearing. The necklace, earrings, everything.

In the meantime, he took out an album from the other cupboard, and indicated to me to come closer, 'Have a look at these pictures. Otherwise tomorrow when you hear the neighbours talking and gossiping, you'll start complaining. That's why I thought I should tell you about it all myself.'

And one by one he started turning the pages of the album. In some, there was a picture of a girl alone, and in some, with my husband, and elsewhere, with him and his friends. The same girl, in every picture.

As he turned the pages, my husband told me the story, 'We both studied together in Amritsar. Our marriage had been finalized, but then something went wrong. That aunt from Singapore? She had come down especially for my wedding. Many other relatives had also come for it. There was only one week left for the wedding. But…everything is destined. Anyway, my aunt couldn't go back without attending the wedding. She has some personal reasons for that. That's why Mehta Sahib quickly found you.'

I understood some of what he was trying to tell me, but the rest I couldn't.

He placed the album back in the cupboard and said, 'Okay, now go to sleep, the day has been tiring...'

And lying down on the other cot, he turned his face away. Within a few minutes, his snores were vibrating in the air.

I sat for a while in a stupor, on my own cot. Then I too lay down.

In a shadowy sky, dim stars were trying to twinkle bravely. Were these tears mine, or were they falling from the sky?

No, I didn't cry that night. There was no denying that I was unnerved by all that I had had to face that night, was totally befuddled and confused at the turn of events, but all of it had made me so stone-like, that I just couldn't cry.

Life takes unexpected turns and things happen without warning, and yet a forewarning was being given that night, that the doors of my emotions were being shut tight and not only locked from outside, but also nailed and sealed.

That night I remembered neither Beeji, nor Jasbir, nor Baldev.

Looking back, I don't understand why I didn't think of them. My mind should have revolted against it all. I should have fought with them all.

I should have fought with Daarji, that when last year your friend, Mehta Sahib, told you that he had his eye on a boy who was into poultry farming, why did you refuse him? The suggested boy was the son of his doctor-friend, his middle son. But Daarji did not find poultry farming an acceptable profession. His brother was doing an internship in Amritsar after completing his medical studies, but had already selected a girl for himself and they were considered more or less engaged. And now suddenly, when Mehta Sahib had called out of the blue, 'That doctor boy is available now. They are coming to Delhi. Receive them at the station,'—why didn't you ask him about the girl he was earlier engaged to? What had happened to her?

Maybe my father-in-law had sat down with Mehta Sahib and made him call. Maybe Mehta Sahib couldn't refuse him so he spoke to Daarji. But he didn't want to face Daarji, so didn't come to Delhi with them.

Why didn't you ask Mehta Sahib why he hadn't come? And Karnal was not Canada that you couldn't go there to check them out. I had always heard that parents asked a hundred questions before giving their daughters in marriage. Why hadn't you made any inquiries?

I should have fought with Beeji, asked her why had she not even once taken me onto her lap like a mother? When I was very young, why was I not allowed to play? When I was on the threshold of adulthood, not once did you sit down with me to make me understand the changes happening in my body. Why did my garments get soaked with blood? Instead, you had looked at me with amazement, as if I had committed a crime and only said, 'So soon?' So soon what?

Each time that I was caught talking to Baldev or our letters were intercepted, all that was said was, 'Get her married off quickly, otherwise she'll bring disgrace to the family name. This immoral profligate has cut off our nose. Don't know what wrongs of a past birth she has come to avenge by being born into our family.'

Constantly the same refrain, 'I remain so ill all the time, get her married while I'm still alive. What will happen to her after me? Alone how will you...' and she would start crying in front of Daarji.

Listening to all her lamenting, Daarji had begun to

believe, and I, too, had begun to accept, that without my getting married, Beeji would not be able to breathe her last easily. The best way to give her peace of mind, help her be free of all her illnesses, bring tranquillity into her life, was to get me married off.

I should have fought with my brother, that when you used to go to drop me at college, and some boy from my class would ask me in your presence, about something the professor had said, you would look at me as if I had been caught stealing something red-handed, and then relate it in a misconstrued manner at home so that I had to face a lot of flak. What did you want to show by that, that you were fulfilling your duty as a brother to the hilt? Where were you when a stranger was taking your sister to his house as his slave? Couldn't you see then which well they were going to drown your sister in?

My whole life I kept tying rakhis on your wrist. What protection did you give me?

I should have actually fought with everyone.

Once in my childhood, when my Dadaji and I were taking a walk on Shimla Pahari in Lahore, a nail in my shoe started pinching me. The whole way my Dadaji had refused to listen to my pleas to check the nail which was pinching me, neither did he pay attention to my tears, nor stop to ask a cobbler on the way to remove or hammer it in, and the nail continued to bite into my foot. When we reached the top of the hill, a stranger saw me crying and asked me the reason, so I told him about the nail. With the help of a stone he hammered it into my shoe. When we reached home, Dadaji told everyone that I had been talking to a stranger. Daarji slapped me so hard that I fell against the rack of utensils in the kitchen. And he had given his royal decree, 'Be warned, if after today you ever talk to a stranger again, I will kill you!'

Now how did you send me away with a total stranger? Go, take her, do whatever you like with her. She is your property now.

༄

I don't know what time I slept that night. Did Jesus Christ manage to sleep the many days He was on the cross? I did manage to fall asleep, finally.

When I woke up in the morning, the merciless light of the day was piercing my eyes. I stood up in a panic.

Oh Lord! How did this happen? A clear, bright day had dawned. What must everyone be thinking, that the spoilt girl from Delhi is still sleeping even after the sun had come up?

I quickly got up, and neatly folded the bedclothes on both the cots, and placed them on the cot inside the room. Then I thought, should I let the other cots remain outside or bring them in?

I heard the loud sound of footsteps climbing the stairs and my heart started to beat wildly, stabilizing only when I saw it was my sister-in-law. She came into the room, smiling naughtily.

'Why Bhabhiji, up so early? Okay, come and have your bath. Take out your clothes from your trunk and bring them down with you.' I nervously opened the trunk to do so.

Suddenly, as if she had just remembered something, she exclaimed, 'Oh, I had almost forgotten! You can't take the clothes out just yet. First my aunt and all the other relatives will choose clothes for themselves from your trunk. Only after that can you take out anything for yourself. It is a custom.'

Custom? Auspicious? The clothes for all the relatives had

been placed separately in one of the other trunks as part of the dowry, with each of their names on them. They had sent us a list. I had packed them myself in gift-wrapping paper. Sarees and suits for the ladies. A Kashmiri pashmina shawl as well for each close relative. For all the aunts, an article of jewellery. A woollen suit-length, a shirt piece, tie and handkerchief for each male member of the family.

And not only relatives, my father-in-law had added the names of his close friends (some well-known personalities of Karnal, and some of his patients as well) to this list.

But my mother had taught me this much before coming, don't ask any questions. Agree to everything quietly. You have to keep everyone happy. And the biggest lesson, that the house to which you're going as a bride, you should leave it only on a bier—this has been the custom of our family. And this also, that woman represents the Mother Earth, so like the earth should be able to bear all crosses with equanimity.

So I remained silent.

My sister-in-law said, 'Do you want to go to the bathroom yet or not?' and started laughing raucously.

She took me downstairs. But before going to the toilet, I touched my father-in-law's feet, then my mother-in-law's, and then Buaji's also. While I was touching her feet, I felt that everyone was laughing.

It was only Buaji who gave me blessings from the depth of her heart, 'May you have a long life, find happiness, be blessed with your husband, lots of money, and worthwhile sons!'

When I touched Buaji's feet, my sister-in-law burst out laughing, 'Oh, it will be my turn next! I'm not less than Buaji, am I?'

After that it became a routine, daily in the morning and before going to sleep, I would touch everyone's feet.

My puny thoughts made me think that maybe in this way I could get closer to their hearts.

Every newlywed girl hopes and expects that the house she has entered, the piece of land on which she stands in that house, at least that should be solid. If she manages to make a little space for herself in that unfamiliar house, that unknown family, at least that family would not intrude into her private boundaries. Just a little love, a little respect, a little tenderness, a little affection, this is all that every girl desires.

Every girl, who right from childhood has been hearing, 'Tomorrow you have to go to your husband's house,' or else 'You can wear such clothes when you go to your own house. You can be as fashionable as you like in your own house. When you're in your own house, you can go to the cinema,' and so on, has the expectation that the strange, new house she is going to will give her a hitherto unknown freedom to live her life as she wants.

No girl can ever decide which is her own home. And which another's! A totally confusing concept!

Parents are also strange. To make their own prison strong, they show you dreams of that 'other house'…that 'other house' is going to be your own, you can do whatever you like over there, go wherever you want to. This house is just like an inn, where you are to be prepared to go to the next house, that is, your own house. You have no rights here, neither can you enforce anything here and nor do you have any responsibility. This is your father's house. And after your father, your brothers'. You have to fly away like a bird from this house.

When you go to your house…

When you go to your house…what then?

Whenever they wanted to scare you, they would say, 'Learn some sense, tomorrow you have to go to your husband's house. They will throw you out of the house by your plait if you open your mouth unnecessarily. You'll only get kicks if you raise your eyes insolently. They will leave you at your parents' threshold if you don't know how to cook or take care of the house.'

What should she understand from all of this? Which is the 'own home' and which the other's? Which is that house, where the girl has the right to live her life according to her own choice? Which is that house, where she doesn't feel as if the earth is not sinking beneath her very feet?

Actually, the truth of the matter is that a woman has no home of her own. First she has to live in her father's house, where she is continuously intimidated with the fact of her going to the 'next house'. And groomed and chiselled for her departure.

Then comes her tenure in her husband's house. Husband, whom she has to regard as the Divine Lord and Master. His house, where she has to go as a bride and can only leave it on the funeral bier. Where her husband has the full right to rape her whenever he chooses to do so. The law gives it the name of 'conjugal rights'.

And whenever he feels like it, he is at liberty to kick his wife out of the house.

༄

That's why when I used to wake up in the morning and while going to bed at night, I would touch everyone's feet. Maybe in this way, I could create a secure place for myself with all the blessings that I would collect.

When I think about it today I realize that even the blessings given are all for their sons. 'Sada suhagan raho'—that is, may our son have a long life. When you become old, may he still be alive. 'Putrvati bhav'—that is, may you bear sons for our son. Sons, who will take the family lineage forward.

21

Early in the morning, Buaji would make the mash for the cattle while humming her daily prayers. The whole night the buffalo would remain tied up to a hook in the lane outside, along with its calf.

In the morning both would be brought in and the buffalo given a bath. The calf would also be bathed every few days. It was Buaji's task to feed them and she would do it very lovingly, talking to them affectionately.

The calf was kept a little separately from its mother, so that he didn't drink up all the milk.

While the buffalo was eating, its halter was tied to a hook. Whenever she moved her head, the bells around her neck would tinkle.

She would look with sad eyes at her calf, whose bucket of mash would be placed a little away from her.

As the buffalo ate up her quota of mash, Buaji would go on chanting and stroking the buffalo's back with her rough hands, also oiling her horns. Sometimes she used to make garlands to place around their necks. Then everyone would make fun of her, 'Why Buaji, are you going to send her to her bridal house?' And some times, 'Are you trying to bedeck the calf to be a bridegroom?'

༄

Bua! Everyone called her Bua.

'Bua…just wash these few clothes and dry them…Bua, please sweep the floor from here…Bua, don't sit idle, cut the vegetables please...Bua, please knead some dough...Bua, you haven't heated the earthen oven yet? When will the chapattis be made?...Bua, today there was very little butter, are you sure it didn't dissolve in the buttermilk?...Bua...Bua...'

Bua's chores would start before the sun rose, and maybe she finished them sometime after everyone went to sleep. At least I had never seen her tasks coming to an end.

At night when I climbed the stairs behind my husband to our room on the terrace, I would surreptitiously look at Buaji. I used to feel guilty, I don't know why.

She used to do all the work within the house. Only for milking the cows did someone come from outside, morning and evening. After milking them, he would place a bucketful of frothing milk outside the kitchen door, the onus of the disbursement of the milk falling back on Bua.

Considering her age and relationship, everybody naturally called her Bua, but my father-in-law, who was actually her brother, also called her that. As if her name was Bua.

Maybe Buaji had been a child widow or had become a widow in early youth, I never got to know. Anyway, her in-laws had sent her back to her parents' home. Not in Karnal, but in Gujarat, the Gujarat that is a part of Pakistan now. After the creation of Pakistan, many people had come to Karnal from Gujarat and here, from the evacuee property, the houses of the Muslims who had gone to the 'other side', my father-in-law was allotted a big mansion.

Now Buaji had become very old. She was older than my father-in-law. But she looked so aged that people mistook her for my father-in-law's mother, or thought she was his aunt, and so the whole family addressed her as Buaji.

Women usually fade away earlier. Become older quicker. For a woman's form is as delicate as a flower. Everyone says that a flower wilts away very quickly, no wonder that a woman, too, withers fast.

But I also feel that Buaji became old early, because other than the buffalo and her calf, no one else needed her love. Apart from the buffalo and her calf, no one else loved her. The whole day, every day…going constantly through a mechanical grindmill, bereft of any closeness, a woman is bound to get older quickly. When she has no hope of a better tomorrow, has nothing new to look forward to, she's bound to age quickly.

More than half the women in this country age before their time only due to this reason.

∽

Buaji, a little bent, slightly lame. The flesh on her face was like crumpled wastepaper. Her eyes appeared to be deeply sunk into her skull. They were always watering and she was continually wiping them with the corner of her veil.

She was dark-skinned as though she had been baked in the fires of life, scorched and smoky.

My in-laws had clear complexions, you could call them fair. But among the children, only my youngest brother-in-law, Mahinder, had a fair complexion. My sister-in-law, my husband and my older brother-in-law were on the darker side. Even for this my sister-in-law used to blame Buaji and say, 'At my birth I am sure Bua must have been there, her shadow must have fallen on me!'

'Don't talk such needless rubbish. May the shadow fall on your enemies. May my child always live happily,' my mother-in-law would lovingly scold her and caress her head. What she meant to say was, why should this unfortunate woman's shadow fall on her darling daughter, causing her life to be similar to her aunt's! Her daughter would be married off with a lot of fanfare. She would remain married forever. Children would play in her house. She would rule her house. Why should the shadow of such a luckless woman fall on her precious daughter!

The youngest, fairer than all and everyone's darling was my brother-in-law, Mahinder. He was the only one who would talk affectionately to me. One was him, and the second, Buaji. These were the only two people in the whole house whom I didn't fear.

In such a big, spacious house, Buaji used to walk in a cowering fashion, sit in a huddle, lie as if she was a small inconspicuous bundle, and speak in a timid manner.

The whole day her hands used to remain busy. The whole day she would be immersed in some task or the other. Even then, my sister-in-law would laugh derisively at her, saying, 'Bua can't be trusted at all! I told her to grate the radish to make stuffed paranthas. Don't know in which daydream she remains lost, she cut them up. Now we'll have to make a dish out of them. And no one likes to have that dish. So we'll have to make Bua eat only that for the next few days. Right, Bua?'

And Buaji would cringe in embarrassment.

Whenever I saw Buaji, I was reminded of Rohini's mother. She, too, used to sit the whole day on a low stool like a shrinking bundle, in the kitchen of that huge mansion, wearing a white muslin saree. God knows how much pain that pale-faced, simple woman was holding inside herself. No one cared. She spent her days just cooking or roasting or frying. Her very being would cringe at the sound of her father-in-law's footsteps going up and down. At every call, she would run barefoot to her mother-in-law's room.

When the cooking-roasting-frying was over, she would turn to clipping the betel nuts. When that task would be over, she would make papadum and nuggets of dried lentil.

Similarly, Buaji would also never be free. Bathing the buffalo, looking after the calf, cutting and cooking the vegetables, cleaning the kitchen shining-bright, stitching the quilts, repairing everyone's torn clothes, dusting and cleaning the house. And if after that she got time, then in the afternoons she would knead a dough of refined flour and make vermicelli. In the season of fenugreek, she would fragment the branches and dry them on a sheet spread out on the cot on the roof. In the season of turnips, she would make garlands of cut turnip wedges and dry them. She would make pickles and conserves...

Every widowed woman works like a bonded slave for each morsel that goes into her mouth. On her own. No one has to force her to do so. Maybe it's her own feeling of obligation.

'We cannot depend on our husband for anything as he has passed on. He cannot fulfill our expectations. That's why we have to survive on your benevolence. We are living respectably within your walls, beneath your roof, wearing the clothes you have given and eating the food provided by you. Obligated to you, for you have given us sanctuary in your house...

'Oh compassionate ones, those sheltering us, may you be blessed! We, who are imprisoned on silent islands of loneliness. We implore the Divine for your family's peace and harmony, happiness and love.

'We call down benediction for a perpetual flow in your coffers, for the food you give us. We found a safe haven beneath your roof, for that we call down blessings on your mansions, your tall edifices. For the clothes you have given us to cover ourselves, we hold out our hands to ask for fine silk shawls and clothes from the Divine for you and your family...

'We are always ready to serve you all our lives. Till we don't complete the punishment for some negative karmas from our past life. Till the Lord doesn't call us to Him. Till then...

'We'll cook your meals, scrub and scour the utensils, launder the clothes. Cutting-grinding...we will do everything. We'll take care of your children, do all the dirty tasks for them. Will feed them, bring them up. May they be ever blessed...may your children be ever happy. May your sons serve you well in your old age, and may your daughters be happy in their homes. May you always receive pleasant tidings from them. Blessings for the children, blessings for their well-being...'

22

This was the world in the lower portion of the house. That is, the actual house, where all the family members lived, guests and relatives were welcomed. The outer room functioned as my father-in-law's clinic, morning and evening. Though his actual clinic was in the marketplace.

But the world on the roof, in that terrace room, that is, mine and my husband's world, was still on the same track as on the first night. There was no change in that.

The only difference was that, the first morning, that had dawned so late on that open roof in front of the room, had started to dawn very early now.

The whole night I would watch the position of the stars, and try to guess the time from their movements. Though it stands to reason, in a new place, a new house, it takes time to understand their movements as well.

༄

The first morning...My sister-in-law Darshan brought me downstairs.

I wanted to go to the toilet, but my mother-in-law, that is

Mataji, was sitting in the courtyard. My father-in-law, whom everyone called Pitaji, was also sitting there, having breakfast placed on a small table in front of him.

So I first bowed down to touch his feet, to take his blessings. I knelt on the floor and placed my forehead on his feet. He said something. Maybe it was a blessing. I couldn't understand it. I became nervous. What if the veil slipped from my head?

Just then Buaji came limping towards me, 'Oh my! How nicely you have bowed! Bless you! But you don't need to kneel down every time you take our blessings. You can just bend down a little and lightly touch the feet.'

I bowed down to her as well. She gently caressed my shoulders, head and back as she gave me a lot of blessings.

After that day, whenever I touched her feet, she always added two more things to her blessings, 'May everyone in your parental home be happy. May the Lord bless your brother with a long life.'

Suddenly Mataji asked, 'Where are your bangles?' She had seen my bare arms. There was irritation as well as anxiety in her voice. Then she pulled the veil a little away from my neck and said, 'And necklace?' then pulling it aside, 'And earrings? Why have you removed them all?'

I answered softly, 'Upstairs, in the cupboard.' I was scared, I knew I had done something wrong.

Mataji exclaimed, panic-stricken, 'Oh my God, girl, what have you done? You've taken the bangles off yourself? It brings misfortune! Those bangles have to be removed only after at least one month. Go right now, first of all go and put on all your jewellery.'

And then she turned away from me and continued in a complaining tone to my father-in-law and Buaji, 'Just look at this girl! Is she mad or something? Does anyone take off all their jewellery in this way? Especially when the house is full of guests!'

I was quiet. I didn't have the courage to say that it was their own son who had told me to remove it all and place it in the cupboard.

My heart wanted him to suddenly emerge from somewhere and say, 'I told her to remove all her jewellery and keep it away. She's not to be blamed.'

But Raj was nowhere to be seen. Pitaji said, 'Well then, you ask her, whatever she would like to wear all the time, tell her to keep that with herself. The rest should be placed in a box and given to me. I'll go and keep them in the locker today itself. Before going to the clinic, I'll go to the bank.'

I stood there quaking in my shoes. What dimwittedness, what stupidity, I had displayed on my first day in my marital home.

Darshan was laughing at me, 'Bhabhiji, when you get jewellery to wear, then you've to take good care of it also.'

Only Buaji looked at me with sympathetic eyes. I knew that if no one else had been around, she would have hugged me and gathered me to her bosom.

I went back upstairs. I quickly put on all the jewellery again. I removed the kaleeras and placed them in the cupboard before putting on the bangles, then went slowly downstairs again.

Darshan left me outside the door of the toilet. When I emerged from it, I didn't know where to wash my hands. Darshan suddenly materialized, tossing her plaits, and moved to a hand pump near the buffalo trough saying, 'Come here, we wash our hands here.'

I said, 'Oh, please don't put yourself out for me, I'll work the pump myself.'

As a matter of fact at that moment, I was actually thinking

that if I moved forward, I would get the ends of my salwar wet in the water. But Pitaji was still sitting there so how could I pull it up? So I let it get wet.

She started laughing, 'Have you ever used a hand pump before? Do you know how to do so?'

'Yes, I have used it, in Jalandhar,' I replied

'Jalandhar? Lahore and Delhi, these are the two places we've heard that you stayed. Who lives in Jalandhar? Some relative?'

'No, when we were uprooted from Lahore, we stayed for sometime in Jalandhar.'

She remained silent and then tossing her plaits again, moved forward towards the stairs. I, too, climbed the stairs behind her.

When I reached the roof, I was a little unnerved to see a number of ladies sitting comfortably on the cots.

Darshan immediately moved towards one of them and putting her arms around the neck of the fair, heavy-set woman, hugged her affectionately.

'This is our aunt from Singapore,' Darshan said with pride.

Later whenever I recalled that moment, I couldn't understand whether the love and pride was for the aunt or for her being a foreign national? Or maybe for the innumerable gifts from abroad, which she must have brought for them each time she came home? Today I don't recall her face clearly even though thirteen or fourteen years later, this very aunt and her Singapore, were used as a threat for me by my husband. Every time that he wanted to intimidate me, he used to say, 'I'll sell both your daughters to a brothel in Singapore.'

Anyway, I bent to touch the feet of the aunt from Singapore, then turn by turn, of all the ladies present there. Simultaneously, Darshan kept introducing them, 'This is Mamiji, this is Chachiji, this is the neighbouring Auntyji.'

When I had greeted them all, Darshan suddenly sat down on the cot and stretching out her legs, pushed her feet in front of me and said, 'And this is me!' So I touched her feet also. All the ladies started laughing.

'Now open the trunk,' Darshan ordered.

First of all the aunt from Singapore turned the sarees and suits in the trunk upside down and pulled out a saree for herself. Then all the other ladies took out sarees of their choice.

I felt as if a lot of vultures had attacked the trunk, snatching at it. But I didn't feel even a moment's distress. I just thought, it is the custom over here, so has to be fulfilled. Sarees don't matter surely, my husband would buy me more! Besides I wouldn't be wearing so many suits and sarees all at once.

To clothes, to jewellery, I never had any attachment, and don't have even today.

My biggest hunger was for love. I desired that everyone should love me. That they should say, how good is our daughter-in-law, what a great family she comes from. Well-educated, yet not at all proud! Bends so humbly to touch everyone's feet! Girls don't allow anyone to touch their things. And look at her, allowing everyone to take her things so happily!

No, at that moment I was not thinking of my sarees and suits, I was only happy. Strange, isn't it? It was only later that I tried to analyse why I was so happy.

Darshan finally said, 'Okay, now you may take out your clothes, and come and have your bath downstairs.'

The ladies were all descending the staircase. I could hear them talking and laughing gaily as they went down.

I asked Darshan softly, 'Where is he?'

She started laughing, 'Who? Raj? Oh he left in the morning, for the clinic.'

I felt a jolt. On the first day itself, leaving his wife all alone in a strange house…gone already!

I went downstairs in a quandary. How would I come out of the bathroom after taking a bath? How would I tie my saree in such a small bathroom? And where would I keep it while I was bathing?

A very difficult situation. Secondly, the real fact was that till then I didn't even know how to properly tie a saree.

Darshan had disappeared somewhere inside. Buaji was frying something in the kitchen. Not inside the kitchen, but outside in its extended area, in front of the actual kitchen. Pitaji was busy with his patients. I didn't know where Mataji was.

I quietly went upstairs. I put the saree, blouse and petticoat back in the trunk, and instead, took out a salwar-kameez.

I came downstairs and went into the bathroom. I bathed and washed my undergarments, wrung them out and hid them in my hand beneath yesterday's soiled clothes.

Then I remembered my towel. Oh Lord! Where should I wash the towel? There were only four hooks in that tiny bathroom, a low sitting board, a bucket and a mug.

I decided to first go and hang my wet undergarments upstairs. Then I would come back and wash the towel.

I opened the bathroom door to find Darshan standing outside. 'Where are you taking all your dirty clothes?' she said. 'The washerwoman will just be coming, she will wash them.' She took the clothes from my hands and found my wet undergarments beneath them. She started laughing. 'The maid could have washed these as well.'

I slowly went up the stairs. Reaching my room, I wearily sat down on the cot and felt as if I had just returned after walking a great distance, as if I had been on a long journey. I felt drained of all energy.

If, in just having a bath I could feel so tired, what would happen to me when I would have to do other tasks as well? But this tiredness was not due to the effort of having taken a bath. It was a cumulative result of the tension, hesitancy and constraint in creating a new kinship and the resultant effort that is required to make a place for one's self in a new house, new environment, among new people. A fatigue every new bride must experience.

Where was that zeal, that eagerness, enthusiasm, that overflowing happiness associated with marriage, a romantic image of which had taken shape in my heart after reading numerous novels and watching movies? All were conspicuous by their absence.

Instead, there was a deep silence, like the one just before a storm when the sky is dark with clouds and even the wind seems to have been throttled.

I wanted to be accepted in that household. I was ready to wash their feet, press their legs, do the cooking, scrub the floor, wash the clothes, polish their shoes...anything to find a niche in that house, in their hearts.

I only didn't know how to prepare mash for the buffalo. Then I thought, I will learn that as well!

~

In the afternoon, my husband came home. I was sitting with my mother-in-law on the cot in the verandah. Some of the neighbouring ladies were sitting around us, appraising me.

The moment he came, it was as if the whole household had been set into motion. The table was at once set for lunch.

Two dishes, as well as chapattis, were set out, along with glasses of buttermilk.

He quickly washed his hands and sat at the table. Mataji said to me, 'You also go and join him.'

I timorously asked her to come with me. She started laughing, and all the ladies joined in.

'No, no, for today you go and eat alone with him. From tomorrow, we'll all eat together.' Looking at the neighbours, Mataji continued to smile. I hesitantly went inside.

In the confusion, I forgot to wash my hands. But now I had neither the courage nor the time to go back outside and across the courtyard to the bathroom, for he had already served himself from the dishes and was picking up a chapatti.

I looked into the dishes. In one there was mutton, and pulses in the other. I served myself with a little mutton gravy in one bowl, and put some pulses in another bowl. Taking a chapatti, I started nibbling slowly at it.

He continued to eat, as if in a hurry. He seemed to be in the grip of a strange sort of intoxication. A shine in his eyes, a blitheness. Under the table his leg seemed to be dancing.

Suddenly, he said, 'Everyone calls me Raj. Those who are younger, and of course the older people, everyone. You also call me Raj. I wouldn't like to be called Aai-ji, Oh-ji.'

He finished his fourth chapatti and picked up a fifth. He was less restless now, calmer. He asked me, 'And what have you been doing the whole day?'

'Nothing,' I said softly.

'Yes, at least for a few days these ladies are not going to let you live in peace,' he said, gesturing towards the women sitting on the verandah.

Finishing his meal, he went towards the pump to wash his hands. I hastened after him to operate the pump. Then he started climbing the stairs to the terrace. 'Listen a moment,' he called me from the staircase.

I looked towards my mother-in-law, as if to ask for permission. She gave no indication at all of seeing my silent appeal. So I followed my husband upstairs.

'What have you done since morning?' he asked me again when we were on the terrace.

'Nothing,' I replied again.

He started talking about his aunt from Singapore—her husband was a well-known person there. He had received the designation of 'Daatey', equal to a Member of Parliament, from the President of Singapore. The aunt had eleven daughters. In a married life of fifteen or sixteen years, she had had eleven children, all girls, in the hope of a son.

Now her mother-in-law was threatening that she would marry her son off for the second time. Whenever this Singapore aunt came to India, her mother-in-law accused her of getting a talisman from there, to control her son. This time when she was coming for the wedding, she had made the same accusation. Now if his aunt had returned without the wedding happening, would her mother-in-law have let her survive? That's why when things went wrong with the other girl just a week before the wedding, a second option had to be found immediately. It was essential for that aunt's well-being. Poor aunt!

In that moment I felt, that the person who could understand a woman's hardships so well, must be really tender-hearted.

I also felt that a person who could love one woman so consistently for so many years, must be quite remarkable.

But that same person was still a stranger to me. I had to spend my entire life with him. I had to make him my own.

༄

I had always been taught that a man could be made one's own only by negating oneself completely.

'Losing yourself you gain the Divine.' This was the essence of the Gurbani. Even though this thought was for the Lord, for the Divine, I felt as if it could be applied in my case. For my Divine was Raj. The pinnacle of my life. The one ambition of my life.

My identity could remain intact only by his acceptance. Acceptance by his family would strengthen and complete the piece of earth on which I stood. Otherwise it would weaken and collapse. And along with it, so would I. My whole identity would be wiped out. A woman alone had no status of her own. She gained her identity from her previous, and then her later family. That is what I believed. First, in her childhood, whose daughter is she, who is her father, to which family does she belong? After marriage, whose wife is she, daughter-in-law of which family?

.And after that, what offspring has she borne? Has she borne sons or not? If she has, then what sort of boys are they, worthy or unworthy? All this accountability is also on her head. That's how slowly and gradually, her shoulders get bruised, her back gets scratched, deep scars appear on her skin, the hair on her head turns grey, and her neck is always painful.

Raj went to sleep.

His snores reverberated against the walls, the netting on the windows, the mountain of trunks, the roof, the lizard roaming on the roof, the piles of wheat and onions, the mound of bedclothes, the wooden cupboards on the wall, and on me.

23

And so four days passed by. In these four days and nights, he had only once held my hand.

The hunger of the body was still slumbering in some snowy cave. Maybe, because I was still too young. I was well acquainted with the fervour and yearning of love, for I had been madly in love with Baldev. But I was still unacquainted with the passions of the flesh.

Maybe my inclination towards passion was also still unawakened because Baldev had once said that one shouldn't touch the one you loved. He used to say, 'We shouldn't touch our idols, the gilt might come off and stick to our fingers.' And most of my beliefs had been influenced by Baldev's opinions.

It could also be because Beeji and Daarji had always taught that every man was a bestial monster. (Of course, Daarji excluded himself and Jasbir from this label by saying that other than your real father and brother, all men were beasts!) Keeping myself safe from even the shadow of such men was my responsibility.

The fact that Raj maintained his distance, and slept quietly on a separate cot every night, was proof enough that he was superior to such bestial types of men, that he was principled and decent. He would keep tossing and turning while he slept, hitting his legs against the footboard of the cot, writhing... I would watch silently and think, maybe he's feeling miserable. Maybe longing for that girl whom he loved, whom he couldn't marry. I pitied him. Poor Raj!

~

This was my fifth night in that house. Suddenly, there was a banging on the front door. Someone was clanging the heavy knocker on the door.

I woke Raj up, 'Someone is outside.'

He woke up and switching on the light, looked at his watch, 'Who can it be at this time of the night? It's quarter past twelve.'

He stood up and went downstairs.

I heard the sound of the front door opening. And the sound of soft whispers. And then the front door closed. Raj came back upstairs. I stood up and came to the door of the terrace. He said, 'Come downstairs quickly. There is some work.' I followed him down the stairs.

In a basket in the kitchen, were lying a dozen fish. Raj said, 'One of Pitaji's patients has brought them. He said that he had informed Doctor Sahib in the morning that he would bring fish for him. But unfortunately, his car broke down on the way. That's why he got delayed. The fish will spoil by morning. They have to be salted right now. I'll slit their stomachs and you fill them with salt. There is the salt container, bring it here.'

I stood without moving. I had never seen whole fish like this before. Their eyes were open. Those glassy eyes held me mesmerized in a strange sort of fascination.

Raj picked up one of the fish and slit its stomach along the centre, like we split open a bitter gourd.

I could see stars dancing in front of my eyes. Black spots seemed to be rising up, like torn strips of black rags flapping in the dark.

Just then he lifted up something with the point of his knife, round like a marble, completely red, and said, 'Look, its heart is still beating.'

What happened after that, I have no recollection.

I had fallen with a thud. I must have somehow been picked up and placed on the cot, though I was unaware of it all.

When I regained consciousness, Buaji was caressing my

head. Darshan was laughing. I could see my in-laws' faces as if in a dream. Then I saw Raj's face, more angry than worried. His stupid wife had bothered everyone at midnight. Had created a big commotion just because of a few fish!

When we went back to our room upstairs, he asked me, 'Have you never seen a fish being cut before?'

'No,' I said guiltily, as if it was something criminal.

'Have you ever eaten fish or no?'

'Only in Lahore. Daarji sometimes used to order fish from the Capital Restaurant.'

'And mutton? Chicken?'

'Only potatoes and gravy from the mutton dish.'

'Is your family vegetarian?'

'Beeji doesn't have non-vegetarian food, so it's not made at home. Only when guests come, then it's made. We used to have only potatoes and gravy, both myself and Jasbir.'

'Do you know how to cook it, or you don't even know that much?'—his temper was rising every second.

'Beeji was the one to cook mahaprasad.'

'Now listen to me carefully. Tomorrow or day after, Jasbir is coming to take you back to your home. Go with him and learn how to make mutton, chicken, fish, before you come back. When you have learnt how to do so, only then send me a message. I'll come to bring you back here, otherwise stay there.' So saying, he turned on his side, and facing away from me, went to sleep.

Numbly, I continued sitting on the cot, feeling like a criminal, deserving of punishment.

A little later he asked again, 'What have you been eating all these days here then?'

'Gravy,' I mumbled.

It was true, for in his house mutton, chicken, fish, partridge, pheasant, pig-meat, deer-meat were cooked daily, morning and evening, that was all they ate. Till now only once had peas been cooked and once lentils—that's all!

He went to sleep. I lay awake late into the night, feeling I had failed some important exam.

A few days later, Jasbir came to take me home for my first visit after my marriage. Raj talked to him cheerfully, as though nothing had happened.

∾

Back home in Delhi, I asked a friend, 'From where should I learn how to make all these dishes?'

She asked someone else and then got back to me. And so I landed up at Lady Irwin College, to seek admission in the home science course. 'You want to learn only non-vegetarian dishes? That, too, in such a short time?' the girl at the reception said, laughing. 'Here you have to do the entire course which is three years. This is a college, Madam. Not a shop to teach a quick-fix cookery course.'

'But there must be someone who can teach me?'

She thought for a few moments, then said, 'Yes, Mrs Singh sometimes takes crash courses at her home. I'll ask her.'

The next day I took admission in Mrs Singh's course. She lived on Rouse Avenue. It was a three-week course. I told Beeji and Daarji that Raj and his family were fond of eating different sorts of non-vegetarian dishes, so I thought that I should also learn them.

For the first time I saw raw meat. For the first time, I touched it. I tried to shut my mind to it, by making myself believe I was standing somewhere far away.

But the day I saw a whole chicken, without its feathers, neck hanging down...and when Mrs Singh inserted her fingers into its stomach and pulled out its intestines along with other paraphernalia...red and mucus-covered...a darkness began to come in front of my eyes. With great difficulty, I controlled myself and sat down on a nearby chair, willing myself not to faint again. If I had, Mrs Singh would have thrown me out of her class!

I had two aunts, my mother's sisters, and was very attached to one of them. I used to call her Mataji.

Actually I had three aunts, but the third one, Prakash, had passed away years ago, when I was just about three years old. I don't even recall what she looked like. But I remember the hue and cry that had followed her death. In the verandah and courtyard of my Nani's Peer Makki house everyone was wailing loudly.

Her husband had poisoned her, as he was in love with another woman.

My Nani suffered a nervous breakdown due to this shock and never really recovered. She spent most of her time beating a drum and singing the songs that she had sung at Prakash's wedding.

I have based my story, 'This is also History', on this incident. For it had engraved itself on my heart with a burning rod, that a husband has the right to poison his wife and no one can say anything to him, for a husband is a husband. Even if he proffers poison, one must eat it unprotestingly and not even tell anyone. Even with her last breath, his wife should not make a statement in front of the police. Only quietly whisper into her parents' ears that he had given me poison and I took it. What else could I do? When sending me to his house you had clearly said that he was to be my God. That I had to obey his every command. He had said, go to your parents' home or drink this poison. Now you tell me, how could I come back home? How could I let you down? How could I allow either yours or his family's name to be dragged in the mire? While sending me to this house as a bride, you were the ones to say that the house to which a girl goes as a bride, from that very house should her bier depart. For your dignity, for the honour of my father, I ate the poison he offered. No, no, don't worry, it was not at all bitter, he gave it to me in a capsule. No, no, I was not in the least afraid while eating it...

When a girl passes on in such a manner, everyone praises her after her death. All say, 'What a family-oriented girl was she! She let herself become a martyr with never a single complaint!'

Prakash Aunty was the youngest in the family and everyone's favourite. She became even more deeply entrenched in everyone's hearts after the way she had 'sacrificed' herself.

My other aunt was Balwant Kaur, whom I used to call Mataji. Her son was born twenty-nine days after I was born. She sometimes used to breastfeed me as well. In our house, no one used the word 'Mataji'. 'Beeji', 'Baiji', 'Bhabhiji' were the words commonly used to refer to a mother. But everyone told me that when I had just started speaking, Mataji happened to come to my maternal grandmother's house, and the moment I saw her, I addressed her as 'Mataji'. Everyone was very surprised for no one in our neighbourhood ever used this form of address for a mother!

I had managed to hide my feelings from everyone around, but when Mataji asked me, 'Everything is fine, yes, my child?' I could not hide my sadness, though I replied, 'Yes, all is well, Mataji.'

'Then why are you so sad?'

'No, not at all,' I tried to laugh it off.

'Liar! You never lied to me earlier. Tell me truthfully, Raj does love you, no?'

'He will do so, eventually,' I said in a low voice.

'Eventually? What do you mean by that?'

'Actually there was this girl whom he had wanted to get married to. I don't know what went wrong between them. Maybe that's why...'

'That is beside the point now, what I mean is, you two do sleep together, don't you?'

'Yes, upstairs on the roof.'

'On one bed?'

'No.'

'Meaning, till now has he...till now...has he loved you yet or not?'

'No, he's very decent and upright. He hasn't said anything to me so far.'

'He has not even touched you?'

'No, he did hold my hand, once or twice.'

'You're really stupid! Do you get married to hold hands? Even now your Uncle...Don't you feel anything in your heart?'

'No. He goes to sleep quietly. Then after sometime I also go to sleep.'

'If he has not touched you, couldn't you go and sit on his bed?'

I was silent.

The very next day she got a book for me on sex. The book was in English. She must have got it through Mausaji. I was ready to sink into the ground with embarrassment.

She said to me, 'Read this book carefully. And now whenever he comes to take you back, you must hug him tightly on your own. And if he asks you to remove your clothes, don't create a ruckus about it!'

That was my first sex education.

∽

Within a month I learnt to cook everything. To cook, to touch and even eat a little.

I wrote a letter to him. Raj took another eight to nine days to come to take me back.

He met everyone with such affection that I completely forgot the tribulations of the past one month.

When we were alone in the room at night, the only thing he said was, 'I have especially ordered pheasants. To test you and see how much you have learnt!' All Mataji's edicts were of no use! I couldn't summon up the courage to touch him. In the face of an uninviting indifference, what could be done?

∾

In the morning Raj said to Daarji, 'Look out for a place I can use as a clinic here. I want to move from Karnal. My practice there is going nowhere. The whole day I work like a donkey yet am able to cover only the cost of the rent of the clinic and the cost of medicines.'

Daarji said, 'But have you asked your father? Maybe he would want you to stay there and lend him a helping hand.'

'No, there is no need to ask him. You also don't mention it to him. Just arrange something for me here.'

Even after returning to Karnal, he kept on writing to Daarji, with the same request. He was also very mellow with me during that time.

∾

Then one night…in a span of one and a half minutes, I got an insight into the real meaning of marriage.

Maybe I was not ready for it and it caught me unawares. According to the book given by Mataji, Raj should have helped to prepare me for the experience, but he said nothing, did nothing. The only feeling I got from all of it was that it was all very ugly and dirty.

I think they were the most painful moments of my married life, ones which I had been through and yet not.

'A woman should accept everything'. Everyone had given me this advice. So I accepted this as well. There was nothing else to do.

The very next month I developed morning sickness. Everyone kept laughing. I was throwing up all the time, and they were all very happy. I couldn't even digest water.

I must have had a tough constitution. That's why even without eating and constantly throwing up, I remained alive the next six months.

24

It was during this period that Daarji arranged a place for a clinic for Raj in the Patel Nagar area. So we came to Delhi and started living with my parents. The bedroom where Beeji, Jasbir and I used to sleep, was given to us.

Raj took up his practice and to encourage it, Daarji began sending his own patients to Raj. And on my brother fell the responsibility of taking care of all the odd jobs at the clinic. By then he had completed his pre-medical studies but was still underage for admission to medical college.

Raj now had a new demand and ordered me, 'You look for a job for yourself. My practice is very new. If you work, only then will we be able to take up a separate residence. How long can we stay here in this manner?'

I asked him, 'What job can I get?' I really had no idea as to what job I was suitable for. I had never actually thought about a job. All I knew was that till you got married, you kept studying, and once your studies were over, you got married.

Raj had clear ideas about this as well. He told me, 'You

can take up teaching, but you must work only in a girls' school.'

Once I started making rounds of different schools I came to know that for a job in a school you needed to do either BT or BEd., that is, teachers' training. So I took admission for the BEd. course. I was four months pregnant then.

The course was very difficult. I had to leave early in the morning by bus for Delhi University. Classes the whole day, then back home by bus in the evening. It would usually be late evening by the time I reached home.

Beeji would say, 'You're unable to digest anything you eat. On top of it the whole day you're running around. Now why have you taken on this hardship as well?'

I never told anyone that Raj had said that I had to take up a job. I thought, Beeji already remains so ill, why should I bother her any more?

૭

It was my seventh month. My feet were swollen badly. Even my legs were swollen. I used to walk in a bent posture so that my protruding stomach and swollen feet wouldn't be visible to anyone.

Daarji wanted to get my blood tests done. I replied, 'No, Raj will get them done on his own. You don't worry.'

One afternoon, Daarji and my uncle came to my college. They took me to Hardinge hospital. My uncle knew a Doctor Padmavati there. After examining me she said, 'She must immediately be admitted to the Emergency here. She's in danger of kidney failure. And her eighth month is also about to start.'

I protested, 'No, if Raj comes to know I've got admitted into hospital without asking him, all hell will be let loose.'

That night when Daarji told Raj that I had to be admitted

into hospital in the morning, he was furious. He said, 'I'm also a doctor. I know everything. There is no need to go to hospital. She cannot miss her studies for so many days.'

The next morning I again headed towards the bus stop to go to college, like an obedient wife.

'It's only by negating yourself completely that you can gain the respect of your husband.' I was negating myself completely, and was getting annihilated in the process.

∽

Hardly ten or twelve days had passed after this incident, when I started experiencing sharp pains while returning from college in the bus.

The whole evening…the whole night…and all of the next day…it was as if I was standing face to face with my Maker on Judgement Day! Towards evening I was in a really bad condition. The doctor, who had come for the delivery, also seemed to be very scared. My brother went several times to the clinic to call Raj. He didn't come. All he said was, 'I'm a doctor. I know nothing will happen to her.'

At 9 o' clock, my daughter was born. She was tiny, soft like silk, doll-like.

Beeji was worried whether the eighth-month child would survive or not, as she had come one month before her time. Beeji had not even arranged a cradle for her as yet. She got her low woven stool from the kitchen, made a thick sort of mattress with a clean sheet on it, and wrapping the baby in a soft cotton cloth, placed her on it.

Raj came home. The first thing he said was, 'What is it? A girl or a boy?'

In a shrinking way, Beeji answered, 'The first-born daughter is like the Goddess Laxmi. She has been born after a lot of trouble. May the Lord bless her with a long life.' And she went into the kitchen.

Raj entered the room and his first action was to viciously kick the low stool hard. 'No one in our family has given birth to a daughter as a first-born. Where has she come from? Accursed is she!' The stool went and hit the wall with a thud. For a moment I felt as if my last breath had got stuck in my throat.

He stormed out of the room.

Shivering, I got up shakily. I placed my feet on the floor, and it felt as if the floor was not solid but made of cotton. I felt like a boat being tossed on wind-swept seas that would capsize at any moment. With trembling steps I reached the low stool and sat down beside it on the floor. No, nothing had happened to my child. She was fine. She had been miraculously saved.

∾

'What should we call her?' asked Beeji, hugging her to her heart.

'Dolly? How does Dolly sound?'

'That's a very good name. And she's really beautiful. Doll-like!' Beeji removed her from her shoulder and held her in her arms. She looked at her cherubic face and kissed her forehead.

The third day when I was feeding her hidden under my veil, playing with her tiny fingers, Raj walked in. He looked at us both with contempt.

Somehow I gathered my courage and hesitantly said, 'I won't go to college any more. She's an eighth-month baby and needs a lot of care. She can't even drink milk properly, she gets tired very quickly and her stomach is always upset. We'll have to put in a lot of effort to bring her up.'

Raj snapped his fingers, 'Just you watch now, I'll dry up your milk within minutes.' What did he mean by that? I was really scared.

The doctor had prescribed some injections, maybe antiseptic or for strength, I don't remember correctly. It had to be given every third day. Daarji had bought the injections from the market. Raj would administer them to me. On the third or fourth day, the injection that he gave me was not the prescribed one, it was to dry up my milk.

After that Beeji tried many tricks—made a mixture of roasted cumin seeds and jaggery for me, made me eat 'chikriyan', drink at least two litres of milk at a time, all to no avail, for the milk didn't start flowing again.

On the eighth day, in accordance with Raj's orders, I was heading towards my college. I felt broken from within, as if my very soul was weighed down with a burden of a thousand dead bodies, listening to the silent screams of my being.

Daarji, Beeji, Jasbir...all were witness to those disastrous days. But they were incapable of doing anything. I, of course, could only remain silent.

The entire day in college I would keep thinking about Dolly. There was a constant searing in my heart. When my classmates asked me in amazement, 'How did you hide your secret so well for so many days? And now whom do you leave your eight-day old daughter with?' I would feel like crying.

Principal Basu, usually a taciturn person, famous for being a strict disciplinarian, called me to advise, 'In future, of course, I'll make it a point to ask in the admission form itself—"Are you pregnant?" But for the moment I would like to say to you that studies can even be done next year. Right now you should be at home looking after the baby. Somebody told me that she weighed barely five pounds at birth. She must need a lot of care then. No nectar is better than mother's milk.'

How could I tell Principal Basu that I was like an empty well devoid of all nectar? That I didn't have even a drop of milk for my poor baby. That if I left my studies and went home, then my husband would abandon the two of us.

Maybe then even my own parents would not accept us. The very parents, who for the sake of their self-respect, were ready to follow every order of their chosen son-in-law, and day and night were boiling baby bottles and feeding Dolly tinned milk powder dissolved in hot water. Always with the worry in their minds about how much of the milk was being absorbed by the baby and how much of it was being lost by way of diarrhoea and throwing up.

Beeji kept trying different remedies for that—sometimes giving whey water, sometimes water boiled with aniseed and cardamom, sometimes this, sometimes that.

The whole night I would be up, half asleep, bottlefeeding her and changing her nappies and sheets, snatching a nap when I could.

On one half of my bed, a rubber sheet had been spread for Dolly. Beeji used to cover this with a loose cover made of thick but soft cambric material, for if we spread only a sheet on it, it would invariably slide off. The whole night would sometimes just pass in changing those loose covers.

In the morning, I would wash the dirty nappies and covers of the night before. The three clotheslines in the courtyard would be filled with the tiny pieces of cloth, from one end to the other.

Then I would quickly have a bath, get ready, swallow some morsels of food hastily and rush off to college.

The whole day, the sound of Dolly's mewling cries would echo in my ears.

※

I had not chosen motherhood. Marriage had also been loaded onto me and now this baby. Now if, from the core of my being, I felt a love for my baby, what could I do about it?

My life was like a spinning top, whose string was always being manipulated by someone else, according to someone else's whim, and the top just had to spin! When you look closely at a spinning top, all the colours seem to disappear and only a whirling dervish-like object can be seen, with no identity of its own. This was what was happening with me.

I was constantly exhausted, waves of pain would rise from the soles of my feet and twirl like a whirlpool within my head. A desperate lassitude spread through my body, and I felt totally apathetic.

At that time, I really wished that I could contract a malady which at least could be seen by people. Maybe then I would have the right to lie quietly on the bed. An aeon seemed to have passed since the last time I had had a good night's sleep.

And then there was Raj, who didn't even talk cordially to me! Who would only ask after me now and then to keep up appearances in front of Daarji and Beeji.

Since Dolly's birth, he had been sleeping in a separate room.

25

It was a Sunday in the beginning of winter. It was mid-day; Beeji was giving Dolly a massage, and I was stitching a smock for her.

Raj had come home for lunch. He came and stood next to Beeji and catching hold of one of Dolly's legs, straightened it. When he let it go, the foot slipped to one side. He picked it up and straightened it again, and again, when he released it, the foot fell limply to one side. He pronounced, 'The girl is lame.'

It was as if all the life had drained out of Beeji, and so had mine. 'No Raj, babies' feet are like this, soft and pliable like wax. And then she was only five pounds when she was born. There is no strength in her feet yet. Once they are strong, they will straighten out on their own. You don't need to worry at all.' It was as if Beeji was asking forgiveness for something. As if Dolly's foot was a result of her negligence, something for which Beeji was personally responsible.

'No, the foot is completely unaligned. When she grows up, the problem will be mine alone. No one else will take responsibility. A lame girl! What will I do with her?'

Daarji was resting inside after lunch as he always did. No one disturbed him when he was taking his siesta. Everyone spoke in whispers and took care not to make any noise.

But now Raj had complete authority. He was talking in a loud voice, almost shouting. And no one had the courage to tell him that Daarji was resting. In their own house, Daarji and Beeji were forced to cater to all of Raj's whims. I could only stand by helplessly.

Hearing the commotion, Daarji came out into the courtyard. He had overheard Raj's announcement and now intervened, 'Rajji, I'm also a doctor. Nothing is the matter with the girl's foot. It's weak, that's why it doesn't straighten out. We are massaging it daily. It will be fine in a few days.'

Raj flared up, 'I know what sort of a doctor you are. Is homeopathy any sort of medical line at all? You might as well open a mithai shop instead of a homeopathy clinic. It's one and the same thing.'

Daarji's face lost colour. Yet he swallowed the insult and remained quiet.

Raj said, 'I'll put her foot in plaster. It will straighten out.'

Daarji couldn't control himself any longer. 'You'll apply a plaster to such soft flesh! Her whole leg will rot!'

'You don't interfere in my business. Her leg is going to be put in plaster.'

For the first time after my marriage, Daarji took a stand, 'No, not in this house. I cannot allow the baby's leg to rot. Otherwise, the child is yours, you may take her wherever you like and then are welcome to even chop off her leg. But not in this house.' So saying, he went inside.

'How dare you say that! Browbeating me like a bully! Trying to gloat and intimidate me! House...my foot!' With that, Raj stomped out of the house. He didn't come back that night, or the next.

Beeji and Daarji worried, 'What will happen now? We live in Patel Nagar and have opened a clinic for Raj here. Everyone will come to know about the situation. Our reputation is at stake. How will we even venture out?'

While returning from college in the evening, I went to Raj's clinic. He refused to acknowledge my presence and continued sitting there, an angry look on his face.

'Why haven't you come home?' I asked, my voice shaking.

'I have taken a new house. If you want to come you can do so. If you want to bring that girl then her foot will be put in plaster. If you don't want the plaster to happen then let your mother bring her up. That's all!' Raj gave his final verdict.

Perforce, I had to go to his house. There was no other option. Dolly remained with Beeji and Daarji. I continued going to college.

The responsibility of Raj's new household naturally fell on me. From the cleaning, the washing-up, to the cooking—everything had to be done by me.

On my way back from college, I would go straight to Beeji's house. I would play with Dolly, cuddle her lovingly, for a brief while. Then I returned to Raj's place. It would usually be eleven or twelve at night, by the time I finished the housework. I would fall asleep, I don't know when, while completing my college work. Life seemed to be an unending race, without rhyme or reason.

And the never-ending excruciating exhaustion!

~

Till now Raj had touched me only once. And the result of that touch was Dolly.

Despite having given birth to Dolly, my body was still a virgin's. The intensity of desire, the longing for a mate, I was still unaware of that. What was the craving for sex, I had no idea.

Raj's anger increased day by day. The smallest mistake, and I would be at the receiving end of a hammer-like slap. If I tried to save my face, then it would fall on my shoulder. If I saved that, then my back would take the brunt.

Dolly must have been about six months old when one night he came to my bed and in a cold, clinical voice said, 'I want a male child.' And within two minutes left, after planting his seed in the fertile soil of my body, as if he had completed a necessary task.

When I look back, I find it really amazing that in thirteen years of marriage, my husband touched me only twice.

It was much later that I accidentally got to know that he had actually been incapable of impregnating me and had needed to take injections to overcome that weakness and place his seed in me.

In reality, my married life actually lasted only four minutes, and with my new knowledge, it was not at all surprising as to why it was so.

~

I don't know when I actually started feeling the pangs of physical longing.

There was a fire dancing within me. My body would burn in it like a roast in the oven.

But I had always understood that a woman didn't talk about the longings of her own body. Could never even think of talking about them. Keeping silent on this issue was very essential for a respectable woman. She had to wait for the moment when her husband condescended to come to her bed to quench his thirst.

But that moment never came in my life in the thirteen years of my marriage. Maybe I wasn't capable of arousing love in Raj's heart. Maybe also because the girl he had wanted to marry, had come back into his life.

I never tried to find out whether this was the same girl or someone else, the girl whom he had now set up in a house in Patel Nagar, and whom he went to meet every day. When he would be really deeply involved with her or would be in a dilemma as to what to do with me, he would just simply throw me out of the house. When in the next few months, he would get fed up answering people's queries about where his wife was, his children, he would come to Daarji's house and take me back.

This happened eight times in the span of twelve years.

I never felt anger against the 'other woman'. I was bewildered and bitter about my derailed life. But I never felt anger for her, just pity. What was her fault in all of this! It was Raj who had created a mess out of both our lives.

26

The second time when I conceived, I felt a strange restlessness. Was I some sort of container in which whenever Raj desired he would deposit his seed, then tell me, now go, nurture it with your blood for the next nine months?

No, not this time.

I pleaded and cried that I didn't want another child so quickly. 'On the one hand you say you want me to work. Then who will look after this child?' Beeji and Daarji were already thoroughly tired looking after Dolly. Were they of an age to look after young children? How could I look after everything all alone?

After completing my BEd., I started desperately looking for a job, giving interviews everywhere. Once I got a job, I would have to work in a school and also do all the household chores. Now he was also talking of bringing Dolly to our house. So I would have to do all her work as well. And then at the same time nurture a baby in the womb?

Raj declared, 'I can't give permission for an abortion.' And without the husband's permission no doctor would agree. 'What if this child is a boy? Why should I finish him? I also need to take my family lineage forward. My parents have some expectations from me.'

Expectations? From those family members who till today had never even tried to find out where we were! From those, who till today had not even seen Dolly's face? What could I do? He was the owner of my body! I had no right on my own body.

I cannot describe my state of mind in those days. I could not share my thoughts with anyone, for everyone would scold me if I mentioned the word abortion.

I couldn't even share this with my mother, for every mother must have been in the same position of having to bear her children against her own wishes. I couldn't share this with any of my friends either. After having been rendered homeless from Lahore, I had made only one friend, and she was a typical example of a submissive, obedient housewife.

༄

I got a job in a government school in West Patel Nagar. It was at a distance of at least two and a half kilometres from Raj's house. But out of fear I couldn't ask him for my bus fare. There was a small hillock on the way. On the other side of it, there was a narrow path. That path would reduce the distance by about half a kilometre. I would wake up early in the morning, complete all the household chores, then race along that path to reach school on time.

After school got over in the afternoon, I would check a pile of copies for half an hour or so, and then head for home carrying another pile of copies along that same uneven path.

In those days, I used to wear a pair of cheap chappals costing two rupees. I could feel the stones piercing my feet through the thin soles.

In the evening when Raj went to the clinic, I would go to Beeji's house to meet Dolly. Beeji was again ill most of the time. She had hired a Multani maid for Dolly. But the care that a mother can give, can be given by neither a maid nor anyone else.

Whenever Beeji was seriously ill, then it was I who was responsible for sponging her, helping her to change her clothes, washing her hair, combing it, and also supervising the servants and the cooking. Jasbir was doing his medical studies faraway in Amritsar. If I didn't take care of that household, then who would? Who else was there for them? Life was synonymous with an unending exhaustion, an exhaustion which had become an indivisible part of my very bone marrow.

༺༻

Raj had got some medicine from Vaid Mohan Singh for me which the Vaidji said would hundred percent ensure the birth of a son. When he would stand in front of me to make me take it, I would quietly do so. The doses that I had to take during the day, I would throw away and pray to God that if this child is on the way, if I am being forced to bring it into the world, then at least have this much pity on me, let the baby be a girl. I didn't want to give birth to any male. That male would also be like Raj—a younger version. No, I didn't want another ruler over me. Please give me a lovely doll-like, soft as cotton daughter, dear Lord! When they both grow up, we will face the difficult task of living life together, like three friends, a support for each other.

I will not let anyone else make the decisions for their lives. I will teach them to make their own decisions. I will empower them with the strength which I had always lacked. We three would be each other's backbone, supporting and sustaining one another. In this way we would battle all the hardships of life. By making my daughters independent, capable of courageously taking their own decisions, I would also show Beeji and Daarji how to bring up daughters.

My head seemed to be always swimming and I often felt a darkness in front of my eyes. Waves of pain would invade every cell of my body.

Without telling Raj, I went to visit a gynaecologist. She told me, 'There is deficiency of blood, your haemoglobin is very low. If you cannot keep your food down, then at least have orange or mausambi juice.'

I said to Raj, 'Please bring oranges for me. Or else give me the money for oranges. The doctor has told me to have juice.'

'Juice?' He looked at me contemptuously. There was derisiveness in that look, an insult, as if a beggar woman had demanded the crown in alms.

My salary at that time was barely two hundred rupees. I had to hand over the whole amount to Raj. And every morning he would give me five rupees, for the household expenditure. I had to keep an account for those five rupees. How much I spent on vegetables, on pulses, how much on spices, on kerosene oil for the stove, on matches, on bread and on flour. Raj checked this account every few days. On Sundays most definitely the account would be checked. He would see when was the last time I bought a matchbox. How long had the one kilogram of onions lasted. How much kerosene I had bought. The slightest mistake, and I would get a severe scolding.

When I stuck to my demand for oranges, he flew into a rage and ordered, 'Go to your father's home if you want oranges.' And shoved me out of the house in the clothes I was standing in, banging the door shut in my face.

That was my first exile! Interred as at Kaala Paani! Go, wherever you can find shelter. Hush, hush…go from here!

'Is this your father's house?' These words were always at the tip of his tongue. 'Is this your father's home that you're keeping two lights on so late to check your copies?'… 'Is this your father's house that you have finished a matchbox within four days?' Meaning that I could do whatever I liked in my father's house, but not in Raj's.

Was this really true?

In Daarji's house, I used to feel mortified by my very existence. I always felt as if each morsel that I swallowed was in reality a morsel of sand.

Actually, the doors of that house and the hearts of the inmates of that house had always been open for me, though it had never been evident to me earlier. During the periods of exile, they became even more loving and gentle. Daarji himself would squeeze out the juice and make me drink it. Like when an expensive glass article develops a crack, we handle it with great care so that it doesn't shatter into bits. Still the feeling would always be festering that…

No, no one would say anything in Daarji–Beeji's house. That was the whole thing, nobody said anything at all. Never mentioned once the holocaust that was echoing every moment in my veins, fluttering in my ribs. Nobody would talk about that struggle, which was screaming in my head like thousands of vultures. If someone did want to take the responsibility to talk, then who would do so? As it was, who was there in the household who would talk to me about what I felt or thought, even before my marriage?

When I think back today, I realize that right from my birth till adulthood, if someone spoke to me it was usually to order me not to do this or not to do that.

The same was happening in this house. The same had happened in that house!

∽

My position in Raj's house was even worse than a chair. Because I was under strict orders that 'you have to dust yourself, wipe yourself, repair your broken legs on your own and also the torn seat. And always have to be ready to present yourself for someone to sit on.'

My position in Raj's house was even worse than the utensils, because utensils are scrubbed, washed, dried and polished. They are kept neatly in the cupboards. I had to scrub, wash and keep myself ready all the time so that whenever Raj required it, wanted to use me, he could do so. I had to be ready and available.

All the time it felt as if there were burning embers in my heart. And my inner flesh was slowly getting roasted on it. Forming kebabs. And those kebabs too, would burn to a cinder.

Sometimes I really felt as if I could smell the odour of burning flesh coming from within me.

———

27

About six or seven months later Raj came and took me back, to his home.

In between, Candy had already been born. Candy went with me, and Dolly remained with Daarji and Beeji.

Again and again Raj would make me realize that I was absolutely worthless, as I had given birth to two daughters. What is the value of a woman who gives birth to only daughters? It was very magnanimous of him that he had taken rubbish like me back into his home. I should be really thankful to him.

Beeji had sent the Multani maid she had kept for Dolly along with me, and had hired another girl to look after Dolly.

During the school break I would come home to feed Candy, riding a hired bicycle. It cost two annas to hire it for one hour. I had been riding a bicycle since my childhood in Lahore. It is said that once you learn how to ride a bicycle, you don't forget it lifelong.

But no, I had forgotten how to ride. Or maybe exhaustion had set in so much in my bones that riding the cycle was a truly difficult task. It was impossible to climb the sloping road on the little hillock between West and East Patel Nagar. I would start breathing heavily.

Many a time I would tumble off the bike and would look around guiltily, to see how many people were laughing at me for having fallen off.

With scratched and wounded knees I would get back on and start pedalling the cycle again.

After feeding Candy, I would go back to the school. At half-time, when all my colleagues would be having chapattis or sandwiches or fruit, or gossiping, I would be giving two annas to the cycle stand owner, and race, hungry and thirsty, back to school to do my duty.

The most peculiar thing is that when time screams, howls, sings dirges, mourns as it passes, it gives rise to two kinds of anomalous experiences. For both these experiences are truly opposite to each other. At that time, when we are actually passing through those torturous moments, it feels that though morning has come, we will not be able to survive till the night. Will definitely lose the thread of our breath somewhere in between. Ours, and times as well! If it's night, morning will not come. Even if it does, we won't be there to see it.

Every moment, every second is passed on tenterhooks. Sundering us into two parts as if with a sharp saw. Leaving us bloodstained.

And when you look back and see, then no day, no moment, no event ever comes back to you from the garbage heap to which time has reduced it. One day dissolves so insolubly into the next, that later on it appears as just one mountain-like mass of black ugliness. And nothing else. Definitely that mountain would have innumerable depressions and fissures, and many snakes, scorpions, lions, cheetahs, pigs and deer would be living in its dark caves. Maybe ferocious flesh-eaters would be hunting down smaller animals. Maybe at the top of that mountain there could be an old tree atop which an eagle was nesting. There may even be more nests of birds in the bushes and trees on the mountainside. A whole world may be forming and dissolving every moment of time.

But from outside it would appear only as a lifeless, black, stony pile!

Can you identify the causes of pain and analyse them? When it is exploding like a roaring thunderstorm, then all analysis becomes pointless. Just the awareness of a piercing scream remains with you. That, too, seems to be stuck in your throat, fluttering like a wounded bird in your ribcage. Those years were somewhat like that.

∾

Then I used to feel that with my patience, my silence, my sacrifices, obedience, I would one day or the other attain my Lord and Master. Would win over his heart. Would make him my own.

But patience, faithfulness, obeying every order with a bowed head, in the hope that some day you could win another's heart, is all a total sham. A pseudo tonic that every mother presents her daughter as a precious legacy. And this same tonic is given by one's religion, one's society, and even by one's traditions.

I was earning myself, yet every morning I would have to ask Raj for five rupees, like a beggar woman.

My two daughters were the only tangible justification for my existence...the fundamental source of my life. They were the ones to create a rock-like stability for the trembling earth beneath my feet, were the orbit of my life! But sadly, I had no time to play with them, cuddle them, or indulge in childish prattle with them.

Neither did I have any longing, any yearning or desires left in me.

Not one, not two, but thirteen years passed like that. In those thirteen years, my very being had shrivelled to become microscopic. It was concealed within my body, like a troublesome, imbecile dolt, coiled up covertly, within a perfectly fine, wholesome green peapod.

I could not look the women of the neighbourhood in the eye. I didn't have the courage to speak to any of them. The more the probing eyes of inquisitive people tried to dig out hidden secrets, the more I would shrink deeper within myself and take refuge in silence.

But sometimes, when Raj said something hurtful to me, I would feel as if my heart would burst, and all my protective shields would crack and break. I would cry uncontrollably and beat my head against the wall and injure myself.

Then suddenly, seeing the terrified, sobbing faces of my children, I would gather them to my bosom and retreat to my room. Meaning that room that Raj had condescendingly bestowed on us three destitutes out of the kindness of his heart.

There was only one bed in that room, a bed that had been brought from Beeji's house. On that bed all three of us would sleep huddled together, many a times, hungry.

In every turbulent relationship, tension inevitably builds up, and this was happening in our relationship as well, growing day by day.

I would often feel like an acrobat trying to balance myself on a tightrope with the help of a bamboo pole. No one seemed to have any link whatsoever with my life, my death, with my tense, brittle nerves. Below the tightrope, was an indifferent crowd, mere spectators.

On either end of the long pole in my hands, helping to balance myself on the tightrope, were my two daughters.

Without them to give me this balance, I would have fallen to the ground, my bones shattered into bits and my head split open, my blood staining the hard, heartless earth. They were the ones who were not only my support system, my anchors, but also my raison d'être to stay alive though it broke my heart to see the murder of their childhood.

If I had fallen, they too, would have fallen along with me, and shattered to bits like delicate porcelain flower vases. It was this fear that propelled me to rally all my strength and willpower, so as not to let myself fall, break or go mad or even die.

༄

I was being ground as fine as kohl powder. To see how finely it had been ground, it was enough to take a pinch from the mortar and rub it with the fingertips. But, if one looks at it rationally, there is nothing strange in being ground in this manner.

It is the lot of every woman to be ground. Minutely ground, sieved and refined by passing through a muslin cloth, she is then imprisoned safely in the dark chamber of a kohl-container, so that when applied to the eyes, doesn't sting or irritate.

At the top of a kohl-container, there is a small hole which is tightly closed with the help of a small needle-cap. When someone wants to beautify their eyes with the kohl, then only for a split second the tiny door of that dark chamber is opened, a minute part of the powder is applied to their eyes, and again that chamber is tightly closed with that needle-like top. This is the fate of many women, there is nothing peculiar in this.

The kohl-container is what is considered to be her protected, respectable, acceptable by society, rubber-stamped, rightful place. And she is always taught that her dignity and respectability can be safe only in this container, that is, her house. Her identity doesn't exist if she cannot be regarded as someone's daughter or someone's wife. And if she ever tries to break free of that identity, her very being would be as ephemeral as a straw, worse than even the garbage on the street.

It would indeed be a remarkable thing if that finely ground woman, imprisoned in the kohl-container, decided to break free of that grey and suffocating atmosphere, of her dark impenetrable prison, and transforming back into a black, hard stone again, hit back at her every persecutor. But all that that would result in would be that all the neighbours, relatives, her own parents…all those who were at one time her own, would become her enemies, for with her one step of hitting back, she would have completely ruined the family name. She would be challenging the very foundations of society, terrifying them as she took on their preconceived, stamped and certified ideals.

Those people also had to get their sisters and daughters married off tomorrow. If the family had given birth to such an ill-fated, shameful and shameless woman, then how could the other girls of the family be trusted!

They were also right in their own way. They had to stuff their ancient, rotting traditions down the unwilling throats of future generations. The outdated ideals had to be propagated further, or else there would be a black mark on the family name. The entire social structure would be destroyed.

When, to get out of the hard stony walls of that dungeon, I made a small opening by scratching with my nails and fingers, and somehow dragged myself out of it, on coming out I saw that the skin of my whole body had become scratched and ripped. The skin had got left behind while rubbing, chafing against those stones. Stuck to the walls of that dungeon.

When I emerged from that dungeon, without the covering of my skin, only bloodstained crimson flesh, I must have looked really horrible, so terrifying that everyone refused to recognize me. Many would even change their path when they encountered me.

When I walked, I would leave crimson footprints behind me imprinted on the mud.

Seeing those crimson footprints, everyone would get to know, would get a clue as to where I had gone, so that they could stealthily come from anywhere to grab me, bury me, feed my flesh to the vultures, remove every evidence of my being.

28

I have often thought, another name for life is—monotony! And born of this monotony, endless boredom. And after boredom comes ennui. A silent emptiness. The same morning, the same evening; the same cooking, and then eating, day after day. The same gathering and throwing of rubbish out of the house, and then again the accumulation of fresh rubbish, new dusty mud entering again in the house. The same sleeping at night and waking up in the morning. The same hard work and then more hard work. The same washing and drying of clothes and bedclothes, and again their becoming dirty. The same condition of being sleepingly awake and awakingly asleep.

The same brown earth and blue sky. Neither of them concerned with the ups and downs of human lives. The same summer and winter, dispassionately oblivious. The same cycle of seasons, and the perpetual transformation of time into a pile of garbage!

The only bitter difference was that those small things that had given immense pleasure during childhood, despite all the curbs and hindrances, had now lost their magic touch completely. The small, innocent pleasures of childhood. Like guessing the time by looking at the movement of the stars.

Like going on the roof to get drenched in the rain. Like the smell of green gram and corn, especially when they were being roasted on a slow fire, and their lightly toasted sweet taste. Like the rising of the sun after the advent of dawn everyday, and the gentle milkiness spreading on the horizon and the lightening up of the sky. And along with a horizon coloured like fresh watery buttermilk, the first celebratory songs of the birds filling up the courtyards of the sky.

Like the fiery sun moving further and further away while setting every evening. As it set, the crimson red colour would slowly change into ochre, and the ochre, into the colour of burnished brass...

How could anyone dye the sky like a sheet, immersing it in a huge dyer's cauldron and turning it multicoloured with all the hues of crimson, blazing red, ochre, vibrant cerise, flame, fuchsia and purple? Every day. Every evening.

Then slowly, all the colours would dissolve. Evening, with a broom in hand, would sweep up the heap of colours from all over the sky and take them to the western corner, near the horizon. Then even that heap of colours, those confused, rioting colours, would start melting. Hues of pink, red, orange would still be colouring the upper part of the sky, when at the same time, at the other end, it would start turning grey and ash-like.

In that ash-like kohl-coloured sky, a slumberous moon along with a few stars would open sleep-heavy eyes, still filled with the ragged dreams of the day. Akin to those of my chaotic life.

Yes, those were the pleasures of childhood. Like friendship with the animals in the zoo. Like, letting your mind soar with the winds amongst the mountains. Like, the intoxicating smells of far-off forests carried by the wind. Like, books hidden under the pillow to be read secretly at night. Like, writing stories.

This was totally out of the question now, because it was my husband Raj's order that writing stories was complete madness. Unnecessary nonsense! That women of respectable families did not write stories. For if they wrote, the stories got published. If they got published, people read them. And if people read them, they may try to meet the woman. That 'all this cannot be done here, this is a house of respectable people' was his command.

And I didn't know where all the small joys of life had vanished. The stars had lost their shine, and the moon its grace. Daily, life seemed to be dragging along like the broken-down, squeaking wheels of a dilapidated bullock cart. Where was the time to see the rising or setting sun!

Life was not moving forward, it was just dragging tediously. All my relations with life had got snapped. I never went for any wedding or birthday celebrations to my relatives' houses. I had the impression that I was jinxed. If I had not been able to gain any happiness in life, what happiness could I give anyone else?

Carrying the burden of my own crosses, I had no wish to be a part of anyone else's happiness. That's why I never went anywhere. And anyway, where was the time to go anywhere! For me, life was just the name of a blind-deaf race.

29

In 1959, I was transferred to a school in Sarai Rohilla. Such transfers were routine in government schools, but my problem was, to go to Sarai Rohilla you first had to get a bus from Patel Nagar to Dev Nagar, then from Dev Nagar to Anand Parbat, and from Anand Parbat to Rohtak Road. After that, a walk of one and a half miles on foot.

Once I was waiting at the Dev Nagar bus stop to go to the school in Sarai Rohilla. An acquaintance, a writer, happened to pass by and stopped on seeing me. 'What a calamity has befallen!' he said.

'Calamity? What calamity?' My voice felt as if it was coming from afar, through a tunnel. My eyes were glued on the road, in the direction from which my bus was to come. The biggest disaster for me would be if I missed the bus, or if the buses were on strike and no bus turned up.

He said with great relish, thrilled at being able to impart the news to someone, 'Haven't you read the morning newspaper?'

Newspaper? Where there was no time to live, how could there be time to read the newspaper! Many years had passed since I had last read a newspaper, magazine or a book.

'Kennedy has been murdered.'

I thought, so what if Kennedy has been murdered? My bus had still not come. My own murder was happening, on that road. What did I have to do with Kennedy?

Today when I think back, I feel amazed.

I, who today am so hungry for information about the whole world, who has a concern for every morsel of news, be it about rioting, drought, floods, famine happening anywhere in the world, who is as troubled by the hungry and sick children of Africa as the hungry, naked, poor people of her own country, who is as troubled by the situation in Bosnia, Serbia, Rwanda, Kosovo as with Bhiwandi, Ghaziabad, Meerut, Mumbai, Delhi, and the murders of innocents happening in a thousand other small towns, villages and tribal areas, and the disastrous terror of the '84 massacre of Sikhs, at that time was more concerned about my bus not coming than about Kennedy's murder. Where had my bus got held up?

I have given fearless commentaries on terrorists and national terrorism, sharper than daggers and double-edged swords. My arguments about the Punjabi language and script, deviating from traditional norms, once even caused the students of Punjab University to get angry with me and threaten that I wouldn't leave Punjab alive.

For the woman who today is deeply concerned with the incidents of heists, fraud, violence and murders happening the world over, to that woman, Kennedy's murder at that time, did not seem to be a bigger issue than the bus not coming.

The whole of America must be crying for Kennedy. People the world over must have been plunged into grief. Who was there to cry for this tired body standing on this bare, scorching road?

I myself had no connection to it.

Sarai Rohilla. To where there was no proper bus service in those days. Somebody advised me, why don't you go and meet the director of education. He sits in the Old Secretariat. If someone gets a job in a distant place, then they go to meet him to ask for help. They tell him their grievances about commuting to that remote place. Submit an application or something. According to the law, we could get transferred to only within a range of eight to ten kilometres from our residence, especially the lady teachers.

Fearful and hesitant, one day I finally managed to find my way to the Old Secretariat.

After a long wait, I met the director. In a trembling voice I told him my problem, that Sarai Rohilla was too far away from my house. Shakti Nagar was also at a distance, but there was a direct bus service for it. But there was no such service for Sarai Rohilla. It was beyond my means to splurge on a tonga.

'Why? Aren't you married?' he asked me.

'Yes, I am,' I replied, looking down.

'What does your husband do?'

'He's a doctor.'

He laughed, 'Then why do you need to work?'

If a woman was working, then definitely she must be a widow or abandoned. Or she could possibly still be unmarried. Maybe she had been sent to work by her parents, or her brother and his wife, to go and earn money for her wedding, for her bride money. Otherwise which woman would venture out to work leaving her kitchen and the daily routine of her house?

'It's essential for me to do so. My work is my passion. I respect it a lot.' I tried to turn the topic around, but his eyes were more piercing than an eagle's. Maybe, some gossip from Patel Nagar had managed to reach this corner of the world as well, that...

'Oh, what's in a transfer! We will transfer you wherever you want. If you say, it can be in Patel Nagar itself.' He leaned his head against the chair and slowly started rocking it.

'Thank you so much, sir!' I was thanking him with every pore of my body.

'We will just have to sit down and discuss as to who can be shifted where, so that we can create a place for you in the Patel Nagar school.'

'No matter, sir! You please discuss it. How many days will it take? When should I come again?' I asked him.

He laughed, 'I have to discuss it with you only. Let's decide this evening itself. Come to Nanking at seven today.'

Nanking? I was confused. What was this 'Nanking'? I had never heard this name before nor did I know where it was. I only knew the way from my home to the school and from school to home.

He read the confusion on my face and understood my naivete. 'You don't know Nanking? Have you seen Connaught Place?'

'Yes sir. Madras Hotel, where the Central News Agency is.'

'Yes, that's the one. Nanking is right opposite to it. Exactly at seven o'clock.' Saying this, he stood up, indicating that the meeting was over.

My heart was full of anger. What exactly was this Nanking? Some restaurant? Some hotel? What did this scoundrel think? That I would go to him in a hotel to get my transfer?

Was this the most respectable profession? And we were considered to be the ones helping to carve the future of the country! I didn't want to go. I didn't go.

And then it happened, something which in the teaching department, people said, had happened for the first time.

I got demoted. In the same school, in Sarai Rohilla.

Sometimes I marvel at the irony of life.

A few years ago, I suddenly happened to meet the same director again at the India International Centre. I was sitting in the coffee lounge downstairs, drinking tea and reading, when I heard someone saying 'Excuse me', and looked up to see a man standing near my table. His face was familiar, but I couldn't recall who he was.

'Can I sit here?' he asked politely, indicating a chair in front of me.

'Well...' I still couldn't place who he was. Behind his thick glasses, his eyes seemed to be sometimes spreading out like a djinn's and sometimes narrowing like a cat's.

'I was the director of education a few years back.'

'Oh...' It all came back to me in a flash.

'Sit down,' I said. But I didn't order tea for him. This was not his Nanking, it was my India International Centre.

'Why did you leave your job?' he asked as though he was referring to something that had occurred just the day before.

'Because at that time saints like you were ruling there. And at that point of time I didn't know how to deal with such saints,' I laughed.

He seemed embarrassed. 'But I have been keeping track of you,' he continued regardless.

'Really?' I mocked him.

'I have heard that you are bringing out some magazine nowadays. I have also done my MA in economics. Can you not give me any odd job in your office?'

'Give me your address. If there is any need then my secretary will get in touch with you.' (I didn't have any secretary. I had never kept one.)

Like an obedient child he wrote his address on a piece of paper.

I finished my tea, signed the bill, and took my leave of him. As soon as I came out, I threw that paper into the dustbin.

༄

Sarai Rohilla.

I have already told you that I used to get a bus for Dev Nagar from Patel Nagar, for Anand Parbat from Dev Nagar, and for Rohtak Road from Anand Parbat. And then after crossing the road, I had to go past a number of small factories and shops to cross a veritable sea of railway tracks. I had to sprint from Rohtak Road to Sarai Rohilla, and cross that network of steel tracks too at a run, to reach the school on time. Engines were always shunting on those railway tracks, goods trains and fast trains would thunder by, leaving the station to look forlornly after them.

In my mind, I would pray, 'Dear God, may this engine run over me, sundering me into two parts. Dear God, may my body not be identified, so that my daughters may live in the hope that some day their mother will come back suddenly from somewhere.'

Then I would think, Raj would have an excuse to abuse the poor things even more, taunting them that look, your mother has run away with her lover.

All my logical affiliations with life seemed to have gone awry.

Life was the name of an endless race. An endless exhaustion, an exhaustion that was nesting permanently in my very bones. I would wake up at five, wake up my sleeping daughters, bathe them, comb their hair, put their uniforms on, place lunch packets in their bags and also feed them something, then put them back to bed. Their school bus used to come two hours after I left the house, at eight o'clock, and take them to school.

Reaching the bus stop at six o'clock, I would wait for the first bus to leave the Shadipur depot.

Though the school started half an hour later during the winters, the scene at the bus stop was the same. Only the road sweepers, milkmen on their cycles laden with the milk cans, and one or two people heading to work, were around at that hour. The street lights would still be on, their shadows splayed across the grey road. Standing at the bus stop, I would be half-asleep. I would nap on the bus also, waking up with a start every now and then, worried that I may have missed my stop.

30

During this time, one major change had happened, just one change in a long period of thirteen years, and that was, that I was given permission to keep my salary to myself. Even to spend it as I wished. Without having to keep any account of it in any notebook. No longer did I have to beg Raj for five rupees every morning.

Actually this change had not come on its own. In a history of eight exiles, on returning from one of them, Daarji had managed to persuade Raj to let me keep the money I earned.

Raj had said, 'Okay. Then she will run the house, pay the household expenses. I will pay the house rent and the electricity and water bills. Also the telephone bill.'

'And the children's expenses? Their fees? Books and copies? School uniforms?' asked Daarji.

'She will do all that.' Raj announced his decision.

My salary should remain with me—this was the only condition that Daarji had made and Raj agreed to when he came to take me back after a period of almost ten months after having thrown me out yet again. This time when he had thrown me out, the incident had been really humiliating.

It so happened that as usual Raj had had his dinner before us all. After that, I fed Candy and Dolly. As often happened, the vegetable dish and pulses were just enough for them and nothing was left for me. So, as was my wont, I was having a chapatti sprinkled with salt and red pepper along with some onion.

Raj noticed it and said, 'Are you mocking me by having a chapatti with salt-pepper-onion?'

I replied, 'You bought only a quarter kg of pumpkin in the morning. It was not enough and has got finished.'

He said sarcastically, 'There is no talent in your wretched

hands, no management. Everything is always depleted in this household.' I quietly continued to eat. He yelled with anger, 'How can you continue eating your chapattis even after so many curses? How shameless are you! Anyway, it all still comes out of my earnings. How could you sustain yourself without my benevolence?'

I stood up and threw the chapattis into the dustbin.

After that I stopped eating food in that house. I would go hungry to school in the morning. While returning, I would buy two chapattis for two annas from a nearby tandoor vendor. Lentils used to be given free with the chapattis. Reaching home, I would quickly eat this. Soon after, whenever possible, I started having dinner at Beeji's home in the evening before coming home.

When Raj got to know my secret of buying chapattis from the tandoor vendor, he literally kicked me out of the house, 'Are you bent on maligning my name in the whole colony? Go, go and malign the name of those who have given birth to you!'

Each time that I was thrown out of the house, I never told Daarji or Beeji anything. If they asked what had happened, I used to get irritated, 'He has thrown me out, that is all. If you want to keep me, then do so, otherwise you also throw me out. I will go away somewhere. Anywhere.'

Eight or ten months after this incident, when Raj came to take me back, then for the first and last time I told Daarji the whole story of why there had been a fight. I told him that unless things changed in that house, I had no intention of going back. Even if I did, I would have my food at the tandoor vendor. And then when he would get to know it again, the same arguments and fighting would ensue and he would again kick me out of the house. That is how the decision was taken that I would retain my salary, and also take charge of the kitchen expenses.

But the salary that had started at two hundred rupees had only reached three hundred rupees till then. The payment for translation work, which I used to do to earn extra money, was also barely two rupees per page. Somehow with a lot of difficulty, I was trying to make ends meet, but there was no end to the expenses. The children's fees, books and copies, uniforms, shoes and socks, the donations for school functions. And then all the food-related expenses! Daarji would try to give me money on some pretext or the other, like on every birthday he would give four-five thousand rupees, but birthdays were also only three. Yes, Diwali and Baisakhi would come along to help.

∾

The principal of Dolly's and Candy's school, Rajni Kumar, was an old friend of mine. When she was working at Salwan School, I was doing my BEd. from Delhi University. I, along with a few other students, had been sent to Salwan School for a few weeks for practical training.

Sometime later, Rajni had a confrontation over some issue with the management of the school. So she had resigned and had opened a school in her own house in East Patel Nagar on the main road. She named it Springdales School. She contacted all her friends and acquaintances and asked them to send their children to her school.

She was an honest, hardworking and dedicated woman of good character. Born and brought up abroad, she had come to India after she married an Indian lawyer.

One day she came to my house, and picking up Dolly in her arms, said, 'I'm opening a new school. The first five admissions are of my choice.'

'But she's still too small. She can't even tie the cord of her underwear yet.'

In those days elastic underwear was not very popular and was also very expensive, beyond my reach.

I myself used to stitch their undergarments, vests and frocks from soft material, though inexpertly. Or sometimes I would get them stitched on a Sunday from a daily wage tailor, Master Gyan Chand. Dolly was not even two yet while Candy was just two or three months old.

'What is Dolly's real name? I'll have to write it down in the register,' Rajni asked, not to be daunted.

'There is no real name. I have not given her any name yet. When she grows up she'll find a name for herself, of her own choice. For the moment write Dolly in the register.' Realizing the ineffectiveness of my protest, I submitted to her determination.

She started laughing, and carrying Dolly in her arms, got back into her car and drove away.

I didn't want to choose the real names of my daughters. Many a time, Beeji had voiced her impatience at my delay in naming them, saying, what scriptures do you need to consult to choose names? You just have to open a page in the Guru Granth Sahib and read whichever hymn opens up. You can keep any nice name using the first letter of that hymn. Otherwise these stupid English names will stick. And then you need the real names for their admission into schools.

But I insisted, saying that when they grew up they would choose their own names. I couldn't say to her that I did not like the name she'd saddled me with. I didn't like it even a bit. Yet I had to live with it all my life. Any name, chosen by others, becomes your lifelong identity! I found it very strange.

Think about it! There are thousands of Ajeet Kaurs and Ajeet Singhs in this world.

Sikh names...The same name with 'Kaur' added for girls, and with 'Singh' for boys, and the job is done. No creativity or personalization!

I pitied my daughters. It was not their decision to be born in this accursed household. It was just by accident that they had been born here.

Its curse, pain and terror, they were being forced to share all that with me, for no fault of their own. Along with me, they also had to endure their father's rejection, for they had been born as girls, not boys.

Their faces, their features their complexion—they had chosen nothing on their own. The combining of two wandering cells in some dark cave of my womb, had created whatever was their being now.

Man cannot choose anything himself. Not his features, nor his environment, nor his genes. At least they should have the right to choose their own identity themselves.

That is why I decided, when my daughters grew up they would choose their own names themselves. When they grew up they would look for their own identity. Until they were capable of doing this, why should I overload them with some name, some faith, some identity? Because from the name itself you are categorized as a Sikh, a Hindu, a Christian or a Muslim. When they grew up they would decide for themselves which faith could bring peace into their lives, which scripture could provide them the right direction in life. Or which philosophy of life they would like to follow.

Why is a mere label of a faith necessary? Why is the voice of conscience sitting within each person not enough to rouse the voice of his soul? The criteria that one sets up for one's life, the moral codes, were one's belief in them not enough to help one lead a fulfilling and moral life?

From childhood, I had developed a trust in a big, stupendous and Divine Energy. I don't know if this was the result of the environment I had grown up in, or the effect of Bapuji's Sikhism-steeped personality, or the wonder of Beeji's voice chanting the Sukhmani Sahib melodiously every morning, or the effect of seeing Dadaji talking to God like a close friend.

Right from childhood, the habit of reading the scriptures, doing Ardaas, reading the Kirtan Sohila Paath to everyone before sleeping at night had been ingrained in me.

Every morning, when I bowed to the Guru Granth Sahib, I used to feel as if I was sharing all my fears, terrors and sorrows with someone. With Him, who was larger than life, much stronger and more soft-hearted than me. All my joys and sorrows I used to share with the Divine. There was a comfort in knowing that someone was aware of my problems. The belief was strong in me that today or tomorrow, whenever He got time, whenever He felt that I deserved His compassion, on His own He would deal with all my problems.

I had always strongly believed in Him who was Omnipotent. The greatest Sculptor, who had created me, who had also created the whole universe. It was so easy to share all joys and sorrows with Him. Because you could talk to Him voicelessly and wordlessly. This seemed to me to be the greatest miracle, quietly, silently, sharing your heart's concerns with another without anyone being the wiser!

I used to think, there must be some very competent force that could discipline everything so meticulously, that millions of stars were continuously travelling on their set paths, without ever dashing against each other or falling down.

In an infinite universe, millions of stars, the planets, moons and suns, all moving systematically...it seemed a huge miracle to me. Definitely some unseen force was driving them. There was someone who was driving these suns and moons and stars, all bound together in a harmonious sequence.

Otherwise, how was it possible that every night, when a star reached one corner of the overhang of our roof, it was always the same time?

How did the seasons all tie up in an orderly manner to change one after the other?

How could such enormous oceans be contained as if within the boundaries of small bowls? If they were just a little bit naughty, the whole earth would be in danger of being drowned. Who was the one who stopped them from being naughty? Kept them within their boundaries?

Bound in the rotation of seasons, how did the trees shed their leaves? Then, how did the new buds blossom?

I had always been very much aware of the eternal and infinite greatness of the universe around me, right from childhood.

For as a child I had seen and heard Bhaiyaji, my grandfather, jocularly talking with God. I had seen multitudes of twittering birds flocking around him, and had seen Bhaiyaji playfully laughing with them. I had learnt to read the scriptures from him, and it was he who explained their meaning to me. He had his own way of doing Ardaas as well. He first took the names of all ten Gurus, and then he would start his conversation with God. As if a lover was talking to his beloved. Like a child complains about all things to his mother, tells her the activities of the whole day, who he played with, what he studied, what naughty things he did, how much hunger he felt. Baby-talk, which has no order, just rambling on and on. Like friends talking together about random things, gossiping, that is how he talked to God.

But I had no wish to load my thinking onto my daughters at their tender age, at a time when they were incapable of making their own decisions. That's why Dolly's name was put down as Dolly in the school register, and later when Candy was admitted to school, she remained Candy.

When they grew up, while filling up the examination form for the Senior Cambridge examination, they both looked up names for themselves, and chose them. Dolly chose the name Arpana for herself and Candy, Payal. Both the names were free of class distinction or faith, and neither were they hedged in by boundaries.

Often, I wanted to go and talk to Rajni. Both the girls were so intelligent that they always topped their classes. Maybe they could both get scholarships.

But I just couldn't gather up enough courage. My own self-respect was my biggest enemy. Had always been so, and even today, it is so.

Whenever I was kicked out and sent to Daarji–Beeji's house, I was able to save my household expenses. So during that time, I was able to save up almost forty to fifty rupees each month. I could however only save this much with difficulty, because staying in Daarji–Beeji's house, I couldn't stay up late into the night doing the translation work. What could I say if they asked me anything? If they offered to give me the money themselves, I would have been embarrassed. It was bad enough for them to have their married daughter with her two children staying with them.

Whenever neighbours or relatives asked Beeji inquisitive questions, her face would turn red. I used to really feel sorry for her. But in those days, I was too scared, too fearful and timorous, to think of living alone.

Beeji, Daarji, all my uncles, relatives, neighbours, would tell me that if you had had a son, then there wouldn't have been any issue, you could have passed your life in your husband's house; but now you have the responsibility of two daughters...

They're daughters, for their sake you have to accept everything...When they are asked tomorrow, where is your father, what will the girls answer?

They will also have to be married off sometime. How will the marriages happen without a father? Who will give away the bride unless their father is there to do so? Actually Sikhs don't have the tradition of giving away daughters, but during the ceremony, the father does hold the daughter's shoulder to guide her. If the father was not there, finding respectable houses and suitable boys for the daughters wouldn't be an easy task. Without a father, daughters have no respect in society, no place. Without a husband, what's the status of a woman? Meaning without a father my children were garbage...And without a husband I was also garbage...

31

I am not sharing all the secrets of my life with you to gain your sympathy.

It's no easy task to scratch the dried scabs of your wounds, to pass again through the silences of engulfing terrors and horrors, passing through every second of which, every tiny millisecond of it, the only desire is to let this fear swallow you at once, completely. May it swallow your whole being, your body at one go. And let all the trials and tribulations be finished, once and for all.

It's very difficult to relive those struggling moments between life and death, reliving those breaths again, when life seemed worse then death, and callous death seemed to have forgotten you.

More difficult is it to pick from the ashes of time, those burnt out pieces of rafters and beams, that had at one time formed the timber framework of a home. Look for pieces of burnt plaster, which once sat hugging the walls. From those ashes of time, you cannot dig out those lost mornings, evenings and nights which at that time seemed as if they would never pass. That before they passed on, I would pass away.

No, I am not suffering all this pain, all the effort, the agony and grief of once again going through those lanes of death, because I require anyone's sympathy.

As it is, showing sympathy is not in fashion nowadays. Even if someone passes away in the neighbourhood, the neighbours only express their condolences as a formality. Other than that, they neither have time to sympathize, nor the desire, and don't even know how to do so.

Even at the cremation grounds, people just stand quietly, looking at their watches.

Such events like death always happen to other people, what's that to us?

The one trying to empathize normally doesn't have the time to do so, the one at the receiving end also begins to think himself degraded. Dwarfed in front of the other!

ဏ

I am narrating this tale only to introduce you to a shrinking, fearful child who had taken birth in a well-educated, well-off, respectable, middle-class family. That child who was robbed of her childhood only because she was a girl.

First of all she lost her childhood. Then her youth.

In fact, the truth of the matter is that she didn't even know what childhood was. When did it come and when did it vanish, she didn't know. In the same way, when did youth arrive and then went away as well!

These two parts of life at least didn't come into my life.

Even if they had come, I neither saw them nor felt them. On my life, as it happens with thousands and thousands of girls in this country though they are neither aware of it nor think about it, from the very beginning others have had a right.

How I should conduct myself, how I should look, how I should lower my eyes, how speak softly in low tones, never ask any questions! Not only this, what I should study and what I shouldn't, which friend I should talk to, and to whom not, how long I should talk and what I should talk about, and while talking where was the need to giggle like that! All this others had decided for me, always.

This chalked-out life was like an unseen, invisible line drawn around me. The fear in my very being made me aware of its reality. This line was not like a Lakshman-rekha drawn on the ground, but was actually like a line branded with a hot iron into the very thinking and awareness of my being. Sculpted with a hammer and chisel.

But this I had to accept, that my upright and traditional family, did educate me. Among the women of the generation before me, this was considered to be a unique thing, unnecessary and superfluous.

In rare cases, Hindu girls were taught the Devnagiri script so that they could read the Ramayana and the Gita, Sikh girls were taught the Gurmukhi script to enable them to read their Holy Scriptures, while it was considered to be enough for Muslim girls to learn some stanzas of the Quran by heart. These tasks were usually done by the priests in charge of gurdwaras, maulvis in the masjids, and pundits in temples.

By the time my generation arrived, at least in cities, people of status had started educating their daughters according to their position and standard of living.

In keeping with this, I too received some sort of an education in fits and starts.

As I have already told you, my studies were never given any importance, neither was I ever taken seriously. Maybe that's why I myself was never able to take my studies seriously. I dragged on with my studies, just to be able to breathe freely for a while away from the loneliness and claustrophobic atmosphere of my house. Studies, for me, were just an excuse to get out of my house.

My childhood got lost somewhere in between this vagabond education. So did my youth.

Amongst all this there was just one island of peace, in which could be glimpsed the magic of the rainbow in clear blue skies, and that was the fleeting, innocent, pure love for Baldev. A love that just flew away from my hands like a bird.

Then that deaf-dumb, stupid girl, meaning myself, was married off. When I didn't even know the meaning of marriage.

Like every mother, my mother had also said, 'Do whatever you desire in your own home.' Where was 'my own home'? What desire? All that was happening after my marriage, where was my desire included in it?

Earlier, all the restrictions, limitations and boundaries of my life were decided by Beeji–Daarji, now my in-laws and my husband, Raj, were doing so.

I had to give birth, this was also my husband's decision. Where did I need children at that time, who herself was standing on shaky ground, how could she even think about children! I was neither physically nor mentally ready to bear a child. I didn't even know how they were born. How did they get into the stomach, and then how were they taken out of it. Maybe by cutting the stomach? I would feel terrified at the thought of it.

Embarrassed as well. Because right from the start, every girl is presented with a terrifying, ugly picture of sex. Every mother teaches her daughter that men are like brutes. Girls should keep themselves safe from even the shadow of strange men. She must not allow any man to touch her with even the tip of his finger! Such things were never to be acknowledged openly and could only be indulged in covertly within the 'sanctity' of marriage. Doesn't that very veiled deed get publicly announced when a girl gets pregnant? Such a horrible bestial act, which right from the beginning girls are taught to fear, how can they suddenly regard it as a socially acceptable and pure thing?

But I had no right over my body. Had no right, whatsoever, to take any decision regarding myself.

The babies I would give birth to shouldn't be girls, only boys. This was what was expected of me.

Bowing to the royal decree I gave birth to two babies. But the feeling of revolt in my mind made me pray to the Divine to bless me with daughters rather than sons! Giving birth to daughters reduced my value to peanuts—this was my husband's verdict. My in-laws must also have thought the same, because both the times, nobody came from Karnal to see either mine or my daughters' faces!

'You should work and earn bread and butter for yourself and your children.' This was also my husband's order. That work should also be in a girls' school. There was no time to read books, while writing stories had been designated a crime!

'Don't say anything to Beeji–Daarji': this was also a part of my childhood training. 'After marriage you've to go through all ups and downs on your own, nothing is to be shared with your parents'—this learning was part of my inheritance.

Besides Beeji used to remain ill most of the time. Why

bother her more! All these were dilemmas of my own life, I had to deal with them on my own. What could anyone else do in this! This is what I used to think. This is what seemed to be the reality.

Maybe the boundaries of my thinking in such a way had been delineated ages ago. 'Whatever is in my destiny'—this was the actual boundary of my thoughts. Life was somehow dragging on hindered by laboured breathing. That was all that it was.

From such a simple-minded, timorous woman, controlled by her husband and accepting of whatever life meted out to her, when and how a fearless, bold woman, with the courage to take all the decisions pertaining to her life, was born, the story of this transformation, is what I want to share with all.

That uncomplaining acceptance, compromise, ability to amass the milk of life in her breast and tears in her eyes, are considered to be the ideals of a model woman. Every woman is given an elixir of these very ideals. In fact this is the accepted model of a woman in society. That she should be obedient to every wish of her husband.

The husband may be with twenty women if he wishes, sleep with them, but his own woman, that is his wife, should all her life wait for his return with the doors of both her home and her heart open for him, so that whenever he comes back, she should wash his feet and drink that water, be beholden to him because finally he had returned home. The wife's penance had fructified and borne the desired fruit!

After all, a woman after marriage is considered to be the 'estate' or possession of her husband and his family. Her father donates her into a stranger's hands, saying, 'Go take her, after nurturing and bringing her up, we are bestowing our daughter on you. From today this house is no longer hers. From today, it's your house which will be a shelter for her.'

'Daughter, go to your own home...'

If the husband refuses to accept her, does that house remain her own?

Is there any law which tells him that if you don't like your wife, or like someone else, even in that event this house will remain your wife's? If you want to get out of the relationship, then go—leave this house and go. This house belongs to your wife. She is the one who roams the whole day in the house with a bunch of keys tied to the end of her saree. She is the one who sweeps it, dusts and cleans it, decorates it. The whole day she remains busy with the chores in the kitchen. She is the one who has given birth to a child to continue the family lineage, this dynasty.

Then, in her old age, she becomes dependent on her sons for two square meals a day and a place to shelter herself in.

A few days ago, a film on the widows of Vrindavan was shown on television. An elderly, tired-looking woman was narrating in a tearful voice, 'The one who has no husband, no son, her life is a complete hell. Why not dedicate that life at the Divine's feet?'

A few years ago my daughter Arpana, made a series of paintings on the widows of Vrindavan, delineating their pathetic helplessness.

It is in a woman's silent acceptance of even murder, that the respectability of both her own and her in-laws' family lies. She is like a nameless, faceless, invisible yet always present force (like the presence of God) to strengthen the foundation that protects the prestige of the family. The prestige of a family actually has no existence. It's ephemeral. Only so much air!

To understand what it actually is, it is always compared to a man's turban or to his moustache. Just like, to understand the greatness of God, we refer to 'Pir-fakir', 'Guru', 'Aulia', 'Shankaracharya', 'Padre' and 'Pope' in our Holy Scriptures.

If a daughter or a daughter-in-law commits suicide, and if you happen to press your ear against the walls of that house to listen, then you would overhear, 'Oh, this was no daughter of ours, only a curse. A result of some past life karma! She has ruined her father's dignity, reducing it to dust. She has besmirched her brother's honour. Oh Lord, why didn't I throttle you the moment you were born! Why didn't you die at the time of your birth!'

But a woman can be a complete human being as well, like a strong tree, with her feet planted firmly on the ground. Recognizing her own individuality under the huge sky, she listens to the song of life sung by the leaves, with the courage to gather and shelter the nests of birds, revel in the sunshine, the wind and rain, on her own conditions, answerable only to herself, living life to the fullest. This is the first ray of sunshine bursting like the truth from my sombre and sorrowful narrative, like a beam of light, a miracle.

I know that in this country there are millions of women who are more miserable, and in a worse condition than me. Those who work hard the whole day to earn a little money, and that money, too, gets snatched from them by their husbands who then use it to drink. And after drinking, beat up their wives.

Then there are those, who being widowed in childhood itself, have their beautiful, silky hair shorn off like sheep, are given one square meal a day for the rest of their lives, and in return are expected to occupy a servile position in the household. In return for two chapattis, for the faded clothes given to cover herself with, for the roof given to shelter her head (even if that roof is leaking), she is there to serve everyone for the rest of her life. To uphold the reputation of the family and its name, entombed within the four walls of the house, for the sake of prestige, she's buried alive!

The reason she is not given enough food is that she should remain unaware of her other bodily hungers and longings.

You'll find such women wrapped in a white shroud in almost every second family. Quietly chopping vegetables, making chapattis, washing the floor, scrubbing, polishing, washing utensils, gathering the droppings of their more fortunate sisters-in-laws' children, somehow passing the night lying on a mat spread out on the floor, half-hungry, half-asleep, lost in grim nightmares. Menacing eyes staring during the day and menacing nightmares during the night... this is their destiny!

They rise with the first ray in the morning and keep working past midnight. Without any remuneration, a dumb, bonded labour, for the rest of their life.

Or else tempting them with a better next life, they are uprooted from their homes and sent to places like Vrindavan. In this life you have received the result of the bad karmas of your past life—by losing your husband. And when that happens, you no longer have the right to apply vermilion to your forehead, the mark of a married woman, and you lose your right over the keys of the household. In fact, you have no right over anything. All the result of the bad karmas of your past birth!

Now at least improve your next life. Go to Vrindavan and spend your time in worshipping Krishna. He is the True Husband! Leave all your attachments. If the Lord of your life is no longer there, then all else is useless. The household, children, relatives, all! Leave your attachment to all this and place your attention on the Lord Krishna, improve your next birth. Don't worry about your home. Till your children grow up we'll take care of everything, we'll plough the fields, and look after your Lord's business. After all your children are also the beacons of this family. We have to look after them as well, along with our own obligations, be responsible for all their expenses. The duty of marrying off your daughters also falls on us. It is indeed, our big-heartedness that we are doing all this. We pity your condition, that's why to improve your next life, we are sacrificing our own happiness and comforts. We are taking on the heavy responsibility of looking after your land and property, your house, your business and your children.

Those women in Vrindavan feel themselves to be blessed if they are able to sleep on the floor in some dark, dusty corner, boil and eat a fistful of rice, and sing devotional songs in the Lord's name for hours on end. For these long hours of labour they receive only a small bowl of uncooked rice and two rupees. They accept it as their destiny. A covering of wrinkled flesh on a framework of bones, and over it a dirty saree. Young, middle-aged and elderly women!

Then there are those women, who are made to drink an intoxicant, lick hash, apply makeup, dress up like a bride, and then are burned on their husband's pyre. Their sky-shattering screams buried in the noise of loud chants of 'Jai Sati Mata' and the beating of the drums.

Or women like my Aunt Prakash, who maintain their dignity by drinking poison from their husband's hands. Fulfil their duty. Don't let any slur befall their family's name.

Then there is that category of women who are victims of rape. When a woman is raped outside the home, it becomes news, but the millions of rapes that happen daily inside the security of their homes are quietly borne by women as part of their lot. Unwanted sex! Unwanted children!

In a country of learned philosophers, there are millions

of voiceless, helpless women! A country with an ancient civilization. The purity of the culture can only be protected by keeping alive the pure ancient customs. The meaning of the word 'ancient' also applies to a termite-ridden, hollow pile of wood. 'Ancient' may also mean a pool of smelly, stagnant water full of writhing insects, rolling snakes. And it can apply to empty, outdated customs.

∽

And me?

I, too, like one of the daughters or daughters-in-law of respectable, dignified families, was uncomplainingly following these customs, burning on a pyre of antiquated, traditional ethics.

Till one day, while burning, I came to my senses, and descending from the pyre, stood firmly upright on my feet.

That is the history and geography of this story, 'Koorha Kabada'. However hopeless it might be, it's no less than a miracle for me.

I am sharing all this with the hope that maybe, some other woman who is being regarded as useless, unwanted debris, would get inspired to achieve the same miracle. That that woman buried in a deep tunnel under the earth, struggling to breathe, may be guided to see the light at the end of the tunnel.

It is, of course, very difficult. I have already said that when you are regarded as some unnecessary garbage, you actually start considering yourself to be so. Then there is no hope left.

32

My whole life was literally being dragged along against my wishes. The water which could have flown in streams, rivers, waterfalls, joyfully laughing and dancing, spreading greenery all around, quenching thirsts, refreshing the people coming in its contact, was flowing through a rusted, smelly pipe, trying to hide its degradation and stench, shameful of its very being.

The biggest miracle seemed to be the ability to eke out one square meal every day.

My heart ached for my daughters. In the evening, all the children of the neighbourhood would have ice creams or chocolates, while my children didn't even get one orange.

It was immaterial to me, for in my childhood I had eaten a lot of maltas from Bapuji's orchards. Pomegranates from Kabul, casabas, pears, apples, apricots, litchies—I had had such an abundance of these during my childhood, it was more than enough for the rest of my lifetime.

As it was, I didn't feel very hungry. Always remaining hungry had slowly shrunk my stomach over a period of time. If, by chance, I took an extra chapatti, my stomach would get upset. Milk, curds, buttermilk, butter—it was as if I had become allergic to them all. When a thing is not eaten for a long time, it cannot be eaten at all. If eaten, it cannot be digested. It's the same case even today.

~

I passed many years of my married life thinking that all my sacrifices, my penance and my austerities, my loyalty and obedience, my silence and my silently tolerating every injustice, would one day definitely fructify and then... everything would change.

I struggled from one day to the next accepting all hatred and insults, even being looked down upon, making the effort to not let outsiders know about the happenings inside 'my home', tolerating every injustice and yet accepting that person who was dispensing injustice, the one to whom my parents had married me off, all with the fragile hope that one day or the other, he would realize his aberrations and melting like wax, would return to me.

This was the main aim in the first eight years of my married life—to make Raj melt like wax and attract him towards myself. And once he had gathered me in his arms, all the acrimony of those eight years would be washed away. And then, having shed all the tears I had to shed, I would sleep with my head on his shoulder. For a hundred, two hundred, thousand years!

Hugging Dolly in one arm and Candy in the other, every night I would go to sleep with this dream in my heart.

Only this hope that one day my days, nights, months, years that had all turned to ashes, would once again be revived, had kept me relentlessly moving forwards. My patience, my silence would one day conjure up a miracle. My daughters would one day definitely be blessed with their father's love. One day Raj would look deeply at me...and then he wouldn't be able to tear his eyes away. On seeing the pain hidden in my eyes, his eyes too would fill up!

What a strange thing it is, isn't it? Even after enduring so many atrocities at his hand, a woman is still anxious to be accepted into the same man's arms, the one who has hung her upside down in a hot oven, and left her to roast slowly there!

This was the wheel that turned continuously in my mind, in which I myself would be doing the spinning and the winding of numerous threads. Then everything would turn into ashes. Collapse in the face of reality.

When cotton catches fire, it doesn't flare up, just smoulders and slowly, turns into a mound of ashes.

For a long period of about eight years, the lamp of my life burnt fed by my own blood, and only a blackened bit of shard was left at the end of it all, a mute witness to the intensity of the flames. No evidence of that cauterized life remained except a black, burnt-out bit of clay!

∾

But there came a time when from among the ashes accumulated over the years, I rose like a smouldering ember, phoenix-like, gathered and shook myself, like a wild animal shakes the hair on its body, and looked around, with newly opened eyes.

What had I gained from so many years of poverty, hunger, deprivation, patiently and silently accepting every injustice, beatings, insults?

I had spent those burdensome eight years just scratching at the threshold of life. The consequent wounds from the splinters piercing the delicate flesh beneath my nails had become like permanent blisters in my life.

What had I gained by working hard so devotedly?

I suffered a great deal of ignominy, for in front of every patient, anyone who came to him, all the neighbours, Raj would narrate self-created stories to show his helplessness in the face of my stubbornness—foremost on the list being my pursuing a job despite all his recriminations, not even considering his children—completely tearing my character apart, making me the villain of the story.

The more stories that he created, the more I retreated into my shell. Felt more and more belittled, completely dwarfed! Many a times I wanted to just vanish from there, never to be seen by anyone ever again...

The life of both the girls was my responsibility, that was my only reason for living.

Broken with the exhaustion of an endless race, singed with the indignity of being beaten, regarded as a contemptible object of hatred and mockery…Because tucked under my wings were two innocent visages, two frightened, pale faces…

I was that comforting dark cave, wherein they could hide and feel protected even in the face of violent storms. I was that nurturing tree, who though itself burning in the scorching sun, was the only one who could give shelter to the two innocent, tiny beings, hidden amongst its leaves.

I used to think, dying is so easy! But leaving these two poor things alone in this whole wide world would not only be an act of hard-heartedness but also one of cowardice and selfishness.

33

He was a master storyteller. It was incredible, the number of tales he could weave. I don't know how many are still stuck in my heart like nails even today.

Only two incidents are enough to understand that man, or be amazed at not being able to understand him! These incidents actually took place much later. Still what's the harm in narrating incidents that happened later, first? That is what life is all about. Time follows a straight path. But when you look back and see, then time dissolves like water. The wave starting at the back comes forward to hit the rocks at the edge, but many others just turn back due to the confusion created by it.

The first incident.

By that time I had left Raj's house and also that of my parents' and had shifted to a working girls' hostel. As always, I had been uprooted and exiled to Daarji's house. As always, Raj had come to take me back, this time after one year. As always, with folded hands Daarji had said, 'Take her. After all, she's your possession.' And for the first time I put my foot down and said, 'I am not going anywhere now.'

Shouting abuses and threats, Raj went away. Daarji was also very angry, 'If you won't go, then what will you do? Will you stay at your parents' house for the rest of your life? Now your mother has also passed away. You go away to school in the evenings. Who will look after the girls then? Bhaiyaji? Will he become a nanny and a babysitter for your daughters at his age?'

Bhaiyaji was still alive. He must have been around a hundred years old. But he still went to the gurdwara every morning and evening, and even for a stroll, three or four times a day. But Beeji had passed away after a long, lingering illness.

Due to Beeji's illness, I had got myself transferred to an evening school. Now Beeji was no longer there, but how could I get myself transferred to a morning school immediately?

So, Daarji was angry. He was not ready to accept my decision. Raj was also angry. I could not return to his house.

Both the girls would come back from school at four o'clock. I couldn't get back home before six-thirty. That too only if the buses were on time.

Till I reached home, my two babies would be roaming around like orphans. Daarji would get the servant to heat the milk for them and give them biscuits as well. But he kept grumbling and asking me if I thought it was right for him to take on all this inconvenience and hassle at this age?

What was I to do? If I returned to Raj, would anything

change? Would the children return at six-thirty instead of four? Would my job end at four instead of six-thirty? And if I left my job, then who would feed the three of us? Daarji was there to feed us, but I could stay at his home only when Raj threw me out of his. Daarji's house was just a guesthouse. The children's education? Clothes? Shoes and socks?

I knew that Daarji desired that I should return to my husband's house in a respectable fashion. After that, he could sleep comfortably with the thought that his daughter was happy in her 'own house'. He could tell the neighbours, 'She is happy in her own house.'

I had been kicked like a football seven times from Raj's house to Daarji's and back again. This was the eighth time, and I was not ready to get kicked out yet again.

After every kick now, instead of a bounce, there was only a flat, fizzling sort of noise. For after sustaining so many kicks, the stitches on the ball, too, had come undone. Now after every kick, the football could barely roll a distance of a few metres, that too, with a mere whimper!

My decision to not go back was considered to be an unforgivable crime. Daarji refused to even talk to me.

When I began to feel totally suffocated by Daarji's anger and stony silence, I took leave from school one day and found my way to a working women's hostel. They told me, 'Yes we have a room. The rent is sixty rupees per month.

'If you want to eat in the mess, you can get two or three types of meals. The cheapest is "daal-chapatti" or "daal-rice", which is forty rupees per month.'

'Children?'

'We don't have permission to keep children here. Nobody has ever brought children with them. This is only for working women.'

'If a working woman has children, where should she go then?'

'She can take a room on rent, like a terrace-room.'

'But when I go to work, who will be responsible for their protection? What if someone throttled them or kidnapped them?'

This is how Raj always used to threaten me, 'Don't think that you can take the girls and become independent! It is to control wanton women like you that the anchor of children has to be tied around their necks. Where can you go, taking them with you? If you still dare to go then I'll have both your daughters kidnapped and will sell them off to some brothel in Singapore! Understand?'

I could never understand why he always talked of selling them to a brothel in Singapore. Maybe his aunt from Singapore had told him that her husband…or maybe my middle brother-in-law had told him so—for that brother had worked for three years with the uncle in Singapore.

I only knew that the threat would strike fear in my heart. My own insecurities would make me believe it to be a reality.

'Where can I get permission to keep my children with me here?' I asked the hostel warden.

'I don't know, no one has done so till today. Actually, no one has ever asked for it. But yes, if you want to try, then only Minister Sahib can recommend it as a special order,' she replied.

'Minister Sahib? Which minister? Where does he live?'

The warden gave me the name: 'Meherchand Mahajan.'

Oh Lord! He was one of Daarji's patients! If I went to meet him and he got to know who I was, the news would reach Daarji. Then what would happen to me? Daarji would make mincemeat out of me!

I knew he would say, 'No one has ever thought about living

separately in our whole family! Where have you come from to blot the family's name...Has a married girl ever lived alone till today that you will do so? If you cannot accommodate yourself in this house, then go to your husband's house. That's the rule for girls of respectable families. Your parents' house or your husband's. There is no third place for them...He had come to take you back with him, but you were on your high horse. You refused to go. What was this pride for? Don't you know that the honour of a woman staying alone gets besmirched, makes her lighter than straw, worthless? And where will you go with your two daughters? Who will be responsible for their marriages? For the sake of their children, mothers are willing to smoulder like embers throughout their lives. Look at you! Where is your dedication towards your children? The father of these girls is still alive. The women who lose their husbands, and have no one to support them in their conjugal homes, even those mothers don't dare to cross the threshold of their homes and stay put for the well-being of their children. They may even die a hundred deaths every day, but don't let anyone know anything...

'Don't kill us like that, while we are still alive! How have we harmed you? For what crime are you punishing us?'

These oft-repeated words were constantly hammering against the walls of my chest. The same words...over and over again, I kept hearing them. From Raj, from Daarji, from Beeji, and sometimes even from Jasbir's mouth.

Their family...their prestige!

Now there was no other option. So one day, struggling with the crowds in the buses, asking the way, I somehow managed to reach the minister's house.

'Where is your parental home? Your in-laws' home? Husband?'

I kept answering all the questions. From which actually,

all the real answers were missing. My voice shook as I lied, for I had never before told any lies.

Finally taking my courage into my hands, I said, 'Please tell me, if a woman has no established home, and she wants to take care of her children through her own efforts, bring them up on her own, then where should she stay?'

I don't know when and how compassion starts flowing in people's hearts. This is indeed, the biggest miracle of life! The minister eventually passed an order, giving me permission to keep my daughters with me in the hostel.

A few days later, I packed all our clothes in a suitcase, made a bundle of our quilts, blankets and pillows and came to the hostel.

Daarji was not at home when I left. He had gone to his clinic. I wrote my address, gave it to Bhaiyaji, and left.

For the first time in my adult life, I had a room all to myself. A room for myself and my two daughters. It was our home.

It was a home full of poverty. We didn't even have sufficient bedding. There was a single quilt under which Arpana and Candy slept. I shivered all night under a dhurrie with which I tried to ward off the bitter cold of the Delhi winter.

I had arranged for food for two from the hostel. The three of us shared it at each meal. Because it didn't look nice dividing two meals into three in the dining hall, I would go to the kitchen and fill an aluminium container with watery dal and some vegetable with rotis which we ate sitting in our room. I could not look the cook in the eye when he put the rotis in the container. I felt so guilty. Later, I managed to persuade the son of the maid who washed the dishes at my neighbour's room to fetch our meals from the kitchen for three rupees a month. In spite of all that, we called that room our 'home' with considerable pride. We were free to live there as we liked. We could sleep and wake up when we liked. We could read whenever we wanted. No one screamed at us saying, 'Why are you keeping the light on so late?'

Raj kept threatening me that he would take them away, so I had withdrawn them both from Springdales School and had got them admitted into Lady Irwin School, which was very near the hostel.

About this time, I had been transferred to a division of the British Council which dealt with creating television programmes for teaching English to young children.

The feeling had always been with me that the Divine had never supported me. But He must have taken pity on my daughters and got me this transfer, so that I could get them ready in the morning and drop them inside the school gate, on my way to the British Council office located in the AIFACS building on Rafi Marg.

When their school got over at four, they would both sit and wait for me on the lawns within the school gates. I used to reach there about five-thirty, and after collecting them, head back to the hostel.

Crossing that short stretch of road, my mind would be full of so many different fears and doubts. When I crossed that road, I would imagine that a car or van sent by Raj would drag both the girls into it and speed away, or then, that it would crush the three of us and leave our bleeding bodies to the mercy of the elements. I would shiver in fear at the picture this conjured up.

34

I have often pondered about what we regard as women's liberation, the idea of her freedom, where does it start, and where does it end? What are its boundaries and limitations? Could a woman actually achieve complete liberation in the true sense of the word? What way should she adopt to gain this so-called liberation? All the old meanings of liberation were becoming meaningless in front of me.

If a woman works and earns her own living, if she's not dependent on anyone for her needs, then she's capable of throwing off the age-old chains of slavery that she's bound with. This is a generally accepted concept.

But is economic independence, self-dependency, the first criteria for liberation? Nonsense!

I had been earning my own bread for years, and yet all the time I was consumed by an unknown terror.

A husband's beatings, hatred and disgust, again and again being thrown out of the house...I had borne everything, despite earning and sustaining myself and my daughters.

For so many years...for thirteen long years, I kept torturing myself, because I was totally petrified, intimidated by the thought of creating an independent life for myself.

Everyone would scare me with stories of what would become of me if I did. Daarji, Beeji, Raj, my own friends who numbered barely two or three, all would say, what option did I have but to continue to suffer?

And now that I had emerged from my prison after breaking innumerable doors, had left both my father's and my husband's houses, staying independently in a hostel, earning my own living, still where was this liberation? Economic independence alone doesn't allow a woman to experience liberation. Nor is it gained by breaking free of the proverbial seven constraints, leaving a father's and husband's house to create your own world. Neither from fighting life's battles on your own, nor from garnering the courage to live alone by shattering the shackles of age-old social norms.

Breaking the outer handcuffs and fetters does boost your self-confidence a little. A feeling of self-satisfaction does arise at having protected your own dignity. There is an awareness that I am not just a heap of garbage, I am worth more than that.

Confronting and shaking off the ties of both, the parents' and the in-laws' houses, knocking down the well-defined, moss-covered, snake- and scorpion-infested dungeon walls, struggling with the storms outside, standing in the cold, heat and rain under the naked sky, challenging the whole earth and sky with one's puny strength, is no easy task!

Yet in my mind there was no feeling of either freedom or liberation. I was still living in fear—of so many things, still enduring so many hardships. Seeing the unrelenting, inquisitive eyes of passing strangers, I still felt as scared as ever.

In school, and now at the British Council, and in the TV station, wherever I saw a few people whispering together, I used to feel that they were talking about me.

All the time, I felt that Raj was meeting my colleagues, the warden of my hostel, all the teachers at Irwin School, the Punjabi writers, and saying things to them against me, like he used to tell his patients in Patel Nagar, the neighbours and even the shopkeepers and servants. The more he spread tales about me, the more I kept retreating within myself. If anyone tried to dig out details from me, I just wanted to vanish from their sight. I knew that in comparison to Raj, my worth was less than even a straw, totally insignificant. He was a doctor. If any doctor speaks kindly to his patient then that patient starts regarding him as a god, and Raj could wrap his patients around his little finger superbly. He was also blessed with a healing touch. How could his patients then not believe his words?

And me...how could I help anybody? What could I achieve by narrating my story to anyone? I detested sympathy. I always used to feel that those trying to probe and question me were not my sympathizers, just spectators expecting to be entertained!

Due to Raj's cunning machinations, the image that had been created in the minds of the residents of Patel Nagar about me was that of a disreputable, rakish woman, who indulged in all kinds of revelry, and was using her job as an excuse to stay out of the house the whole day, not at all concerned about either her husband or her children.

In the face of this image, I continued retreating into my shell.

And poor Raj, the saviour of the sick and suffering, was tolerating a vixen as a wife, for the sake of his family's prestige, for after all, she was the mother of his innocent daughters...For the sake of his daughters...simple, innocent children...without whom he couldn't survive—this is what he told everyone. 'Poor me! My poor daughters!' And taking out a handkerchief, would wipe his eyes. And everyone would say, 'Oh poor soul! What a god-like doctor! So much money! So much respect! A sinful woman has wrecked the poor man's life. Dear Lord, what sort of Divine justice is this? You have written a shrew into a deity's life! All the result of past karmas. He mustn't have hurt even an ant in this life, he speaks so kindly, how benevolent he is! Oh, this is indeed what is called Kalyug!'

The way I used to avoid the residents of Patel Nagar, I was still avoiding them, and everyone else around me, certain of what they must be thinking of me. Was this liberation?

The only difference was, there were no beatings now. No insults morning and evening. There was no suffocation. I could sleep when I wanted to, and get up whenever I wanted.

What sort of clothes I wanted to buy for my daughters, I could decide that now. I was not dependent on anyone for permission. If there was any limit, any fetters, it was just how much I could work, and how much I could earn to fulfil our needs.

Liberation is not a name for the knocking down of outer walls. It's actually a name for the collapse of a dungeon-like, dark hole in your mind. The foundation of that dungeon has been filled with redundant customs and traditions of a bygone era. Advice passed down from a mother's mother's mother…A conviction that woman has no identity or worth except as a daughter, wife or mother.

Age-old lichen clings to the walls of that dungeon in the mind. With water oozing out of the stones beneath the lichen. Age-old stones, hewn into the foundation. Bats have hung from the roof of that dungeon. For ages! At the slightest movement in the dungeon, they attack, fluttering and beating their wings, and attaching themselves to the object causing the disturbance, suck her blood, pluck out her flesh, and snap her bones before going back to hang onto the roof, upside down!

❦

When Raj's threats began to intensify even more, I took both the girls to Shimla and got them admitted to Auckland House School. But the expense of paying their school fees and staying in a hostel myself, was beyond me.

I didn't have anything that I could sell. Neither jewellery, nor clothes, nor property.

Under the wide open sky, I was standing alone on the sunburnt earth, trying to shield my two daughters with my own shadow. Like a hen hides her chickens beneath her wings. But the problem was that my wings had also been plucked. Only a naked body was left, and from whose pink flesh, even now the blood was dripping. Isn't it an amazing thing, that my body was still warm after having been quartered a long time ago!

ॐ

The principal of Auckland House School was Miss Hakim. She was a very intelligent, elderly lady, probably an Anglo-Indian.

She had spent her whole life in Auckland House School. She had joined as a teacher, and now had become the principal.

I explained the whole situation to her. The story of two innocent buds born from the cracks of the broken walls of a broken-down house, two buds who were my daughters.

I showed her all their report cards right from childhood. Both had always topped their classes.

'Miss Hakim, you are welcome to take their test. If you give them admission then I'll quickly go to Delhi and get their school-leaving certificates. I didn't bring them, as I wasn't sure if they would get admission here or not.' She said, 'Why should I test children who have got such good marks? Go to Delhi and get their school-leaving certificates. And clothes and things also.'

She handed me a long list of things: six uniforms, four sweaters, two coats, six pairs of woollen socks, six pairs of white cotton socks, two pairs of school shoes, one pair each of walking shoes, one pair each of sports canvas shoes, twelve handkerchiefs, six pairs of undergarments, two party-wear frocks, a special dress each for the annual function. Quilts, pillows, bedsheets, blankets...

When I saw the list I panicked, but she must have understood my dilemma from my expression, for she herself deleted a number of items from the list.

I realized then that though I couldn't stand sympathy or pity, there are times when you have to accept them. Yet the heart becomes heavy.

When I was about to return, leaving my daughters in the school, I could see the pain and bewilderment on their faces. I tried to make them understand that the separation was only for a short time. The moment their father's anger cooled down, and he stopped threatening us, I would take them back to Delhi. Nothing is more heartrending for a mother than when she sees the silent pain in the vulnerable faces of her children, or experiences the helplessness in innocent eyes brimming with unshed tears, looking huge on downcast, defenceless faces.

Comforting each other, we all wept together. This was another grief-stricken milestone in our lives which we had to face together.

I wrote and gave an authorization to Miss Hakim that whenever the children's father wanted to meet them, he could do so. Only he shouldn't be allowed to take them out of the school premises. Within the school, he could sit with them as long as he liked, talking to them.

An old friend, Anang Paalji, a well-known official of the Himachal government, was appointed by me as their local guardian. He had been through so much adversity in his life that his heart had become as soft as a flower. He had a special soft corner for children. He was bringing up his four daughters on his own. He would wash and iron their clothes, get them ready, pack their lunch with his own hands, and then drop them at school in his car and bring them back as well. He would help them with their homework and their studies. He had kept himself away from the social life of a high government official and was completely devoted to his daughters.

When I asked him to become the local guardian, he laughingly agreed, 'I'll consider that I have six daughters rather than four from now onwards. I'll take good care of them both. Whenever I take my daughters for an outing on Sundays, they'll go with me. I'll even look after them if they fall ill. You don't worry at all.'

I wrote a letter to Raj informing him that both the girls were studying in Auckland House School in Shimla, and that whenever he wanted to, he could go to meet them there. I even made Miss Hakim write to him that he could come to the school and meet his daughters whenever he liked.

I also sent messages through some of his friends that he should mete out my punishment only to me. His poor, innocent daughters had not harmed him in any way. If he went and met them lovingly in Shimla, they would forget the bitterness of their childhood days. But in three years he never visited them even once!

When he was crying in front of the residents of Patel Nagar, lamenting that God knows where his wife had hidden his innocent daughters, both the letters were in his pocket, the one from me and the other from the principal.

Everyone pitied his condition. 'Poor Doctor! What sort of a mother is she that she has snatched the children from their father and hidden them. How the poor man is crying for his children. Which father doesn't long to meet his children? What a pitiless woman she must be, who can do this.'

Whenever Dolly or Candy would fall ill, they would beg the warden not to telephone me. They knew that it wasn't easy for their impoverished mother to come to Shimla. And if she knew they were ill, she wouldn't have been able to stop herself from going to them. It was the rule in the school that only twenty rupees could be given as pocket money to each child every month. Many of the girls who were better off, of course had more money. But I really liked this rule of giving only twenty rupees, for giving more than that was beyond my capacity.

That money was meant to be used for going out on Sundays, for skating, and for going to a movie once a month. And also to have ice creams and chocolates.

But Dolly and Candy didn't go with the other girls of the school for Sunday outings or to watch movies; or to go skating or to have an ice cream. Sometimes making an excuse of a headache and sometimes of a stomach ache, they would stay back in the deserted school. In this way, they saved their pocket money.

With the money they saved, they bought shoes for me. They asked the Chinese shoemaker, whose name was Ta Tung, to make shoes from the softest leather, for my tired feet. After many years, it was because of them that I could wear such luxurious shoes. My wonderful daughters!

They were also experiencing poverty along with me. Contributing their mite to my struggle, suffering my destiny along with me.

I was the poverty-stricken wife of a rich husband. My children were a wealthy father's penniless daughters.

༄

I got to know from someone that Raj had taken his sister and her husband to Shimla for a holiday. They were staying at the Grand Hotel. They were planning to stay there for eight or ten days.

My heart beat violently. Would he go to meet Dolly and Candy? What if he said something bitter to them? What would happen then? Would he beat the two in front of the whole school?

I called up Shimla and spoke to my daughters. I tried to make them both understand, 'If your father comes to meet you, don't get upset. Talk to him happily. Show him your school. Don't even mention any of your problems to him. After all he's your father. Even lions and tigers don't eat up their young ones, on the contrary they protect them from all dangers. Forget the past. Whenever he used to beat the two of you, he did it to upset me, because he knew it would cause me pain. He only wanted to torture me. It's with me that he has some issue carried over from a past life. Some debt that he's claiming now. How can he have any enmity with you two? If he brings chocolates then say thank you to him. Act sensibly, otherwise he'll say that your mother has filled both your hearts with hatred. Dolly, Candy, talk to your father like loving children. Just don't go out of the school with him. Have you understood? Mummy loves you very much! Children don't need anything else, do they?'

He stayed for fifteen days at the Grand Hotel, but did not go to Auckland House School, just half a kilometre down the road, to meet his daughters.

Not even a bird in Patel Nagar knew that his daughters were in Shimla. And he stayed there for fifteen days, ate and drank and made merry, and returned without meeting his daughters staying just two furlongs away.

When he returned, the same old drama—eyes full of tears…the same sympathetic dialogue from the people, 'Poor Doctor! How he's pining for his daughters…And that hard-hearted woman…'

35

The second incident.

It happened a long time later.

After two and a half years in the hostel, in 1968, a few of the women staying there were allotted flats in a new building opposite the hostel, built for the UNCTAD Conference. The flats were meant only for government employees, and were allotted to those who had put in an application for it, and then had chased the files, wearing out their shoes in the process.

The building was then called 'UNCTAD Building'. The name 'Curzon Road Apartments' was given to it much later.

By that time I had started a magazine called *Rupee Trade* and had resigned from the education department, so I was no longer a government employee. But my friend Toshi, who was still working in the education department, teaching in a government school, had been allotted a flat in the UNCTAD Building, and agreed to rent it to me. It was a beautiful two-roomed flat. These flats had been built for foreign guests. And it has always been a tradition in India that whether there is enough to eat at home or not, a lot of money has to be spent on foreign guests coming for international conferences, to create a good impression.

First spend a lot of money on them, feed them mutton and chicken, serve them champagne, then stand in front of them with a begging bowl, asking, from the donation box you have created for backward countries, please put a fistful of charity into our bowls. In the name of your excellent dinner…In the name of the champagne and Scotch…in the name of all your outings in limousines……and in the name of seeing the Taj at night…

In the working girls hostel, the first thing I had done was to buy 100-watt bulbs to replace the earlier ones. Because at Raj's house I used to be cursed for switching on even a 40-watt bulb. Raj would taunt me, will your father pay the electricity bills? Many a night I had spent outside our home sitting under a street lamp to either check papers or translate or just study.

Now after moving to the UNCTAD apartments, I made enquiries at the bank about their loan schemes, especially how to get a loan to buy an air-conditioner.

In those days, Lal Bahadur Shastri's son, Sunil, was an employee at the Connaught Place branch of the Bank of India. Much later on he became the chief minister of Uttaranchal Pradesh. Maybe he's still a minister somewhere. If any of my friends or acquaintances become ministers, I don't go to meet them—because after gaining that position, they start thinking that whoever is coming to meet them is doing so for a selfish motive. Sunil had read a few of my stories in a couple of magazines, *Nai Kahaniyan* and *Dharamyug*. So he would show me a lot of respect and used to call me Didiji. Taking the responsibility on himself, he got my loan sanctioned.

The first thing that I bought with this loan, for which I paid the instalments over the next three years, was an air-conditioner. It cost five and a half thousand rupees, in the summer of 1968.

Isn't it a strange thing? The one who didn't have enough money to buy food, who used to eke out days on an eighteen-paisa milk bottle and half a bread loaf for twelve paisa, who used to save every pice for the children's school fees, uniforms and any illnesses, who would literally scratch out a living, what did such a one want with an air-conditioner?

It was because at that time, I had become prone to fever. I would feel as if my whole body was burning in an oven.

I thought that if I had an air-conditioner, I could continue working despite the fever

Though my garb may have been that of a destitute pauper, my temperament was, and still is, that of royalty. A royal disposition had been conferred on me, friends! The heart longed for comfortable luxuries!

I stayed in that flat for two and half years. When Dolly and Candy came home during the holidays, they found the flat very small. Maybe it was the effect of the spacious environment at school. Also, one of the rooms was my office. All the staff—the steno, typist, designer, lay-out person—sat in that room. The other room was our living quarters. In that one room, the three of us had to live, sleep, eat, drink, fight, talk and love each other. The girls had to study in that room, and Arpana had to make her paintings on old newspapers; long telephone conversations had to be carried on with friends, secretive talks with a lot of smothered laughter. A mother maybe as good a friend as she likes, but growing girls still have some things that they like to share only with their friends.

In 1970, a book I had written for the Russian embassy was published. Through the kind offices of my old friend, Darshan Singh, I got eight thousand rupees for it. A full eight thousand! I felt like Queen Victoria!

I immediately took a flat on rent in Greater Kailash. Three thousand was the advance rent for three months, and five thousand for renovating and furnishing the house. I possessed only a few pieces of furniture—a bed, a couch, below which I kept all my utensils, and on which I would sit the whole day, doing all my translation work, writing articles, and even sleeping on it at night, one cupboard for books, a kerosene and an electric stove. I put all these things in the servants' quarter and gave that room to a family, whose daughter would clean my flat, to live in. When there was enough money for food, then she would even cook the food. She would also wash the clothes.

We shifted to the new house on September 1. Four bedrooms, one of which became my office. We each had our own bedrooms. A nice big living room, a huge kitchen. A lawn in front. A garage and a servant's room above it. I enjoyed cooking in the kitchen where everything was arranged neatly and derived great pleasure out of having my lawn laid with special Calcutta grass. Buying cuttings of roses and cactus plants from the nurseries, a Swedish-style sofa set from Ravi Sikri and a green carpet for the living room were such happy activities. And when I ordered a writing table for myself and put 100-watt bulbs in each room, I felt that all my sufferings had been vindicated.

∾

It was the fifteenth day in that house, September 15.

The tailor, Gyanchand, was stitching curtains in the house. He told me, 'The material for the curtains is a little short. Please get another six metres.' So I went to buy the cloth from South Extension and returned around one in the afternoon. The moment I came in, my typist, Harkrishan, told me, 'Just now Daarji called up to inform that Raj has passed away. You have to reach Patel Nagar at once. At Daarji's house.'

For a few minutes I couldn't recollect which near or distant relative of Daarji was called Raj. Maybe someone from Bhera. In Lahore too, all our relatives would come to us, either for court cases or hospital-related issues. Maybe someone had come for some such purpose to Daarji's house.

With all the work and hassle involved in shifting to the

new house, I had not been able to go to Daarji's house for many days. Normally I would go to his house at least once a week to meet him and set things in order there.

Raj? Who Raj?

I couldn't associate my husband's name, Raj, with someone who had passed away, not even in a dream! A strong, energetic man like Raj. Who, when he walked seemed to shake the earth. Who, when he spoke made the wind around him shiver. Who, when he was at home, could reduce the three of us to talking in whispers. We didn't dare speak in a loud voice. Whose terror made the very earth and the sky tremble! Surely, the Raj who was dead, couldn't be this Raj!

I reached Daarji's house in Patel Nagar. He had been waiting for me. He looked troubled and his eyes were red.

Had Daarji been crying? I felt astonished. Why had he been crying? Crying for a person who was not even in our lives? For whom we had died long ago?

I suddenly realized that my eyes were also moist.

We both went down the lane behind the house, crossed the road, went through the back lane of the next block, to enter the house in the middle of the lane.

This was the house where she lived. The one whose name I had not even tried to find out. The one whose face I had never seen. Or maybe I had seen her face in the pictures that Raj had shown me on our wedding night in Karnal. Or it was possible that she was not that girl, but someone else. I didn't know. I still don't know.

He had created such a miserable image of himself in the minds of the people that he had everybody's sympathy. They said, poor man, what can he do, where will he go? Wherever he can find a few moments of tranquillity, naturally he will go there. He acknowledges her as his sister, she is the one who feeds him. At home, there is nothing...Across the courtyard there was a verandah, then a big room. In that room, Raj was lying quietly.

A person who always used to roar like a lion, how could he be lying there so quietly?

The women were craning their necks to see whether his wife, the wife who five years earlier had left him 'to run away with some lover of hers', would cry or not on seeing his inert body.

The lifeless body was covered up to the neck by a sheet. His arms were folded across the sheet.

I was trying my best to control my tears but I could not. I wept.

I had faced a lot of misery with him, but still, I had spent that time with him.

Just then I heard the whisperings among the women sitting there, 'Oh the poor soul...For the past four or five days he had been under so much stress, he would start crying while talking...today was the court date...the last hearing...for the children's custody...couldn't tolerate that shock...the poor thing had a heart failure...'

Court? Date? Custody? What were these women talking about?

༄

A woman sitting next to me, gently raised my head resting on my knees and softly spoke into my ear, 'What was to happen, has happened. Now you go and take charge of your house. Your father-in-law has sent your brothers-in-law to come and take away all his belongings. They're already packing it up. Go, go and take charge of your house.'

My house? Which house? That house, where Raj used to live? Though just his body used to be present there not his heart, because his heart lived in this house.

That house? In which I was not living now out of my own choice. The house that Raj had never let me think of as my own. It was like a guesthouse from where I would be ejected every few months, and then be recalled whenever he felt like it. Now because I myself had refused to go back to it, what right did I have over that house?

But how strange were these people! My father-in-law was seated in the verandah, surrounded by the other men. His face looked very peaceful. All were saying—the father is as saintly as his son was.

I was astonished. The lifeless body of his son was lying in the room behind him, yet he could think of sending his two other sons to his dead son's house to seize all his possessions, in case his wife turned up to claim them!

I also saw my mother-in-law sitting surrounded by a number of ladies. I went and touched her feet as always. She pulled her feet back and started wailing loudly.

I gathered my courage and approached my father-in-law. On seeing me he stood up. I bowed and touched his feet. He stood there without saying a word.

I said softly, 'Pitaji, that is not my house, it's your son's. You're the only one who has a right over it. You can have everything packed afterwards, any time you like.'

He kept quiet, as if he hadn't heard a single word of what I had said.

I tried to recognize 'her' from among the crowd of women, the one in whose house Raj had breathed his last.

People were saying, 'He came home perfectly fine last night. But he was distraught. For today was the court date. He told us, the judge had to deliver the final judgement today, whether the children were to stay with the mother or the father. She is his sister after all, so she consoled him and kept him involved in conversation, distracting him from his sorrow and persuading him to have dinner. Seeing his distress, she thought he may harm himself in some way. So she didn't allow him to go home at night, made him sleep here in her house. He woke up in the morning and went to freshen himself. She went to the kitchen to make tea for him.

'After freshening up he came back and lay down on the cot. By the time she brought the tea, he was gone.'

Through the corner of my eyes, I once again tried to make out who that 'sister' was from among the crowd of women. But I couldn't recognize her.

Even if I had been able to make out who she was, what could I have done? Maybe I would have hugged her and cried for her, because she was the one who had lost her husband.

I had been a widow for many years. She had become one only today.

༄

Slowly, the whole tale emerged. Raj's last drama!

He had told everyone September 15 was the date on which the judge would pronounce his final decision. But on September 15, the Highest Judge up there had given His last verdict!

The story he had created two years earlier was that his wife wanted to get married again, so had filed for divorce in the court. If Brecht or Chekov had heard his story, they would have marvelled at the fertility of his imagination. In a very methodical manner, he would get 'dates' from the court. Every two or three months, he had a 'date'. Before each 'date' he would shed tears in front of his patients, neighbours, anyone who came to meet him, that on the day of the 'date', she, meaning me, would be present in the court. That he couldn't bear it any more, and so on.

For the first ten to twelve 'dates', he told everyone he was contesting the divorce. He had hired the topmost lawyers. On the day of the 'court hearing', he would go missing from the clinic for half the day, so that people would believe that the poor doctor had gone to court to face the problems created by his vixen of a wife.

Then in the evenings he would recount every detail of what had happened in court that day, what his lawyer said, what my lawyer said, and what the judge said.

He would even describe the clothes I was wearing, the makeup I wore, how boldly I stood there. He told them that he tried to talk to me outside the courtroom—asking me, 'Why are you bent on dragging the family name in a court! You go and live with whichever lover you want. We have never had a divorce in the family. Why do you want a divorce?

'Think about the two innocent children. Tomorrow they also will have to be married off. If they have to bear the stigma of their parents' divorce, then how will they get married? Take this case back. Let my daughters remain with me. I will bring them up myself. I will educate them. Who else is there in my life? You don't even need them. For your own licentiousness you have thrown them away in some far-off hostel. There they're going astray and here I am pining for them. Have some mercy on them and on me as well.'

'But, sir, all this was like water off a duck's back! When a shameless woman is bent on doing something...'

And the listeners would shake their heads and say, what times we are living in! And sympathize with the poor doctor wholeheartedly.

Now for the past five or six months he had been telling everyone that he had also agreed to the divorce. In fact he had told the judge that he had always worshipped his wife. If getting a divorce would give her happiness, then he would not stand in the way. Please give the decision in favour of a divorce, but I beg of you to return my children to me. She wants a divorce because she wants to remarry. You can take it in writing from me, I'll not get married again. I will only take care of my daughters. Please give their custody to me.

So now for the past six months or so, the 'dates' had been for the custody of the children.

The judge had to pronounce the final decision for the divorce and custody on September 15. 'That's why for the last few days the poor doctor had been so disturbed, very depressed. God knows whether the poor man was even eating anything or not,' everyone said.

People also said, 'Such a lion-like body, look how it has been undermined by this deep sorrow. His was certainly not of an age to pass on. It is grief that has carried him off so early. How much he was pining for his daughters! He has, indeed, achieved martyrdom in his distress over his daughters! He must have had a heart attack just thinking that what if the judge rules in her favour and gives the custody of the girls to the mother…'

All were whispering these thoughts. Only I, my daughters and Daarji knew what a huge conspiracy this was on Raj's part, by which he had gained everyone's sympathy. He had played the best drama of his life before exiting from it.

ϡ

These are just two examples of the thousands of dramas and fabrications that Raj used to invent against me and share with everyone.

These two examples of poisonous viciousness that he had spread against me are enough to show that to protect myself against the accusing eyes of the world, I had to retreat into a dark well within myself. I did not know what else to do, I couldn't even talk to anyone about it.

Only one lady, a neighbour, knew what was in reality happening with me, because from the terrace of the second floor of her house, everything that went on in our house could clearly be seen. Though I had never spoken to her, I was aware of her silent sympathy, and for that I am truly grateful to her. In fact if she had tried to voice her sympathy like the others, I would probably have run away from her too.

I was so broken from inside that I turned away from even genuine sympathizers, mistrusting their sympathy as a farce. So much so that when even Beeji or Daarji asked me anything, I would respond bitterly, 'Nothing is the matter with me. Can anything happen to such an insensitive stone that I am? The house that you have chosen for me, I am only trying to live in that house, in whatever way I can cope. What's it to you? What's it to anyone?'

But this neighbour of mine had created such a bridge of sympathetic silence between the two of us, that there was no need of any question being asked, nor the need to answer. This exchange was totally soundless, yet with an element of deep care and concern. For me, it was like discovering a trove of gold coins buried in a pot beneath the earth.

This was the same woman who had whispered softly into my ear while sitting next to Raj's dead body, 'Child, go and take care of your house. That is your house after all, yours and your daughters. Your brothers-in-law are clearing it out completely.'

I gave Raj's house to his parents. All the things in it. I put my signature to reams of papers, the car papers, insurance papers, share certificates and whatnot!

My thinking was that the man who, as a husband and a father, in his lifetime, never gave a square meal, nor clothes, nor school fees, nor books, to either me or my daughters, touching or taking anything of his or even his money after his death, was equal to a crime for me.

Everyone said, 'You're a stupid woman! It's all rightfully your daughters. If you don't want to take anything then don't do so. Why are you depriving them of their right?'

But the logic that people have, or even the logic of the whole world, has no connection to the logic of the heart. They're miles distant from the logic of the soul!

I had no wish to become a vulture, seizing and scavenging everything from a dead man, that which he had never given when he was alive. He had regarded the cold iron of Godrej almirahs and bank lockers to be a more secure legacy for old age than warm beating hearts.

36

We continued to live in the house in Greater Kailash, which we loved. It was airy and well-lit, and we were no longer cramped, as we had been in the flat on Curzon Road.

Dolly, that is Arpana, would stay in her room the whole day, making paintings and writing poems. Right from childhood, she had been a little shy, keeping herself away from the inquisitive eyes of visitors was one of her habits.

First in the Patel Nagar house and then later at the Curzon Road flat, she had kept a small wooden stool for herself in the bathroom. If any visitor came, she would lock herself up in the bathroom, and would keep reading, sitting on the stool. Her speed at reading was also amazing. She could finish a 400-page novel in a day and a half!

Candy was the total opposite of her sister. She was outgoing, very happy meeting people and could talk for hours with her friends. She was also very fond of reading—novels, stories, poems, everything. She had the ability to keep the light of life burning like a lamp with her verve.

What can be said about those who have gone...the less said, the better! Their memories can only come back to haunt.

∽

As soon as we had shifted to our new house, we received a visit from a group of eunuchs. Clapping their hands loudly, dancing and singing. I tried to make them understand, 'I have not bought this house. I have just rented it.'

They said, 'Oh! But it's new for you, isn't it? You're lucky to have it. Live happily in this house. We have just come to bless you. But we will also take what is due to us, money, clothes, you have to give us that. That's our right.'

I laughingly agreed and said, 'Okay come, come inside. Come and sit in my new house and have tea with me. Then I'll see what I can give you.'

They looked at me as if they couldn't believe their ears. And then looked at each other in an amazed fashion, as if to say what can we do with this crazy woman!

'Folks, you have to come in and have tea. Letting guests go without serving them tea is against our tradition,' I told them.

A lot of gulfs got bridged over tea. As soon as the commercial perspective changed, they told me a lot of things, as though chatting to an old friend, 'No one allows us inside their houses. Our place has always been at the threshold of the house, even though we come for an auspicious reason, to give blessings or to take what's due to us. But everyone tries to chase us away, as soon as possible. What's more, even our shadow falling within the house is considered to be ominous and unfortunate.'

They laughed as they told me all this. It was their lot to endure the brunt of all indignities, and yet they could laugh gaily. A lot of courage, daring and practice must be needed to do that. Is that not so?

Masculine voices, masculine features, yet dressed as women...Yet they bore this cruel trick of nature with gay fortitude, were even forgiving towards the Divine for his forgetfulness in their case. I thought, they are truly large-hearted to be able to laugh so spontaneously, brush aside the harsh punishment of nature so casually. I asked them, 'Isn't it easier to sit in one place and earn your living rather than going from house to house?'

In return, they questioned me, 'Is that possible? To be born in this form means to live a kind of life already set for us. Present yourself at every auspicious occasion. Give your congratulations, laugh and dance and entertain others as well.'

'Meaning you have to gladden other people's hearts even though you yourself...'

'Well, we also keep laughing and dancing all the time along with them.'

'Have you never wanted to do anything else? Stay in your own home? Stay at one place?'

'We do have our own home. Who says we don't have a home? We all live together. An elderly person who lives with us, is our Guru. We also cook in our home, clean and wash up, take care of our Guru, massage his legs to relieve him of pain.'

'Would any of you like to live here with me, as a member of this household? The work will be the same—cooking meals, cleaning the house, washing clothes, and instead of the Guru, massaging our heads and feet. We are three women in this house. And there will be one small dog. We haven't kept it as yet, for earlier our house was very small. But now we'll keep one.'

'Keep a black dog,' they were quick to advise me.

'Why, why a black one?'

'It's considered to be auspicious and fortunate.'
'Whomsoever we love, becomes fortunate.'
They continued laughing.
'Now tell me. Give an answer to my question. Who will live here with me?'
'Oh, who keeps us in their homes, Ma'am! We congratulate them for their good fortune, receive their largesse, give them blessings, and then turn back from the threshold of their house. This is our destiny.'
'Well, I have invited you within this threshold. Tell me now, do you accept? Is anyone from among you ready to live with me?'
They were all quiet, looking at each other. Cooing and babbling amongst themselves, like pigeons, laughing out loud at times. Or casually lifting the ends of their skirts, they would abstractedly stroke their cracked heels.
I brought some cream from my room, and pulling the nearest foot with a cracked heel towards myself, started applying the cream.
'Please let it be. We will...'
'But who has told you that you people can't do any other work? I don't think you know but the Mughal Emperor Akbar's minister was also like you and also two of the officers in his army.'
They were astonished to hear that. 'Really? Minister? Officials in the army?'
'But of course.'
'Then why is a cowardly, unworthy person, who has no courage to face up to anything in life, considered to be like an eunuch?'
'That's the very thing. All people's hypocrisy! If once a notion gets set about someone, maybe even without rhyme or reason, it becomes a myth, an ingrained tradition. Society is full of such unreasonable myths.

'Now cats keep roaming all over the place as they do not stay inside the house like pet dogs. So if a cat, while roaming around, happens to cross your path, what's so ominous about that? Nevertheless, people give up and turn back home, believing that now that a cat has crossed our path, what we're going for will not fructify!

'What myths and superstitions are making you belittle yourself? In what way are you a lesser human being than others? It's only that you can't produce an offspring. What else do you lack? You are great conversationalists and have such entertaining and perceptive insights! You think faster than a frontier mail. You can utilize your brains for other things as well. After receiving an education, you can also become a doctor, lawyer, collector, a general in the army, writer, painter or even a singer. You can be anything you like! Even now it's not too late.'

I was speaking on and on, and as I was doing so, all the laughter vanished from their faces and they grew serious and downcast.

That's the whole thing, until you understand life, as long as your life is lost in unfathomable mists, there is no issue. Issues arise when you start understanding things. Comprehension begins to expand the boundaries of your limited thinking. And it's this comprehension of things that gives rise to an inner tussle which further rouses an unbearable smarting against the order of things.

'But we have been told only this, that kings and emperors used to keep eunuchs like us to guard their palaces so that the ladies of the harem were completely safe from the desires of other men. For they had no such fears from us.'

'That is also correct. But from the whole of history only one aspect has been told to you. I am telling you the other side of the story. Just think, being born as a eunuch is a small oversight of nature. That oversight also happens when a child is born sightless, or with some limb missing, or mentally deficient, or in some other way deformed. Some cannot even support their own head, or feed themselves, or sit or walk properly, a lifelong burden on their parents. You people are much better off than those poor burdensome souls. What is there that is wrong in you? You're definitely more strong than me. Now tell me, which of you is going to stay with me? You can consider my house as yours and do all the work. Even cook our meals for us.'

'Okay, we'll think about it and let you know,' they said, and left.

One day, less than a week later, the doorbell rang. It was afternoon.

Right from the beginning, despite living in our own home, we were always afraid of what dangers may befall us. Until we had reassured ourselves by looking through the 'magic eye', we never opened our front door. At night, too, I would make doubly sure that all the bolts were drawn properly and everything was locked. I would even get up a number of times at night to check the bolts, because the three of us were alone at night. My daughters' forlornness, born of the deprivation of not having a father figure in their lives, had always been a heavy weight on my chest, a weight as heavy as Mount Everest.

That afternoon, I peeped out through the 'magic eye'. A short man was standing outside. A dark, pock-marked face, drops of sweat streaming down his cheeks. He wore blue trousers and a red T-shirt and there was a large, heavy bag in his hand.

Putting the chain on the door, I opened it slightly. 'Who are you and what do you want?' I asked.

He smiled, showing tobacco-yellowed teeth. Jerking his hips a little, he said, 'You haven't recognized me?'

I suddenly recognized him from the jerk of his body, its movement and the drag in his throaty voice.

I quickly opened the door.

When he had come along with the others, he too, had been wearing feminine clothes. Then I had hugged them all enthusiastically. But now he was wearing a man's clothes. I couldn't welcome him by hugging him now. Laughing, I moved aside and let him enter. He entered the house as if he had always been living there with us. It was just a few days since he had come with the others, and now he had returned. His name was Kanhaiya.

He stayed with us for about four years. It was a strange surrender on his part. He was ready to even lay down his life for us. Everyone used to say, you must have a past life connection, otherwise who gives up his life like that for someone else!

When he wore male clothes, did his hair like a man, we used to feel completely protected. After all, there was a man in the house now, Kanhaiya!

But whenever he felt like, he would wear women's clothes. Sometimes he would wear a skirt and top, sometimes a saree, and at times a salwar-kameez. He would bind up his hair and attach a false bun, apply kohl to his eyes, lipstick, bindi, blusher, earrings, bangles, toe-rings...Then he would say, 'Now I'm Radha.'

When he presented himself as Kanhaiya, all three of us felt hesitant in allowing him to massage our heads. But whenever he became Radha, we would, without hesitation, sit and eat with him, laugh, play, gossip, get ourselves massaged, have our hair oiled!

It was only much later, after another tragedy struck our

lives, that he left our home. When the very atmosphere of the house seemed to have frozen, how could anyone possibly dwell in an abode of snow? And so he left. But that is a story that belongs to a later part of my life.

37

I would go to meet Daarji almost every Sunday. Each time he would ask me, 'Have you found any good match for Arpana?'

Sometimes he himself would talk to some friend or relative about it and then tell me, 'The boy is a lawyer. The boy's father is also a lawyer. Very famous lawyer! Earns in millions! Has his own bungalow.' Or, 'The boy is a doctor, soon to go abroad. His parents want him to get married before he goes. Shall we meet them?'

A Mr Sehgal lived in the neighbourhood. He also used to continually matchmake and would suggest prospective bridegrooms, one after the other.

Then one day a dear friend of mine, Rajinder Singh Bedi, a talented writer and filmmaker, also suggested a match. His daughter's brother-in-law. I told him, 'I don't want to get her married as yet. She has just finished her schooling and she must go to college.' So he said, 'You can delay the wedding for some time. You must consider the fact that they do not have the support of their father. If you come across a good match then there is no harm in finalizing it. And this match is as good as being in the family. No questions will be asked! Besides, I'll handle everything.'

It was true that I myself would worry whether the girls would be able to get married without the support of a father. What if the prospective in-laws asked me, their father has passed away recently, why were you living separately all these years? How would I answer them? Dowry? Where would that come from? How would they get settled in life? This is what everyone warned me about. 'You have the responsibility of two daughters on your head. How will you handle it all alone? Don't waste your time in thinking too much. Sitting with your eyes closed will not resolve the issue. If something goes wrong tomorrow, then?'

'Goes wrong?' That would conjure up innumerable things that could go wrong. What if someone kidnapped them? What if they got involved in a love affair? What if one of them became pregnant? These were the fears that plagued me night and day.

In this apprehensive frame of mind, fearful of the consequences, I hesitantly accepted someone's proposal when they said, 'He's my nephew. An officer in the navy. If you're willing...'

The boy's family came to meet us. But it was not Arpana, but Candy, whom they liked, for Arpana was taller than the boy.

I objected, 'How can I agree for the younger one? Besides, she has just taken admission in a course in French Literature.'

But Daarji, my aunts, uncles, neighbours, all said that these were unnecessary arguments. If the younger one gets married first, then what is wrong in it? It will still be half a burden off your shoulders. Be sensible. They don't have a father to depend on. It's only you who has to take this decision.

Candy also agreed, for the boy assured her that there would be no interruption in her studies. She could continue her studies after marriage. Candy said, 'People in the forces are usually open-minded. They are not conservative like ordinary folks. Then, as everyone says, you'll also be relieved of half your burden. So let me be married.'

My daughters also felt that they were a burden? How did this thought get into their minds? I had never thought of them as burdens nor had I ever said so to them. They were my soulmates, friends, confidantes, my all-weather companions. They were the wings with which I could soar to unbelievable heights. They were the two achievements of my barren smoke-blurred life. The only genuinely worthwhile result of so many years of struggle.

In fact Arpana had stood first in all of Himachal Pradesh. Now was the time when they could do whatever they wanted to. We had only recently started going for walks together. We used to go to see films, plays and art exhibitions. In the evening we would sit and discuss the books we had read. And tell each other about any interesting bits we had come across in those books.

Now, due to the presence of Kanhaiya, I didn't even need to worry so much about them whenever I had to go out of Delhi on work. But whenever I did have to do so, I would make it a point to call them up daily and we would chat about anything of importance. It was just recently that we had discovered that we were complete in ourselves. We didn't need anyone else in our lives.

Then, where had this feeling of being a burden come into their heads? From the very winds swirling around us? Whether they are told verbally or not, girls have a sort of third eye, even a third ear! From the environment, from the sighing winds, from people's assessing glances, they can perceive everything, sense everything, apprehend it all.

A hard-working mother struggling with poverty, and the fear of being alone at home. I don't know when these things got integrated into their system and started circulating in their blood. I had always tried to protect them from the harsh realities of life. What can pierce the tender hearts of children and continue to fester there, no one can comprehend.

Many a times I longed to find a way by which every wretched mother could once again keep her child safe and shielded in her womb, inviolably protected from all misery!

Because when we are living life, we are not chronicling it date-wise, like a historical document. Living life is actually like walking along uneven paths, raising the dust with our footsteps. One step falls here and the other elsewhere, leaving one totally disoriented at times.

Yet there must be many who carve out avenues for themselves after much thought. Those who live their lives according to a plan.

We are told everything about Madagascar, about the agriculture system in Ethiopia, the sledges of the Eskimos. We are also told what is the square root of a+b. And that there are some unseen, imaginary lines on the surface of the earth according to which the weather and time change. And that in our orbit, which star is rotating at which speed at a given time. But no one tells us anything about our inner world. Our feelings, our fears and terrors, anger and loneliness. Or even about the effect of this savage world on our children who are such an intrinsic part of our lives.

We are left standing alone amidst the ruins of our dreams. Our children too, at times, must be feeling as if they are also standing all alone on a pile of their own tiny wishes and equally tiny moments of happiness.

Why wasn't I able to protect them better from the hardships and sorrows of my life? I had no answer to this, I could only bear the guilt.

Why did I allow this awareness to arise in them, that I would be relieved of their burden only after they were married off? I could at least have done this much—like I had given them the freedom to choose their own names, I could have also given them the flexibility of choosing their own partners, loving whoever they liked. They could have brought their friends home. To relieve themselves of their loneliness, they shouldn't have been forced to think of marriage as the sole panacea.

∾

What was it that made me quietly accept Candy's decision? Was it because of my own fears and insecurities? Or was it more because of my biggest fear of being inadequate in settling my two daughters?

Children don't only take a body from their mother, nor just her features, they also absorb her sorrows into their system. They participate equally in all her misery and problems. Especially daughters.

We may think as much as we like that we have hidden all the fights happening in the house, the beatings, fear and terror from our children because they were locked up in a different room. Or that they were then too young to understand anything. But no, the fragile soil of their hearts absorbs everything. The fear getting amplified every moment in the fragile, tender and delicate soil of their vulnerable hearts!

38

Candy got married.

She was hardly my age, the age at which I had got married, eighteen. I had decided then, that whatever had happened to me, I would never let the same happen to my daughters.

But when does whatever we want happen? In the flow of changing circumstances, we're swept along like forsaken straws, like defenceless, dry leaves, unaware of what is actually happening.

The wedding happened. But there was no glow that is usually evident on a new bride's face. Candy looked sad, as though lost in her own world. Whenever I asked her if anything was wrong, she would laugh it off. Forced laughter. But I was a mother. She was a part of my very being. It was my blood which was coursing through her veins. The deep melancholy that was filling her heart, burgeoning in her very soul, was searing me from within.

One thing is clear, in fact, a universal truth. Children reared amongst the tribulations of poverty, are so softhearted and sentimental that as long as they can bear it, they avoid giving pain to another individual. They conceal their every distress, every unhappiness, every grief, even physical discomforts as much as they can.

But finally she poured out everything. In fact, circumstances forced her to do so.

Her husband was undergoing a number of treatment procedures—from the Medical Institute, from Hamdard Dawakhana. He had some sort of illness that had rendered him unfit to even consummate the marriage. My child was still untouched, a virgin, despite being a married woman.

Those were very critical days. A lot depended on how things would turn out.

I pleaded with her, 'Come, Candy, let's go to a lawyer. Your marriage can be annulled. When there is no marriage…'

But she was firm, 'No, I'll bear it all. Till the time Arpana gets married, I'll have to tolerate all this, otherwise what will people say…'

This is how the dread of people's opinions scares and debilitates. Our very breath gets constricted, suffocating us, and we're not even aware of it.

These were my weaknesses—my own fears, my compulsions, my own wretchedness…and they overwhelmed me.

My crime was beyond forgiveness, the crime of listening to and accepting that immature child's decision.

In the end, though, the tensions and friction in her husband's house became impossible to bear and, as I had done years ago in my own marriage, Candy moved out to a hostel in Jawaharlal Nehru University where she continued her studies in French. But she stuck to her decision not to get divorced or have her marriage annulled, until Arpana got married.

∽

I have taken the story of my life to the end of 1974.

Today when I look back, I wonder, was it really me who used to tremble so much with fear and terror all the time, crouching fearfully in some dark den of life? A whole era had passed, and yet was that all I could in reality do— tremble, timidly clutch my two daughters to my bosom, and desperately try to hide from life?

No! That was my last birth.

When doomsday came, a catastrophe happened, the whole world, all the suns and moons and stars got extinguished, then it was me who was Hazrat Nooh, and it was also me who was Hazrat Nooh's boat, in which holding Candy's bundle of pain to my bosom and concealing Arpana beneath my veil, I crossed from the edge of darkness to the fringe of light on the other side.

Crossed over to this other birth!

Arpana and myself. And Candy amalgamated into the two of us.

From the ashes of the old Ajeet Cour rose Phoenix-like this completely independent Ajeet Cour. In one lifetime I have lived two lives.

The tale of this reborn Ajeet Cour is also spread over

several years. If you consider it superficially, then it's actually no big thing. But on the other hand, at a profound level, it's in truth, something very mystical.

That someone could remain alive for so long even after dying, and create a whole new universe for herself with her own hands, be alive after experiencing the very depths of despondency and degradation. That is the story I will tell if life gives me some repose, some leisure time, and the pen sustains my literary aspirations.

PART TWO

The Ocean and the Seashell

39

Whenever I look back in time I see a whirlwind of red hot fire whose flames leap out of my feet and reach right up to my head. I want to go on dialling the number one zero one. When you dial this number people from the fire brigade come down to douse the flames. Mentally, I dial this number at least fifty times every day.

I am devoured by these flames every day and more so at night. To be consumed by them is the fate with which not only my forehead but my whole body was marked on the night between the 14th and 15th of August many years ago. For seven days afterwards someone seemed to continuously scrape my flesh to carve out this destiny for me. It has been more than thirty years now but the anguish within me remains the same. Perpetual pain has become a part of my being.

Each time I look back, I can see an extremely beautiful young girl who looks like a flaming torch rushing down two flights of stairs. It is a living fire stepping down the stairs. I feel the unbearable heat of the fire not only on my clothes but also on the flesh of my body and it is as though it is I who is going down those stairs enveloped in flames.

It is not in me to ask someone who is not close to me to come and help me in an emergency. She too would have refrained from calling out for help on that staircase in an alien place.

On the evening of August 14, 1974 I was engrossed in work at the press when Arpana called up from home. Sounding agitated, she said, 'A call is coming from Paris but the line is not clear and I can't hear a thing. Please come home quickly.'

A telephone call from Paris? Why?

I stuffed my papers in the file with shaking hands. Getting

into the car I instructed the driver, 'Home, and please drive fast.'

Candy had gone to France about two months ago. She was doing her MA in French at Jawaharlal Nehru University. Having topped the list in the MA Previous exam, she had won a short-term scholarship to take up a course or write her research paper in France. The choice was hers and she had decided to write a thesis for which she was touring all over France. She wrote home almost every day and we had received a letter only the day before. It was a long letter and it had come from Vichy where she had arrived after visiting several chateaux, art galleries, museums and churches at different places. Vichy is famous for natural springs of health-giving and restorative waters to which people from not only France but all over Europe throng. They drink the water of these springs and bathe in it for good health.

She had written from Vichy. How was she calling from Paris? Had she come back to Paris today? But why did she call? She was not one to make a long-distance call unless something was seriously wrong. In fact, she would rarely talk about her worries to me thinking they would upset me. My funny child. Surrounded by a thousand questions, I reached home.

'Didn't you hear any voice at all at the other end?' I asked Arpana.

'I could not hear any words but the voice sounded like Kajjan's,' she answered.

'Kajjan's voice? Not Candy's?' I was surprised, at a loss to understand what could have happened.

Kajjan was our neighbour's son. We lived in the same house in Greater Kailash. His family occupied the first floor and we lived on the ground floor. It was a newly constructed building and we were the first to move in. My two daughters and I had helped the new tenants to carry their luggage up. As a result our relationship had started off on a pleasant footing

However they were very different from us and over a period of time we stopped relating to them the way we had done earlier. They lived in a world of their own where they had a thriving business in diamonds. A ceaseless noise marked their day. It started with the frying of puris for breakfast and stretched on till late in the night accompanied by bouts of drinking and card playing.

Since we lived on the ground floor, we were subjected to an interminable hammering on our heads all the time. Heavy footsteps on the stairs, the noise of cars starting and doors opening and shutting disturbed the silence of the night. You could hear the raucous voices of their two servants talking as dozens of pots and pans clanged in the kitchen. There was not a corner in our house where we could escape the noise. The women of the family chewed paan and played cards with their friends in the room above the rear of our house while the menfolk created a racket in the front. They were only playing cards but the atmosphere that was created was of an arena where ferocious wrestlers fought desperately.

Disturbed by the noise I would often leave the house and go to a park nearby. I could see all the houses in the neighbourhood sleeping like children at night. Only the upper part of our building would be ringing with loud voices, the clattering of glasses, clanging of utensils and stamping of feet as harsh lights leapt out of the windows.

'Oof! What bad luck!' I would think.

In the morning our lawn would be littered with trash thrown down from the house upstairs. Scraps of paper, banana skins, cigarette stubs, bits of broken glass and other junk would be strewn all over the place. It was disgusting to see the blotches of paan juice on our lawn. They treated our lawn as a garbage bin but every time I would try to speak to them about it, they would react so aggressively that my day would be ruined completely.

In that house full of loud noise lived a quiet and totally different young man. His name was Kajjan.

Candy and Kajjan talked about books, listened to music and went for walks together. Because there was no room for books and music in his own house Kajjan sought a retreat in ours, which was full of books and records.

Kajjan used to say that he had no interest in the diamond business and the money that his family had. He wished to do something else. He wanted to be independent. 'Candy, someday I'll make myself worthy of your friendship,' he said once.

After two years of a deep, innocent friendship he went off to France to make himself worthy of her. Candy was like that. Even I had to make a special effort to make myself worthy of her friendship.

It was this Kajjan who was trying to contact us over the phone from Paris. Our hearts pounding, Arpana and I sat by the phone awaiting his call. Time seemed to have come to a standstill.

We waited from five till eight in the evening. Finally I asked his family for Kajjan's contact number. The number they gave me was of Vichy from where Candy's letter had come only the day before. She had mentioned that she was staying in the same hostel as Kajjan.

Irrespective of the fact that the call had come from Paris, I booked a call for Vichy. The call would not go through and I spent half the night begging and pleading with the telephone operators and superintendents but to no avail.

After midnight the phone rang again. It was Kajjan at the other end but we could not hear what he was saying.

The call I had booked materialized at a quarter to two in the morning. It was routed through London. The operator at the London exchange said that her counterpart at the other end spoke only French and they were unable to communicate with each other.

At about half past two Kajjan called up his own family. I ran upstairs. Now the line was clear and I could hear what he was saying.

'Candy got burnt in an accident,' he said.

'What?' I felt the earth shaking under my feet.

'Please, Aunty, there is nothing to worry about. She is on the mend,' he said.

'But when did it happen?'

'On the twelfth,' he answered.

'On the twelfth? And why didn't you inform me till now?'

'She told me not to tell you. She said you'd get upset. That is why,' he said.

'Where is she?' I asked.

'She is in the hospital. Please do not worry, Aunty, please do not worry at all. She is getting better,' he said.

'You have called to ask me to come there, haven't you?' I broke down.

'Come if you wish to,' he said and added, 'but she is improving.'

'Where is she? In Vichy?' I asked.

'No,' he answered, 'I am calling from Lyons. We have brought her here.'

'I am sure it is something serious, beta. Otherwise why would you move her to another city.' I was beside myself with worry.

'There is a special hospital for burn cases here. That is why we have brought her here,' he answered.

'I am coming. Please tell her I'll be there soon.' The

line snapped. Weeping, suppressing our sobs, Arpana and I supported each other as we climbed down the stairs.

It was an endless night. We were both extremely restless.

The next day was a holiday and all offices were closed. I spent the whole day racing around on the deserted streets of Delhi trying to contact ministers, officers of the Reserve Bank and the French ambassador. Finally I boarded a flight that took off for France at three-thirty in the morning.

Only one thought occupied my mind as I sat in the aircraft. 'Tell her I'll be there soon. Candy, I am coming. Wait for me, my child.'

I don't remember how and when I did it, but I had packed the small prayer book Sukhmani Sahib, with my luggage. In Sikh scripture, it was the psalm of peace. For a long time my relationship with God had been as quiet as the one between a couple who have been married for ten years. If something wonderful happened in my life, I would look at Him and lower my eyes in gratitude. And when something went wrong—which was oftener, I would sulk. If He was not concerned with my well-being, why should I speak to Him?

However, I was acutely conscious of the fact that in spite of all that had gone awry in my life in the past, it had never been like the present crisis. I was desperately reaching out to hold on to something, be it a tree, a crumbling wall, even the very air between my outstretched arms.

It was as though time stood still. The terrifying night seemed to have grown innumerable nails with which it was piercing me. Someone seemed to have placed a huge rock on my chest. Every time the plane landed on its way to Paris I would notice bright lights and the normal movement of people and think, 'These lights and all these people do not know about Candy. If they did, they along with the entire universe would stop short in their tracks.'

I tried to read the Sukhmani Sahib but the printed words seemed to dissolve into boundless waters. Alternately, they seemed to crawl onto the vast stretches of desert sands. I saw them sitting down, standing up or moving around by turns but could not identify even one of them.

Memories of the day, May 27, when Candy had boarded the Air France flight, came rushing back. She was dressed in a stunning black outfit. Seeing her in it my neighbour had remarked, 'Why is she wearing black for a journey?'

'I don't know. She got the fabric and asked the tailor to stitch it especially for the journey. She took me to the market this morning and hunted high and low for this red and yellow Rajasthani dupatta to go with the black suit,' I had answered and laughed indulgently. Then turning to Arpana, I had asked, 'Isn't she looking beautiful?'

'She is beautiful,' Arpana had answered. She adored her sister but occasionally she resented the praise people lavished on Candy.

Candy was busy with her last-minute packing, when she remembered she had left her housecoat in the hostel.

'You can take mine,' I said.

'Oh, thank you!' she said and hugged me.

Candy had this way of putting her arms around me and planting little kisses on my face on the smallest pretext. If I looked sad she would quietly come and snuggle against me at night and say, 'I can't sleep, can I lie down beside you?' I would be aware that she had come to sleep in my bed not because she could not sleep in hers but because she was concerned about my wakefulness.

Her departure for France was somewhat peculiar. Her scholarship was for a duration of two months and the air tickets had been delivered. She only had to get the date of the journey entered in them. Originally she was to leave on

May 15 but she would take me to the Air France office every day and get her departure forwarded for the day after the entry in the ticket. Eleven days were spent in this uncertainty.

'It is rather funny, Candy,' I told her one day, 'that you should waste eleven days like this. Other people your age would be impatient to take off if they got a chance like this.'

'Don't you know why I am not going?' she asked, putting her arms around me. She answered the question herself, 'I'll go when you too can come with me!'

'Funny girl,' I said caressing her glossy black hair. 'You go ahead and pave the way for us. All three of us shall go together next time and you'll be our guide. Don't you think it is a good idea, Arpana?' Arpana nodded. Candy started fussing like a child and whispered, 'I don't want to go away from you.'

'You are crazy. No one misses such a good opportunity to travel abroad. Only six weeks are left for you to avail of your scholarship. You have wasted fifteen days hovering around your mother! You'd better run off now!' I urged her.

'Okay, I'll leave on the 28th,' she said.

'But I have invited those Hungarians to dinner on the 28th. How can I go to the airport to see you off?' I asked.

'You are sending me all the way to France alone. Can't I go alone to the airport?' she argued.

'Of course not, you can leave on the 29th then,' I suggested.

However, someone informed her that very day that her scholarship would be cancelled if she did not reach France by May 30. As a result she got her seat confirmed for the very next day, May 27.

And so she boarded the plane in her jet black salwar-kurta complemented by a red and yellow Rajasthani dupatta in muslin. Her hair was tied in a plait twined with a tasselled parandi and she wore an enormous vermilion bindi on her forehead. She had wide, expressive eyes and her face was serenely beautiful. She wore a chunky, oxidized silver necklace and tiny silver bells tinkled on her anklets as she moved around the airport to complete various formalities. Hundreds of admiring glances followed her wherever she went. My bosom swelled with pride to see her looking so gorgeous.

It was a never-ending journey from Delhi to Frankfurt to Paris. I don't think anybody has ever gone on such a long journey before. I was oblivious to the time of day or night. It was like a journey from infinity to infinity, without an end.

There was a gentleman waiting for me at Paris airport. My friend Kamal Bakshi from the Ministry of External Affairs had phoned the Indian embassy in Paris on the 15th and they had sent someone to provide moral support and to help me board the connecting flight to Lyons. Before he spotted me, I had exhausted myself trying to contact the embassy over the phone. I didn't even know where to convert my dollars to local currency. Confused, I noticed a telephone at one place. I thought it was the Lufthansa office and since I was their passenger, they might be able to help me. The officer on duty there was a Frenchman who just could not figure out what I was trying to say. I tried to look up the number in the telephone directory but that too was in French. Distraught, I was wandering here and there in that huge terminal when the gentleman from the embassy approached me and asked my name.

At a time like that, even a small gesture is amazingly reassuring. He informed me that the First Secretary from the embassy, Dilwari Saheb, had gone to Lyons in the morning. That made me very anxious.

'Why has he gone there?' I asked, 'has my daughter's condition worsened?'

'It is not that,' he answered, 'we received a call from Mr Kamal Bakshi from Delhi in the morning. He had made a personal request to take care of your daughter so the ambassador has sent Dilwari Saheb to Lyons.'

'But do you have any idea how she is doing?' I asked anxiously.

'Look, the accident took place on August 12. It is the 16th today. If she is okay till today, God will help her get well soon,' he answered.

'God will have to help her recover,' my heart said determinedly.

He helped me check in for the flight to Lyons and left. There were two hours still to go before the flight took off. My legs could not support me any more so I sat down on a bench. But my mind was racing here and there like a deranged animal in a jungle. The wilderness where my mind was wandering was all aflame and there was no possibility of escape from it.

The flight was announced and I boarded the plane. At Lyons airport, Kajjan and a tall Sikh gentleman were waiting for me. Kajjan bent down to touch my feet and introduced the gentleman, 'This is Dilwari Saheb.'

'How is Candy?' I asked.

'Waheguru will help her recover,' Dilwari Saheb said in a steady voice. I felt somewhat reassured. 'I hope there is no danger to her life,' I said again. 'Pray to Waheguru,' he said, taking my small suitcase from my hands. I suddenly felt weak in the knees. I held on to Kajjan's arm and put my head on his shoulder. All the self-possession I had shown through the long journey gave way to uncontrollable crying.

'Say Waheguru,' Dilwari Saheb tried to calm me down. 'Shall we keep this luggage in the hostel first?'

'No. Take me to my daughter first.'

Hospital. A tall, white building like a fortress. You couldn't see a single human being outside. Deadly silence prevailed over the place. Walking up the stairs was like scaling the walls of a ruined building.

Upstairs was a small corridor consisting of more steps. Four or five doors which opened into the corridor were all locked from inside. There was a telephone on the wall. Kajjan lifted the receiver and said something in French into the mouthpiece after which he replaced it on the cradle.

The three of us sat down on a small bench. Half an hour passed but no door opened. Kajjan said something on the phone again. He seemed to be pleading with someone. He repeated the word *'merci'* several times which was the only thing I could understand.

After what seemed like ages, the upper part of the door which looked like a window, opened. We saw a man in a white coat on the other side. He must be a doctor, I thought. Kajjan explained something to him pointing in my direction several times. Perhaps he was saying, 'Her mother has come from India. I know it is not the visiting hour but she has come from a great distance. She just wants to catch a glimpse of her daughter. Please be kind to her.'

The doctor listened to him patiently, closed the window and went back.

After a long wait, the door at the side was opened. Kajjan held me by the hand to help me get up. Dilwari Saheb, Kajjan and I entered the door which led to a gallery. On the left side of the gallery was a wall of thick, opaque glass and on the right a row of rooms which were separated from the gallery by huge glass windows bolted from inside.

We walked past six or seven rooms and then stopped short. I could see Candy lying on her back on a bed by the glass window. She looked beautiful as usual. Her face was fair and bright with eyes luminous like moonlight and the diamond stud glittering on her pretty nose. Her black hair was spread luxuriantly on her pillow.

'Candy,' I whispered.

Kajjan picked up the receiver of the phone fixed on the wooden wall and handed it to me. I saw that Candy was smiling.

Inside, the nurse on duty placed a small receiver close to Candy's ear.

'Candlou, how are you, my child?' I asked.

'I am fine, Ammi. How come you are here?' she asked.

'I learnt that my daughter is unwell, so I have come running to be with her.' Fighting to hold back my tears, I tried to put a smile in my words. The effort was like holding my voice by the shoulder to prevent it from faltering.

'Did Kajjan call you up? I had told him not to bother you. I am going to be all right now,' she said serenely.

'I know you'll be all right, that is why I have come here. Once you recover, we'll both go visiting...' my voice trailed off.

'Where?' she asked with a smile. There was trust in her voice, and enthusiasm and reassurance. Mother has come and now everything is going to be all right.

'Wherever you'd like,' I answered.

'I was going to Greece on my way back to India,' she said. *Back to India.* Hearing these words, I felt my stomach constrict.

'We'll go to Greece, then,' I said quickly.

'No, we won't go to Greece,' she said.

'Why not?' I asked.

'We'll go to London,' she said.

'All right. We'll go to London, get well soon. I am sitting

close to you—very close. So close, as if you are lying in my lap,' I said.

'But these people will not allow you to come close to me. They won't let me place my head in your lap,' she said sadly.

'It is a matter of just a few days. When you are better we'll be together day and night and soon you'll be fighting fit,' I said encouragingly.

'But how about the visas for London?' she asked.

'You should not worry about them,' I said, 'Dilwari Saheb will help us get the visas. Do you know who telephoned him? It was Kamal Bakshi.'

She smiled. Then asked, 'You'll stay with me, won't you?'

'Yes of course, my little princess. I'll stay here, close to you, day and night.'

Her nurse came and said something to her which made her look sad. Then she asked, 'Have you eaten, Ammi? Please give the phone to Kajjan.'

I handed the receiver to Kajjan. He was still talking to her in French when we noticed the doctor in the white coat near the door of the corridor instructing us to leave with a motion of his hand.

Kajjan said, 'Let us go, Ammi. Candy says I should give you a meal first and let you sleep after that. She says that you must be very tired after the long journey.'

'But why? Can't I sit here in this gallery through the night?' I asked.

'What would you do here?' Dilwari Saheb asked.

'I'll stay near my child. It'll make both of us feel good,' I answered.

'We can't do that,' Kajjan said gravely, 'that doctor would be angry. The nurse on duty is also getting impatient. We cannot afford to annoy anyone here.'

'It is against the rules of the hospital,' Dilwari Saheb added.

I looked at Candy helplessly and waved. She smiled, I could see her thick eyelashes fluttering.

We left the hospital. Dilwari Saheb said, 'If you think my presence would help, I'll come with you to the hostel where Kajjan has arranged for your stay. Otherwise I am booked in a hotel.'

'That is very kind of you. But you need not trouble yourself,' I said.

'Let me come to the hostel and read from the prayer book to you,' he offered again.

'No thanks. My heart is not in it,' I answered.

'He is the one who gives strength and courage,' Dilwari Saheb sighed.

And my whole being bowed before Him as I uttered inwardly—'Keep giving me strength and courage. I need your protection so much.' Outwardly I asked Dilwari Saheb, 'There is no danger to her life, I hope.' I was apprehensive.

'Look, why don't you leave everything to God? He alone knows what is best,' he said.

'What do you mean?' I asked and added, 'At this moment the most important thing is that she should recover, that is all.'

'That is the most important thing according to your understanding. How can we know what He considers proper in the circumstances? For example, if she survives how do you know whether her hands would move or not, or whether she would be able to walk? Do you think she would still want to go on living? And what would you do if she survives in such a state?' His tone was kind.

By now I was really frightened. I stood up trembling and said, 'You are not telling me the whole truth. What did the doctor tell you this morning?'

'As a matter of fact, she is burnt very badly,' he answered quietly.

'But didn't you see her face just now? And her eyes? To me she looked just fine.' My voice seemed to be stuck in my throat and I quaked inside. But I was imploring Dilwari Saheb, Kajjan and my own words to give me a little reassurance, a little hope.

Dilwari Saheb said again, 'We admire her courage. She is a little tigress but even the doctors have no control over the third degree burns that she has received.'

'What is third degree?' I asked naively. In answer, Dilwari Saheb said, 'You should repeat the name of Waheguru. He alone gives succour. And do not worry about the degrees now. If you wish, I can come and recite the Gurbani to you.' I thanked him again but told him he should go home since he had been with us since morning. 'Maybe you can recite from the prayer book to me tomorrow,' I said. I was quite defeated.

Kajjan took me back to a student hostel where he was staying. He had booked a room for me there. He asked if I would like to eat, but I wasn't hungry. 'Okay then, let us have a cup of coffee,' he suggested. He left and came back with coffee in two paper cups.

'How did it happen, Kajjan?' I asked.

'She had come down from Paris a week back,' Kajjan began in a voice choked with emotion. 'We were going to Greece. We were planning to leave on the 13th. Her scholarship was to end on the 14th. We had obtained Greek visas with great difficulty as there is a lot of political disturbance there.'

'If that is so, why were you going to Greece at all?' I queried.

'I'll tell you why,' he said and continued, 'There was a cook in the canteen of our hostel in Vichy. His aged parents live in Greece and he could not get in touch with them due to the tension between France and Greece. When Candy got to know of this, she offered to take his letters, deliver them to his parents, carry their answer with her and mail it to him from India.

'The day the accident occurred I was away at work. I returned at about three o'clock in the afternoon. She was packing her luggage in her room and was still dressed in the lungi-kurta she used as her night dress. I asked her if she had had lunch and she told me she had been writing a long letter to you after which she started her packing. I laughed and told her that she would reach India before her letter. Then I suggested that we go out and eat in a café. She protested that she hadn't even had a bath, and besides there were some green peas and tomatoes in the room which she wanted to cook the way they are made in your house. I told her to forget about the peas and tomatoes and heat some water on the stove for coffee. In the meanwhile I would go and get some food from outside. So I left. When I returned I noticed a fire engine parked outside the building and a crowd of people nearby. Her room was on the third floor but she was lying on the landing of the first floor, screaming, "Get me a sheet" because her clothes had all been burnt away. She was yelling at the firemen, "You ought to be ashamed of yourself. Get me something to cover myself with first instead of demanding my passport! Don't you see that I am naked?" I ran in and came back with a bedsheet with which I covered her. We took her to the hospital in an ambulance where she was given first aid. The doctors said she was burnt very badly and they did not have the equipment to handle such serious cases. They recommended the hospital at Lyons that specialized in burn cases and made arrangements to send her here. She was brought here in a helicopter. When her stretcher was being placed in the helicopter she told me not to inform you about the accident as you would get worried. She said she would tell you herself when she recovered. But when the doctors said...' Kajjan's voice trailed off. He lowered his eyes and paused for a moment. I felt myself growing cold. He resumed slowly, 'I called you up in alarm.' He stopped talking, placed his head on my knees and started crying bitterly.

With great difficulty, I managed to regain my composure. Poor boy, he was hardly older than a child and Candy loved him. He was her beloved friend. My heart filled with tenderness. Lifting his face, I wiped his tears and said, 'Everything will be all right. Now I am here, aren't I? Candy will get well. Haven't you noticed how brave she is? You'll see, she'll recover through sheer willpower.'

After a while, he got up and went to his room.

The next day Dilwari Saheb went back to Paris.

Kajjan and I spent the whole day sitting in the deserted lobby of that fortress of a hospital. We were allowed to 'visit' Candy for five minutes at nine o'clock in the morning and five minutes in the evening. From a distance, across the glass wall, over the phone.

'Did you have dinner? Was your bed comfortable? Have you brought your woollens?' Candy made several queries in a row.

I didn't have the heart to ask her anything such as, 'How did it happen, my child? How did your clothes catch fire, my Candlou? Where does it hurt? What do they give you to eat? Are you in pain?' I did not want to remind her of the traumatic accident. She should not think of those terrible flames at least during the brief moments she was sharing with me.

Candy's composure and smiling manner gave no indication of her pain and suffering. It seemed as if she had just scalded her foot or knee after which she was resting and she would recover in a day or two. Then we would go and tour Europe, chat over cups of coffee, sit in the sun, listen to music and go home to Arpana. My head buzzed with a million thoughts, like bats blinded by floodlight, striking helplessly against each other. But a strange invisible control made me speak in platitudes—lies that I desperately wanted to believe in. 'We'll go sightseeing and return home to Dolly,' I said. 'No, Ammi. We'll ask Dolly to come here and then we'll tour together. How can she stay alone for so long?' Candy said. Was she also playing the game, mouthing soothing lies?

During the 'visit' in the evening, she said, 'You have been wearing this saree since yesterday. Haven't you brought any luggage?'

Controlling my tears with difficulty, I answered, 'Oh, oh, I did not remember to change.' How could I tell her that I had neither washed nor changed nor eaten anything since I had arrived.

I had only been saying to God, 'Look, I have not committed any sins all these years. To my knowledge, I have not even hurt a fly. But if I have unknowingly caused pain to anybody, please do not avenge it by punishing my child. Please let me suffer for my sins. Please be just. Have mercy on me if you can. Forgive me, Friend. I have been punished enough. Please forgive the rest. Bless my daughter and help her get well. She is going to be nineteen on the 26th of November. This is no age to go through such suffering. At this age she should enjoy herself. You know how she has spent her childhood sharing her mother's poverty and how she had to face her father's temper and hatred. Things have just started getting a little better. It is only now that we can afford to relax and enjoy life a little. Our greatest strength is that we have each other as friends.

'The friendship I enjoy with my two daughters has given warmth to my life and dispelled the pain from my existence.

Please God, do not take us away from each other. If ever I have done a good deed, please bless me for it by helping my child get well. You are benevolent. Please show compassion to me.'

At such moments I would hear the voices of my inner sanskaras. With God's grace, the lame can scale the peaks of the mountains and the blind can not only see but have the knowledge of the whole universe illuminate their eyes. God's will can create land in the middle of the sea and inundate the land with deep waters.

Then Candy said wistfully, 'I think it'll take two months for me to recover completely. I asked the nurse and she said so. Where will you stay for two months? How will you arrange for so much foreign exchange?'

'Don't tax yourself with these niggling worries,' I answered, 'I have made all arrangements. Your uncle Jasbir has written to all his friends in London, the US and other places. They'll send us as much money as we need. Then our embassy has assured me that they'll arrange for the foreign exchange.'

'Okay. Let me talk to Kajjan.'

I handed the receiver to Kajjan. He talked to her in French so I could not follow what he was saying.

She looked at the nurse with a smile and said something. The nurse also smiled. I asked Kajjan what she was telling the nurse. He said she was telling her that she had beautiful eyes and so did her mother.

Controlling our tears we came out. Five minutes were gone all too soon. We saw the doctor standing behind the window opening into the corridor. He looked cross. He said something in French to Kajjan. His tone was harsh and impatient. Kajjan seemed to be appeasing him or maybe he was apologizing.

'What is the matter?' I asked softly.

'He is asking why we are hurting her so much. Talking is bad for her. Excitement, too, is bad.'

'But why? She is getting better, isn't she?' I asked. Kajjan conveyed my question to the doctor. In response he protested vehemently and kept saying something over and over again.

'What is it?' I asked Kajjan.

'He says that she suffers much pain when she speaks. She keeps talking to you bravely and does not let you know it but the effort of talking hurts her very badly.'

'But...' I was surprised and upset at the same time. 'How come she looks so relaxed? She seems all right. Tell me how badly is she burnt?' I was really scared.

Kajjan was the interpreter between me and the doctor. Quietly, he told me, 'She is burnt completely neck down and her injuries are grievous. The doctor says all that skin simply cannot form back.'

Stricken, I implored, 'Please graft my skin on her body. Can't plastic surgery be performed?' The doctor smiled at me as if I were an ignorant child. I persisted and said, 'Tell me why it can't? I promise I'll lie down quietly and you can remove the skin from my legs, arms, back and stomach and graft it on her body. I am sure her body will accept my skin. After all she is my flesh and blood. Of course she will accept my skin. How long will it take? Two, four or six months? I don't care how long—I'll keep lying quietly.' I could not hold back my tears. Folding my hands in entreaty, I placed my forehead on the window in front of the doctor.

The doctor left. Kajjan told me, 'He was saying that he'd have to wait for her burns to heal. Then he would see.'

I may not have followed what the doctor was saying but I clearly understood the message his expression conveyed. In simple terms he was saying, 'We'll see if she survives.'

I sank on the same bench as before and cried, feeling utterly helpless. My child was right there—just a few feet away, but all the doors were closed—doors that were white like shrouds.

The corridor was deserted except for our presence. I was sitting on that bench worn out and crushed and crying my heart out. At times I felt I did not even have the strength to cry.

Time seemed to be moving with feet that were bound to millstones. I felt as though I were being ground under their stationary weight.

Late at night, leaning on Kajjan's arm, I returned to the hostel. On the way, I was puzzled to notice people on the streets walking as though nothing was wrong. Didn't they know about Candy?

I spent the next six days totally oblivious to my bodily needs like bathing or using the toilet. I had no appetite and sleep eluded me.

'Please Candy, please get well. I can't live without you,' was the refrain my heart repeated night and day.

'Please save her life, please my Satguru' was the only prayer.

On the third day, as on the other days, we went early in the morning and sat on the same bench. I felt dejected and defeated. Hope was dying slowly in my heart.

Kajjan lifted the receiver of the phone on the wall and spoke into it several times but the cold, white walls around us remained unresponsive.

At length the window opened. A nurse appeared, looking irritated. Arms akimbo, she came and stood in front of the window. Pointing towards me, Kajjan pleaded with her in French. She answered more angrily than before and shut the window.

'Why was she so angry?' I asked.

'She said today is Friday, the visitors' day, and visiting time is three to five, so why were we pestering her since morning,' Kajjan answered.

'Visitors' day? What do you mean?' I asked again.

'Relatives come to visit the patients only once a week, from three to five every Friday,' he explained.

Suddenly I realized why we hadn't seen anyone here for two days. There were other patients in the hospital. They too had relatives, friends and others who cared for them. Why didn't they have visitors? What kind of custom was that? 'Why only once a week?' I asked.

'Because people here do not have time. In the event of a patient's death, people keep the body in a morgue for days and bury it when they are free.' A shiver ran down my spine. 'Please don't talk of death,' I sobbed. Kajjan put an arm around my shoulders and we kept sitting there. We had nowhere to go.

The door opened at about noon. I noticed a tear streaking from Candy's eye down to her cheek. In alarm, I asked, 'What is it, my child?'

Sounding like a small child, she complained, 'This nurse does not give me water. My lips are parched with thirst.' Another tear rolled down the side of her face. My heart quaked, 'What shall we do, Kajjan? Whom should we tell?' Then to Candy, 'Why don't you ask the nurse?'

'This nurse is very bad. She said she has to attend to other patients, too. And in the morning she said "You black people."' Candy's voice was full of tears which she was trying to hide from me as I tried to hide mine from her. But the one tear streaking down her face had carved a deep furrow on my heart. I did not realize then that that furrow would throb with pain as long as I lived. She could not wipe that tear, nor could Kajjan or I.

'Please get me some juice. And cherries,' she said after a while.

'Which juice would you like?' I asked tenderly.

'Lots of juices, apple, pineapple, orange,' she answered.

From across the glass panel, the nurse motioned to us to leave.

We went to the market and bought six bottles of fruit juice. Cherries were out of season and impossible to come by. For me Lyons turned into a wasteland because I could not get what my daughter had asked for anywhere in the city.

At that moment I did not realize that for me, all the cherry orchards of Kashmir would be laid waste and whenever I saw cherries, I'd want to set fire to those orchards.

Back in the hospital, we handed over the bottles of juice and some fruit to the nurse.

At three o'clock visitors with packets in their hands started arriving. The door was opened and I went inside. My heart sank to see Candy crying. She asked, 'Haven't you brought juice for me?'

'But we gave the juice to the nurse in the morning,' I answered.

'But no one gave it to me,' she complained.

'Why?'

'I don't know. The doctor who comes in the morning says I should not drink water and the doctor on night duty told me I should. But I am very thirsty now.' Her lips were pale with thirst. The red lips which had kissed me, with which she smiled and dragged pensively at cigarettes, the lips which sang and which spilled cheerful laughter as she danced Kathak, were parched and I could see white thirst on them.

Kajjan went inside and contacted the nurse who was receiving and arranging the packets from the visitors. She poured the juice in a feeding cup, then went inside and held it to Candy's mouth. As Candy sipped the juice, she caressed her hair gently. After a while she returned to the window and started talking to Kajjan who turned to me and said, 'She has lost a young daughter. She says she can understand what you are going through.'

Weeping, I noticed that Candy was listless even after drinking the juice. She also looked very nervous. I tried to talk to her over the telephone. Her voice came haltingly over the line. She just said, 'I had bought two coats for you and Dolly. They are lying in my suitcase.' Her tone had the finality of a last message.

It was impossible to control myself any longer. I was crying in front of her. 'You'll give me the coat with your own hands once you get well. I'll wear that coat all my life, Candlou. You and I shall wear it by turn. Please, my child, get well soon.' I do not know if she could follow what I was saying for I was sobbing uncontrollably.

She was lying close to me and yet she was so far. My pampered child. I had worked so hard all these years to raise her and now she was slipping out of my hands. However, I refused to believe that she was going to die. I had the false assurance that I was there and hence nothing would happen to her. No gods could subject me to such tyranny.

After a while she spoke, 'That's all. I am tired now.' She closed her eyes.

Still crying, I sat down on the floor of the corridor. Suddenly, I thought of Sukhmani Sahib. I said, 'I am going to read the paath to you, Candlou,' and started reciting a prayer in the mouthpiece of the phone.

Jah maat-pita, sut, meet, na bhai
Man uha nam tere sang sahai.

I must have done the paath for about five minutes which was about as much as the tears would permit me. A feeble voice reached my ear, 'That is enough. I can't listen any more to it.'

She opened her eyes slightly, looked at me and closed them. Her eyes looked like twin sleeping lotuses.

Supported by Kajjan, I dragged myself back to the hostel. I booked a call to Arpana and one to my brother, to tell him to come and save my daughter otherwise his being a doctor was of no use.

I also booked a call to the Indian embassy in Paris and sent a telegram to Dilwari Saheb, 'Please save her. Please ask the doctor in charge to take special care of her. Please save my child.'

The call to Delhi came through and I found myself crying and imploring Arpana to 'go to Gurdwara Bangla Sahib and arrange for an Akhand Paath. They say that no harm befalls a patient as long as the paath is on.'

At about nine at night Dilwari Saheb called up from Paris. 'I have spoken to the senior doctor over the phone. He wants you to come and meet him,' he said.

'What does this mean?' I asked, 'Is there danger to her life?'

'You should repeat the name of Waheguru, Behenji. Prayer is the only help we can give her. Only Waheguru knows what is best for the child,' he answered.

Kajjan and I returned to the hospital and met the senior doctor. He looked very angry. He flared up when we approached him, 'The call from Paris came when I was having dinner with my mother at her house. What do I care about embassies? Who are they to trouble me like this at this time? What can I do if your daughter is dying?'

Suddenly he threw open the lower part of the door and

in a gruff voice asked us to come in. I do not know how and when it happened but I found myself holding his feet and placing my head on his boots. 'Please don't be annoyed. Please save my child, please, doctor,' I begged. Kajjan, acting as interpreter, told me that the doctor was saying even God could not save her. She had third degree burns all over her body. Because her face was not burnt we did not have an idea of her condition. He was wondering how she could talk to us. He was surprised that she had survived so long. He thought it was a miracle.

Even in that distraught state, I thought that my child was performing a miracle with all her willpower so that her mother would not suffer. After all she was her mother's friend.

Kajjan said the doctor was asking us to change into sterilized clothes and go and meet Candy.

'No, Kajjan, we should not do that,' I argued. 'If something goes wrong he'll blame it on us.'

But the doctor handed me a set of sterilized clothes, held me by the arm and pushed me into a small room to change. I put on the clothes with trembling hands. As I came out, he held my arm roughly and guided me towards the room where Candy was.

My daughter was lying on the hospital bed surrounded by bottles of glucose, blood, oxygen and God knows what else. I bent down and kissed her face and forehead. She opened her eyes and said something with her parched lips but I could not understand what she was saying. I could give up the rest of my life in exchange for the words which I could not understand at that moment.

'What is it, my baby?' I kissed her again. For the first time in our lives, I was so close to her and yet she hadn't put her arms around me. Helpless, she just lay there.

Suddenly the doctor lifted the cage-like contraption

which, covered with a sheet, was placed over Candy. An overpowering stench of burnt flesh hit my senses as I looked at her body. She was roasted like a potato from her feet up to her neck. If only someone could have replaced me with her at that time, I'd remain indebted to him for ten rebirths.

Then it was my turn to feel the fire engulfing my body and I am burning in it till today. I have been roasted on live coals since that moment. 'That's it. Get out now,' the doctor ordered.

Shaking with silent sobs, we left Candy's room. The doctor said, 'This is exactly why I did not want you to come inside. You will never be free from this stench. We have to train for long years to tolerate this smell.'

'Will you save her, doctor?' I implored him. I was sobbing, terrified by the approaching footsteps of death, but he moved away.

We came out. No one was there to close the door. I told Kajjan, 'Let us sneak into this deserted gallery. I'll sit quietly against that glass panel, close to my child.'

'Won't they be angry?' he asked.

'If someone gets annoyed it can't be helped,' I answered. We went back and stood silently near the glass panel. Kajjan brought in a chair and a stool from outside. We spent the night sitting there and feeling helpless. We were watching life trickling like sand through the fingers clasped in a tight fist. How a loved one recedes into oblivion step by step and you remain standing there. And you still remain alive, alive with such obstinacy.

Maybe she was unconscious. She was being given blood transfusion, oxygen and glucose. The diamond stud glittered on her nose as she breathed with difficulty. I noticed little tremors in the depression at the base of her neck. Her breathing was laborious like the effort that goes into hauling a vessel full of water from a deep, deep well.

The very air in that gallery was still and mute. You could see darkness playing an intriguing game of hide and seek in the corners. A palpable tension stretched between the two ends of the corridor and was ready to snap any moment. And in the middle life was being squeezed out of my being by degrees. Time just refused to pass. Like a roadroller it was moving excruciatingly slowly and crushing everything in its way.

The cosmos was reduced to a putrid stench, a suspended breath and endless helplessness.

And then it was dawn. Milky white light crept in through the glass panes. I was surprised that the day could progress. Wasn't the sun ashamed of itself?

Kajjan said, 'Someone may see us. Let us leave this place quietly. They won't take care of her if they are annoyed.' Shattered and dragging my feet, I followed him out of the corridor. Out of the hospital with its walls that were unashamedly white. White, the colour of innocence and mourning. We sat down on the bench.

'Will you have tea?' he asked.

What he said made no sense to me. Tea? For whom? Day? For whom? Outside? For whom? Everything had lost its meaning. We spent the day sitting on the bench. I wondered how the day turned into evening.

Several times during the day Kajjan pleaded on the phone but no one came. Just once a nurse appeared at the window. She informed us that the patient was completely unconscious and wondered what we were doing there. I felt sorry for the nurse, thinking maybe she had never had a child and never stayed awake through the nights with it. Maybe she had not spent her days hovering around her child like the earth orbiting the sun. Maybe she had never understood the meaning of life through the existence of her daughter. How ignorant she was and how deprived!

Later in the evening a doctor came and said, 'Please go back to your hostel. We'll telephone you.' He went back immediately.

Kajjan said, 'In case they need to telephone us, they'll contact the hostel. They would not know we are sitting here. I think we should wait for their call in the hostel.'

Phone call? What would they say over the phone? My mind was a total blank. Questions arose in my mind, and then slunk away in fear, before I could grasp them.

Maybe I already had all the answers surrounding me. They crowded around me, but I was refusing to recognize them. I remember nothing about that treacherous evening soaked in blood and pervaded with the stench of decomposing flesh: just a sensation of limpness, helplessness, of suspended breathing and violent sobs, only a feel of meaningless tears of defeat which cross the bridges of time and visit me even now.

Back in the hostel, I sat down to recite the Sukhmani Sahib. With helpless determination I thought nothing could happen to Candy as long as I read from the scriptures and the Akhand Paath was on in Delhi.

ॐ

That night...Candy's last night...

I was sitting on the bed in the hostel room, reading the Sukhmani Sahib. My heart was brimming over with pent up emotions. It felt as if my very being had melted and was draining away like liquid wax.

Just the day before, the doctor had lifted the tent-like covering to show me her seared body...oh, that golden body!

All of a sudden a thought came to my mind, that even if she recovered, would she be able to walk with those shrivelled legs? I had a vision of her sitting in a wheelchair, sobbing inconsolably! How would she eat her food with those burnt hands? Would she be able to learn to live the life of an invalid? I knew deep down that she would not.

Then, I thought, would she be angry with me for saving her, to live such a terrible life? She, who had always wandered blithely around the house, filling it with the musical tinkle of her anklets. She loved to perform Kathak. She would walk contentedly on the grass till late into the night, saying, 'I'm enjoying the darkness.' The moment she heard a favourite tune, she would put on her ghunghroos, ready to dance!

How would she survive, without dance, without the tinkling of the anklets! How would she survive…

If I truly loved her then I should let her…Let her what? Die?

A scream escaped me!

I bowed my head over the Sukhmani Sahib and surrendered myself to the Highest Authority. 'Whatever is best for her, only You know My Lord, My Creator. I only know that I cannot see her in this pain, and neither will I be able to bear it if she won't want to live even though alive. My dear Lord, My Divine, please take her into Your hands! The path which is free of all difficulties for her, please take her onto that path!'

In that moment I let go of all that propelled me to hope. Called it quits!

The boat, which for days I had been trying to push upstream against the flow, I now abandoned to the raging storms. Surrendering everything into the hands of my Lord, I don't know when I fell asleep.

They say, Jesus Christ was able to sleep even on the cross. Despite the nails in His hands and feet, His body drenched in His own blood. Was He really able to sleep?

Today also when I think back, I am unable to understand whether I had done the right thing or not? Was that decision right or not? Was it a decision for me to take or not?

That night, I myself released the ephemeral hold I had on her hand, literally letting go of it in the air, the hand I had been clinging tightly to!

Why did I leave it? Why did I call it quits? Why did I tear down all the sails? Why did I abandon my boat to the strong winds and the stormy seas? Just because I loved her tremendously?

Loved her, that's why I couldn't endure the torment she was going through. Loved her, that's why I couldn't see her living her life as an invalid, writhing in pain.

The night passed. Actually it did not pass, it cut through my flesh and through the space around me. That is how I spent the night.

༄

The morning glow was spreading when the doorbell rang. I got up, flustered. I didn't know when I had dozed off.

'Hurry up, Ammi. Let us go to the hospital,' Kajjan said urgently.

'Why? What do they say?' I asked, nervously pushing my feet into my slippers.

'Just this, that her condition has deteriorated.' Kajjan ran down the stairs.

Hospital. Kajjan was talking into the telephone on the wall as I stood leaning against the back of the bench, trembling.

The window opened. The doctor shook his head in a helpless manner.

'What?' I screamed. He spoke to Kajjan and Kajjan turned to me and told me that Candy had passed away five minutes ago.

'Do you want to see her?'

Do not scream. No, no. This is a hospital. No. Be silent.

Quiet. I must have been conscious even in that dark hour. Otherwise how could I have those ideas?

They brought Candy out from the inner room on a stretcher. She was sleeping peacefully. I kissed her on the forehead and the lips. Her lips were chapped and white with thirst. The tears that had flowed from her eyes had dried in streaks on her temples. 'Do not abandon me, my child. I will die without you. How can I live without you.'

Once, she had said, 'I sometimes want to commit suicide but change my mind thinking of how you would survive without me! So I tell myself, let me stop thinking of dying because I have to live for Ammi.'

And now?

As I looked at her it did not appear like a last meeting. It seemed a temporary parting like the one at Delhi airport on the night of May 27.

They took her away.

I do not remember what happened after that.

I do not know when Dilwari Saheb arrived from Paris. I only remember that he sat by me and read from the scriptures. After a while he said, 'You have to be brave. It won't do to lose courage. You gave birth to her and you have to perform her last rites.'

I had given birth to her. That was right. Now I would perform her last rites. Who else would do it? He was right. I stood up quietly.

Dilwari Saheb took me to an unfamiliar office where a woman was in charge. He talked to her at length in a persuasive manner then came back to me. He said, 'See how Waheguru helps the believers! She told me that they keep the bodies for as long as fifteen days and switch on the furnace only when eight or ten bodies are collected. But I have offered to make full payment and persuaded her to prepare the furnace tomorrow.'

Whatever he was saying did not really register. Even the words 'Waheguru helps the believers' sounded incongruous to my ears. Mechanically, I put my signatures wherever he asked me to.

The woman in charge showed me her arm which carried scars of burn injuries. She told me when she was a little girl her clothes had caught fire from a lighted candle but her father had been there. He hugged her hard and extinguished the flames. In the process he too had received minor burns.

If I was with you my child, I too would have hugged you hard to put out the flames. I would have shared your burns and your pain.

The entire night was spent like a bad dream. She cannot die. It is a lie. People are telling lies. How can she die? She was brimming over with life. She was intoxicated with it. She lived each moment so intensely. She used to sit on the lawn and smoke in the darkness at night. When I asked her why she was sitting alone in the darkness she would reply, 'I like it. I am enjoying the darkness.'

Usually, she stayed awake till late in the night. She would say, 'Such gorgeous gloom and silence—this is the right time to read poetry. Why should I waste it by sleeping?' How could a girl who captured and squeezed each moment of life in her hands die like this? And she was so beautiful. She still had to taste the springtime of her life.

Through that interminable night, I seemed to be floating lifeless on the black waters of gloom. I remember nothing. Absolutely nothing.

The next day I was being taken somewhere supported on one side by Dilwari Saheb and on the other by Kajjan. I was not aware of it but my feet must have walked, one lifting after the other. That is how I must have reached that freezing chamber with huge steel drawers on all sides.

In the centre, Candy was sleeping peacefully in a wooden coffin. The same moon-like face, the broad brow, enormous eyes now closed with thick fringes of silken eyelashes.

I knelt down to kiss her face. I kissed her forehead and her icy cold lips. Someone had wiped the white thirst from those lips. Her tears had also been wiped. Her hair had been brushed and arranged neatly. I wondered where my daughter was going all dressed up, wrapped in white sheets that did not belong to her, in an alien city, after having her mouth and eyes wiped by hands which were not related to her.

Kajjan pulled me by the hand and said, 'She is not lying in a casket, she is lying in our hearts, Ammi. This is not Candy. Candy lives here now.' He placed his hand on his heart.

Dilwari Saheb was saying, 'Behenji, this is only dust. Don't be enamoured of it now. Pray to the Waheguru to give her shelter at His feet.' I must have been listening otherwise I would not remember his words. I must have been outside that coffin. That is how I am writing these words today.

But I swear that I was locked inside that casket when the nails were driven in to close it.

The casket was placed in a black van. I don't know who had placed flowers on top of it.

The van entered a lovely garden. Dilwari Saheb and Kajjan helped me out of the van. 'We have to walk to the building out of respect for the dead who are lying buried in graves here.'

I must have walked. That is how I reached the inner room of the building. My daughter ahead, and the three of us following her. I, who had borne her and who was her mother and friend. Kajjan, the one who shared her friendship and love. And Dilwari Saheb who had come to perform only an official duty but who was thoroughly moved in sympathy with me. He was the one who did the paath and offered the final ardaas.

I caressed the casket and whispered, 'Goodbye Candy, we'll meet again. We'll meet very soon, my child.'

The casket was placed on a raised marble platform. A small, wooden door opened onto the platform. To me it was not a casket, but my daughter's doli which was being taken away from her home. The casket slid gently through that little door. Dilwari Saheb and Kajjan escorted me out. I have no memories of the place where I was taken. Wherever it was, I just sat there inert.

In the evening we went back to the same place. The official there handed over a small wooden box closed with red seals. Inside that box were Candy's ashes. Holding the box to my heart, I came out of the building.

I saw men and women sitting silently on the benches, their heads bowed down. I felt that I too, would be sitting on those benches with them, my hair growing white and my face wrinkled with age, till the last day of my life.

I am still sitting on one of those benches in the graveyard of Lyons. In truth, I keep sitting there day and night, my head bowed down. The sun goes up and then sets. People come and go back after leaving their loved ones there. I take care of them all because they live in proximity to my daughter. They are her neighbours.

40

I seem to have run out of breath after climbing up a huge, treacherous mountain.

Any breath can be the last breath.

I sit hiding in a cave of the dark, menacing, mountain.

Embarrassed about my naked, raw flesh, because my skin has been peeled off.

Because this skin can never grow back.

Because no one can remove the nails driven through my hands, feet and forehead.

Often it seems that nothing is left in my life after the death of my child. Now that Candy is gone, no shred of life should really remain.

But life, after all is life. Diseased, leperous, it goes on limping even when a whole limb is amputated from its body.

Shameless, brazen, obstinate, this life.

I had been hit by other disasters before. Before this trial by fire. But those disasters lost their meaning in Lyons.

Life itself lost its meaning.

Why does one live? Why does death snatch away a significant part of one's body? Why is it so painful to lose a child?

Why does pain run like an underground stream in both life and death?

Life! Bits and pieces of old, useless, discarded scraps of cloth, shabbily sewn together to form a rag. To form a multi-coloured, multi-patched quilt to wrap oneself in.

A dirty, faded quilt with a thousand slashes and a thousand pieces, the colour of mud. Like a beggar's robe in which dull, sleepy colours seem to be complaining and apologizing at the same time. The wandering mendicants who sing and roam the streets are dressed in such robes. The Baul singers, the Sufis, the beggars in tattered rags!

After Candy's death I had a strong impulse to cast away the rag that life is. To fling it away, to burn it.

But I couldn't. How could I make Arpana an orphan? She was all I had left in the world, my precious child!

Then, one day, I thought I could perhaps share the pain with you. For afterwards, neither the rag nor the wounded being wrapped in it would remain to narrate the story of this life. Of a life that is nothing but the din of pebbles in an empty tin drum.

However, none of the incidents that happened before have any meaning any longer. They are empty, hollow, vulgar.

Yes, true! But how can I give an account of my life without talking about those shreds, tatters and patches that have gone to form it?

As a matter of fact life always remains unconcluded. Words have no power to capture the pain and trauma. It is not possible for mere words, powerless words to dive deep and retrieve the anguish which has been lying at the core of my being for such long aeons.

ல

Wait a moment. Allow me time to swallow the flames stuck in my throat.

Let me take a draught of fire.

Just wait for a while.

I will tell you about a few more patches of my life. The patches scattered on dry, sandy, brown earth.

Like shards of splintered glass from the windscreens of two vehicles colliding head-on in an accident on a deserted highway, dark and desolate, under a kohl-dark sky.

These patches are from a time long ago, long before I perished after my encounter with death, my own death in Lyons, where half my body is still buried in the cemetery.

41

Suddenly, penetrating through that excruciating solitary anguish, I felt, as if someone was calling from afar. The plane had landed in Mumbai.

I was puzzled—why Mumbai? Didn't I have to go to Delhi? There must have been some awareness, a thin thread of consciousness still alive, that's why my mind acknowledged that Arpana was waiting for me in Delhi and I had to go there.

They told me, you'll get a connecting flight for Delhi in three hours. First your luggage...Customs...immigration...

'Luggage? What luggage? Where is my wooden box?' I screamed. The air hostess stroked my shoulders soothingly. 'You seemed unable to carry it. It must have been very heavy. We have kept it safely. You'll get it soon.'

'No, oh no! Don't place any weight on it. In it...my child is there in it!'

The air hostess looked at me strangely. There was disbelief in her eyes, and fear—the kind of expression people have when they come face to face with an insane person.

Then I was standing in front of the Customs counter. The officer asked me, 'What's in this box?'

'My child.'

'Children's toys?'

'No, no...'

'It's key...?'

'She has got burnt.'

'The key...?'

The air hostess opened my bag and taking out a letter handed it to the Customs officer. The same red seals that were on the box, were on that letter also. Where had it come from? How did it get into my purse? How did this girl know?

I got so exhausted thinking all this that I couldn't actually ask any of these questions. The Customs officer read the letter and then put an X sign on the box with white chalk. He kept the letter with him.

Placing the box on my lap, I sat on an airport bench for three or four hours, waiting for my connecting flight to Delhi.

∽

Delhi. The moment I got off the plane, I saw them all. Arpana, distraught, her face streaked with tears. Daarji, Jasbir, my friend Toshi, my aunt and others...

Arpana and I held each other and wept. Tears were streaming down our cheeks like scalding hot lava.

How someone helped me into the car, who sat with me, I have no recollection of any of them. All I could see was Arpana clutching me and sobbing. And Daarji's quivering lips, the silver in his beard, his eyes brimming with tears.

I was so unaware of what was happening, that I did not even know when someone took the box from me. But when I suddenly saw the box in someone else's hands, I leapt forward and grabbing it, placed it on my lap.

'This is Candy. I have brought Candy with me. Look, this is Candy. This is our Candy.' I kept caressing the box, stroking it tenderly as I used to stroke and pet Candy. Then Arpana placed her head on the box and took it into her own arms. I can clearly recall that moment, it is frozen in time for me.

∽

I don't know how many days, weeks passed. Maybe three or four months had gone by. There was no periphery for this endless pain. It was like a bottomless abyss.

Suddenly, one day I heard Arpana screaming.

For so many days and nights, so many weeks, months, she had been crying quietly. She could understand my sorrow and tried her best to console me. Like a mother she would cajole me into having food. Effacing herself in the face of my grief, she would roam forlornly from one room to the other, buried in her own grief.

But that day, it was evening I think, her patience gave way. She started screaming, 'You only loved her! You loved only Candy! Oh, why didn't I die in her place!'

I was shocked into silence. I had been sitting at the bottom of a dark well, in total darkness. On hearing Arpana's scream, I looked up. That was the moment when I came out of the well and gathered Arpana to my bosom, hid her in my arms. Like a wounded chicken she hid her face in my bosom and cried without stopping, her whole body trembling.

'My child, how would you know, how many pieces a mother's heart is divided into! How would you know, that each piece of her heart is hidden in the bosom of every child that is born from her flesh and blood. When a mother creates a child from her own flesh and blood, she hides a piece of her own heart in its bosom. That is why when her child faces even the smallest difficulty, strong winds start brewing in her bosom too. A mother of a hundred children grieves as much at the loss of a single child as the mother who loses her only child. No greater sorrow can be created by the Lord, as when a mother sees her child pass away in front of her eyes. He can't think of a more earth-shattering deeper hurt than this.'

He? Who 'He'?

If He actually existed then wouldn't His world shatter on perceiving so much torture, so many atrocities happening? If He, an epitome of compassion, was in reality somewhere, wouldn't He have wanted to lament on seeing His children endure so much wretchedness? Wouldn't the skies and the earth get submerged in the deluge of His tears?

Mothers have to undertake their last journeys on their children's shoulders. If a mother has to take her child to the crematorium or graveyard, then it feels as if time, too, breathes its last by getting buried in a deep, dark den. Storms thunder. Doomsday comes. Earth and water get amalgamated into one another!

In those stormy winds, the very doors and windows of your inner world are torn and thrown aside.

'My child, the dust of those storms has got stuck in my throat. Hush now! Forgive me. From today onwards I will live only for you. Who else can I call my own in this wide world?'

Arpana's scream seemed to have jolted me awake from the deep gloom into which I had fallen, and I started looking for a reason to stay alive, some support to keep me alive.

I had to stay alive. For Arpana. And I had to protect her from all those sorrows, which Candy and I had had to face. I was full of remorse for Candy. I regarded myself as her culprit. Why didn't I save her when I had the chance? When she could have been saved! Why did I leave that delicate life to struggle alone on the slippery path of marriage, to fall and become bloodstained!

And now I was feeling like a culprit for Arpana's state. Why had I not gathered her dark despair to my bosom, all these days, weeks? Why did I leave her all alone to struggle with her miseries singlehandedly? Why did I go on accepting selfishly all her mothering, all the love that she added to each morsel she put in my mouth, her loving fingers caressing my head to help me sleep, her gentle hands combing my hair.

She was also in need of someone to feed her, coax her lovingly to change her clothes, bathe her, wash her, brush her hair. We both had had to cross that fearsome jungle, whose very terror had settled into our hearts, whose thorns had pierced the soles of our feet, whose thorny bushes had scratched and wounded our bodies.

Arpana's eyes fluttering in her fearful, pale face! I saw the tears brimming in her eyes, and gathered her to my bosom.

༄

That was the moment, the pinnacle, where the old Ajeet Cour died, and from her ashes a new Ajeet Cour rose, Phoenix-like!

The way straws are swept up by violent storms, all my fears and terrors were also suddenly swept away.

The most essential thing was life, Arpana's life, which I had to protect at any cost. The most essential thing was to teach Arpana to live on the strength of her own convictions.

It was most important to hear the voice of your own conscience and rationality. After losing so much, it was only now that I was listening to that voice.

Sometimes I think, that was the pinnacle when I became liberated in the true sense of the word. Free of all the fears and terrors of conforming to traditions. Free and emancipated!

That freedom was Candy's gift to the two of us—to myself and Arpana. In her ultimate departure, my daughter had taught the dear ones she was leaving behind, how to live life.

I had never felt liberated even when I was earning my own bread. Neither when, breaking all traditions, I left behind the protection of both Daarji's and my husband's houses, nor when I was single-handedly bringing up my daughters, educating them. I was always surrounded by fears and terrors.

But now...now...despite being shattered into bits, scattered all over like shards, I still felt completely integrated, for with her courageous martyrdom, Candy had taken all my fears and terrors along with her. Now I'm not afraid of anyone or anything. Nor do I give permission to Arpana to be intimidated or overwhelmed by anyone. What a huge price I have paid for this liberation, only I know.

From that moment too was born the Arpana of today, whole, complete, a fearless and energetic Arpana, who, like a sturdy tree is standing with me, next to me. Whose roots go deep inside the earth, whose branches, wrapped in tender leaves, soar into the blueness of the sky, fanning out in the golden breeze beneath the fuchsia sunlight, laden with the scent of exotic flowers and fruits, dreaming mystical dreams, and then transmuting those dreams with vibrant colours onto her canvas.

When she is talked about and appreciated in both her own and foreign countries, and her work is acclaimed, when she gets invitations from all over the world to hold exhibitions of her paintings, when the tears generated by the destructive bombing of Hiroshima fall compassionately on her canvas, and the resultant execution of harmonious colours depicting peace finds a permanent place on the walls of the Museum of Peace in Hiroshima, then it feels that the effort in creating this story of mine, has not been a waste of time.

At least in her, there is one remarkable masterpiece which I have independently created from my completely liberated soul, my emancipated personality.

Candy is present in both of us. Clinging to us like the air around us. Hidden within us. Amalgamated into us.

42

After six years, my landlord said he needed the house back for himself. The government had introduced a new law according to which employees who had their own houses had to vacate official accommodation. House owners were using it as an excuse to evacuate their old tenants.

By then I had been through a thousand storms. Candy's

room had been abandoned for she had gone far, far away from us. She had had the walls of her room painted black and with a brush in her hand, had herself painted a fiery red sun on one of them. On the cream-coloured door of the room, she had sprayed red and black paints. Little streaks of colour had run to mingle with each other. Candy used to say, 'These are black and red tears!'

Saying these words as a joke, she did not realize that not only that door, but also her mother would weep those black and red tears all her life.

I had told my landlord we would move out by March. However, till the end of March I had not found a place. I had met a number of real estate agents and visited several houses after seeing 'To Let' advertisements in Sunday newspapers but I drew a blank everywhere. Every landlord asked me peculiar questions.

'What does your husband do?'

'He has passed away.'

'Oh! How many people shall stay in this house?'

'My daughter and myself. And periodically, my father. He stays with me and my brother by turns.'

'What does your father do?'

'He is a doctor.'

'Why don't you stay with your brother?'

This question always annoyed me. I would answer, 'I have my independent occupation. Why should I stay with him?'

'What occupation?'

'I am a journalist.'

'With which paper?'

'I am a freelancer but I also run my own journal.'

'But how would you pay the rent for this house out of your earnings from such work?'

The emphasis on 'such work' clearly implied that he did

not think much of my kind of work. I owned no factory or business, did not work in an embassy or corporate house, so where would I get the money to pay him the rent? To him I was just a down-at-heel freelance journalist.

'I can afford to pay the rent. That is why I have come to see your house,' I would answer angrily and the story would end there.

My friends advised me not to get annoyed with the landlords. They argued that their houses were their property and they had to satisfy themselves about the credentials of their prospective tenants. They suggested that I should try to impress them, instead of losing my temper.

I had only one thing with which I could impress anyone. And that was my pen, which was of no consequence to the landlords. And yes, I had another thing which Daarji had bought for me some years ago. It was a commercial flat in Nehru Place. I was always anti-property. I considered property to be the axis of the lives of the bourgeois. However, I had no answer to Daarji's argument that I would need something to fall back on in my old age. The flat had been rented out at Rs 1850 a month. During my subsequent house-hunting I started mentioning my commercial flat to the house owners.

But once the question of finances was resolved, they would move onto a different argument.

'But why do you need a four-bedroom flat for the two of you?'

'I need a room for my study and office. My daughter will have her studio in the other. Then we'll need one as our bedroom and one for my father when he comes to stay with us.'

'But even then...such a large house for the two of you does not make sense.'

'We need a large house where we can write and paint

with freedom. For us it is as necessary as going to clubs or races or drinking Scotch whisky is to others. We do not go to clubs or to races. Nor do we drink Scotch. All we want is to live in a large, spacious house. That is our necessity, comfort and luxury rolled into one.'

'All right. We'll think about it and call you up later.'

In March I asked my Greater Kailash landlord to give me one more month.

I still could not find a house. But true to my word, I vacated the house at the end of April.

Dumping my belongings in the garage of one friend, I shifted the office to the house of another who was a woman MP, and with just a suitcase, moved in with my friend Toshi.

Finally, when I found a house in Neeti Bagh, the landlord made me put my signatures at more than half a dozen places. I signed all the papers with my eyes closed. Taking advantage of my desperation, he had prepared an agreement for three years which was to land me in a mess later on. It was an unpleasant tussle on one side of which was my shrewd, cunning landlord who was a lawyer himself. On the other side was I—naive and completely ignorant of complicated legal procedures.

As a matter of fact, construction of the house had stopped midway. I had often passed by and noticed it. Standing at the edge of an open forest, it looked deserted and desolate.

Every time I enquired about the house at the real estate offices I was told that it had been in that state for a long time. They conjectured that either the owner had died or it was disputed property but they had no definite information about it.

One evening I went on my own to make enquiries. There was a decrepit old man shabbily dressed, sitting on his haunches and cooking something on a makeshift brick chulah. I asked him about the house. He looked hard at me and answered, 'We'll let this house only if you can pay two years' rent in advance. We cannot complete the construction otherwise.' I requested him to let me see the house.

There were two flats, one on the ground floor and another on the first floor, and he showed me around both. I liked the first floor better. He gave me the telephone number and address of the owner.

Before leaving the place, I gave the man a tip of five rupees which he accepted with a little salute.

I learnt later that he was my landlord's elder brother.

With difficulty I managed to scrape together enough money to pay the advance rent. After making the payment to the landlord, we started shifting to the flat on the first floor. We could not do it in one stretch because the house was still unfinished. When the work on one room was completed we would move some of our things there. It took about two months for us to settle down and feel at home in that house.

After we had shifted into the house my landlord told me, 'It is just a formality but it is always good to draw up a formal rent agreement.' I agreed.

When I was signing the agreement, I noticed it was for only three years, whereas my landlord had all along told me we could stay there all our lives provided we paid the rent on time. When I questioned him about it, he answered, 'It is only a formality, Behenji. Documents have to be drawn up in legal language. Rent agreements are no exception. It only means that in the case of non-payment of rent or subletting, the tenant could be asked to vacate the house. That is all.'

I was still a bit hesitant. Noticing this, he called out for his son who came out. He said, 'Look, he is my son. My daughter is older than him. She will go to her in-laws after marriage. This boy is studying in the fourth standard. Till he grows up and gets married, I have to let out half of the house anyway. So why shouldn't you continue to live here?'

His wife, who was dressed in a dark blue and red synthetic saree and had her hair tied in a tight bun, was standing close by. From the frown lines on her forehead she looked like a school teacher. I learnt later that she was one and she taught Hindi in a government school. She now said, 'We have spent a total of four lakh on this house. We are indebted to the tune of two and a half lakh. We have to repay our loans from the rent we get. As long as you pay the rent on time, you can stay here for ten or fifteen years. But don't spoil our new floors and walls. We have spent full four lakh…'

Almost as soon as we had moved in, we were faced with a peculiar predicament. My landlady would arrive with different groups of people three or four times a day and show them around our flat without as much as a by-your-leave. Sometimes Goel, the landlord, would bring three or four of his clients to impress them with his house. At times, relatives would come to 'see' the house with his brother whom I had tipped five rupees thinking that he was a chowkidar.

These daily intrusions deprived Arpana and me of all privacy. We could not enjoy the peace and quiet of a home, could not listen to music or read books without being interrupted several times a day. For me the moments of silence when I could read or listen to music were so important that I could not sacrifice them for anything.

But what could I do with the proud owners of a new house? They lived on the ground floor and we upstairs. His children were studying in Dehradun. Just three people stayed in their house and there were three of us in ours. I did not know how long we would have to remain in that house but our relationship seemed to be doomed from the start.

The fact was that they had furnished their house with two string cots covered with gaudy sheets in each room. Our flat, on the other hand, was tastefully furnished with curtains and sofas and books. That was why every time their relatives or acquaintances dropped in they would bring them upstairs to show 'their' house. They would show them round all our rooms, ask them to sit on our sofas and say enthusiastically, 'The house is exactly the same downstairs, the same kitchen, the same large-sized rooms. We have spent four lakh…'

Finally, one afternoon when my landlady landed up with four ghagra-clad women and started showing them around, I stopped her before she could open the door of Daarji's room. 'My father is sleeping inside,' I said.

'So what if he is sleeping?' she countered.

'He is resting. We cannot disturb him.'

'What do you mean? Can't we show our house to visitors from our village? After all, it is our house!' She was furious.

'Of course it is your house but I am not going to open this room now,' I said.

Grumbling loudly, she turned back and left with her companions who waddled like ducks in their swirling ghagras as they babbled aloud in Bhojpuri.

She never spoke to me after that. But the best thing was that she also stopped coming upstairs.

However, it did not mean that I was spared her ill-tempered tirades on the slightest provocation. She would scream if she heard the tap running and raved and ranted if even a drop of water fell downstairs when we washed our floors. This state of affairs lasted for six or seven months.

After seven months my *Directory of Indian Women Today* was published. The foreword of the book was written by Indira Gandhi.

Goel was livid when he saw the *Directory*. The reason

behind his resentment was that he was the lawyer of Raj Narain in his Allahabad case against Indira Gandhi and by then there had been a change of government. The Janata Party was in power in those days and as a reward for being Raj Narain's advocate, Goel had been appointed the general secretary of the Janata Party.

He asked me, 'How could you do this, Behenji? In my own house…' I reacted angrily for the first time and said, 'As long as I am paying the rent and living here, it is my house.'

That was the beginning of a cold war. Quiet on the surface but smouldering inside.

Eventually, I learnt to distance myself from the couple. By that time I had become friends with a family in the neighbourhood. The Mathurs were an extremely pleasant family. Onkarnath Mathur was a lawyer like my landlord but he was good-natured and cheerful. His wife Uma was an excellent singer and their children were very affectionate.

Ignoring the Goels, Arpana and I started enjoying our house.

Once we came to terms with the situation, we savoured the free-flowing fresh air and sunlight, the rooms, the terrace, the blue sky. We loved the ocean of greenery in front of the house and the gently swaying trees reaching up to our balcony.

For the first time in our lives, Arpana and I were living in a house which was tranquil and which felt as though it belonged to us.

I had lived in open and spacious houses in Lahore too, but they were Daarji's houses. Whatever was and was not there depended on Daarji's wishes.

In this house we had whatever we had always wished for. Fresh air, sunlight, space! Beautiful things. Books. Music.

The small jungle in front of our house was cleared later. It was replaced by a lawn laid with lush green grass. From our flat it looked like a pool of emerald water surrounded by tall, leafy trees.

In the beginning, before the jungle was cleared, it was visited by some white birds at the crack of dawn. They looked like herons or some other water birds. A flock of them descended upon the trees and bushes each morning at daybreak. Against the grey-green foliage, their white feathery bodies floated like dreams in a light sleep. Pure, innocent.

At such times, you are intoxicated with the beauty of the dreams but simultaneously aware that they are not real.

The birds stopped coming once the jungle was converted into a park and people started playing football there in the mornings.

The open, wide terrace on the roof was also part of our flat. For the first time after leaving Lahore, we could enjoy the feeling of sleeping under the canopy of a star-studded sky. And all of it was ours.

There was a very large room in that house. Such rooms are referred to as a drawing room by others but in our case, it was of pivotal importance in our lives, the soul of our house. All our time at home was spent there. It was there that Arpana painted, and I wrote stories, there that we listened to music, watched TV, met friends or just relaxed. It was also the venue for musical soirees and gatherings of writers and artists. We held no parties except for such gatherings in our house.

The seating arrangement in that room included a carpet with pretty, Gujarati cushions piled against the walls. It was our favourite niche and it was so spacious that ten people could sleep there comfortably.

The walls of the room were adorned by Arpana's paintings. Books on art were arranged on a small bookshelf. Our music system occupied a corner of the room which was also filled with statues, old iron and copper bowls and other vessels, samovars and ashtrays. Also some lovely bowls and boxes made by Gurcharan Singh, the father of art pottery in India, affectionately known as the 'blue potter', and some flower vases, candlestands and a few antique idols in stone.

On one occasion burglars broke into our house. Arpana was awake and reading at the time. She heard the intruders and woke me up. We called out to our neighbours and the burglars fled.

But we were terrified after that incident. We stopped sleeping in the bedroom. We slept on two cots which we moved into the big room every night. We thought that if the burglars broke into the house again, they would break open the lock of our bedroom on the other side and take away whatever they liked from there. The room where we now slept had nothing of interest to them. Paintings, antique bowls and cushions would be useless to them.

Looking at our home many friends would remark, 'Ajeet seems to be very rich. She must have a big bank balance.' They did not realize how hard we had to work to pay the rent every month. They also did not understand that fresh air, sunlight and beautiful surroundings were as essential for our existence as liquor is to a habitual drinker. That was our need and we maintained it with care and hard work. Money had nothing to do with it.

However, I did not contradict my friends. I rather enjoyed their illusions and their envy.

43

Three years later when Arpana and I were away in Europe for Arpana's exhibition and Daarji was staying with Jasbir, Goel put in an application in the court to have the house vacated.

The application was moved. I returned. The case started.

I was frightened by the very mention of the word 'court' but my friends reasoned, 'Even earlier you vacated your house out of fear of the courts. Don't leave this one and become homeless in a hurry. A court is not a monster and who says you have to fight the case yourself? You can engage an advocate. That is all.'

However, the advocates were not related to me—they belonged to the same fraternity as Goel. First one and then the other charged me hefty sums in advance for the entire case and promptly crossed over to Goel's side.

At the time of letting the house to me, Goel had said that the loan taken for the construction of his house was going to be repaid with the money earned as rent every month. But now he was the general secretary of the Janata Party. Favour-seekers thronged outside his door day and night. He was no longer worried about money which seemed to be pouring into his coffers abundantly.

He would stand outside and discuss the case with the neighbours so that his voice would reach me loud and clear. 'Who does she think she is? I have thrown Indira Gandhi out of power. It won't take me long to throw this woman out of my house. The court is mine, so is the chief justice. Even the prime minister is my own man—he is like a member of my family.'

Feeling scared and helpless, I thought of seeking out someone from the fraternity of writers who could help me. Punjabi poet Pritam Singh 'Safeer' had been a very distinguished judge. I thought of consulting him but was reminded of how he had made a poor man in need of legal help, whom I had sent to him after making an appointment, stand at his gate for an hour and then sent him back without meeting him.

Then I thought of Mahinder Singh Joshi. He lived in Neeti Bagh. He was recuperating at home after a long illness. He said, 'Nothing can be done in this matter. What can you do with a rent agreement drawn under Section 21?' Then he added, 'It is difficult for me to interfere in this matter. After all Goel and I stay in the same area.' By implication he was telling me that a woman without moorings like me would pick up her stuff and leave one day but people like him who had permanent homes could not afford to antagonise their neighbours.

Finally I engaged a third advocate who turned out to be good and sensible. Within a year it became obvious that the judgement would be in my favour. In three years there were no additions to Goel's family through birth or through marriage, so why did he need more rooms? The rule at that time was that you could not have the house vacated if your personal requirements had not grown.

Subsequently my landlord started visiting me every morning and evening. He repeated the same thing over and over again. 'It was my fault that I took a devi like you to court. I cannot explain it to the court but I can confide in you that my wife is quite uncouth and quarrelsome. That is the reason why my son and daughter were sent to school in Dehradun. My daughter has finished school and is in college now. If you vacate my house, I can keep my children on the second floor, at a distance from household tensions and daily bickerings. Then I have my clients, my practice...'

I, me and mine!

I was tired of listening to the same story over and over again. Echoes of his footfall on the stairs agitated me to a degree where I felt that my head would burst with the pressure of the sound.

My cousin Mohni who was an officer in the air force used

to tell us that an officer falling into the hands of the enemy was subjected to third degree methods in order to extract crucial defence information from him. The most painful methods were pulling out the victim's finger nails and the Chinese method of torture which was really strange. The victim's head was shaved and he was made to sit under a tap from which a drop of water fell on his bare scalp every five seconds. After a while the drops of water began to feel like hammer blows and bombs going off on his head at five-second intervals. After each explosion, all his nerves, each pore of his body and his very being would tense up waiting for, and dreading the next. And the five-second gap was as horrifying as the wait after setting off the fuse of a box of dynamite.

It was a method that shattered the morale of the bravest of the brave.

My landlord had chosen the Chinese method for me and my morale came crashing down after a few months.

So, I admitted defeat. He took me to the court in his car so that I would not change my mind. He and I put our signatures on a new agreement.

According to the new agreement I could continue to occupy the house till December 1983.

And after that? A nomadic existence once again? A strange feeling overtook me. The feeling of sitting on a railway platform. I tried to chase away that feeling like flicking away a fly. But it is also a state of vagrancy, to sit inside a house and feel homeless!

ೲ

The year 1983 had seemed so remote at the time of signing the agreement that I didn't even think of that date! So much could happen in the interim. Who knew whether I would survive till that time or not—such were my thoughts.

For a number of years I had been feeling that I wouldn't live beyond a year or so.

How does one benefit by a long life, anyway? Age takes its toll in no time at all. The glow on your face and the lustre of your eyes fade. You lose the will to traverse the world on your feet. Slowly and gradually everything is lost.

But Time after all is Time. Who can ever stop its flow? And so the year 1983 arrived and drew to a close, faster than I had ever expected. My time limit was almost over. My 'home' was in the process of being destroyed, its walls crumbling and its roof leaking. You could see the empty sky with its blue, black and purple colours across the roof. The spectre of homelessness, of vagrancy, loomed before me once again.

Meanwhile rents had risen alarmingly all over Delhi.

I consulted a lawyer once again. He explained to me that mine was a voluntary agreement for it was not signed under a court order or any other pressure. He told me that the case was actually moving in my favour before I signed the agreement. The court had treated the agreement as a voluntary compromise before the verdict.

I put in an application saying that I had signed the agreement because my landlord had stated that he needed extra space for his children who were away in boarding schools and he wanted to bring them to Delhi. The fact was that neither had his children come to Delhi nor did he need extra space. Moreover, he had become a Member of Parliament and had a government bungalow allotted to him. He had this huge house and the government accommodation, too.

The appeal was admitted to Tis Hazari court. My lawyer told me the case would take at least a couple of decades to be decided.

At the same time my landlord moved the High Court on

the ground that I was guilty of contempt of court because I had backtracked on the agreement. According to his contention I should be punished for the offence and the court should pass an order to evict me from his house immediately.

Contempt of court? Which court had been insulted? You commit contempt of court when you agree to a court order and violate it afterwards. But I had gone with my landlord to the court to submit a joint application in which we had stated that we had entered an out-of-court compromise so a court case was no longer necessary. Subsequently the court had closed the file.

The trouble is that the law has neither ears nor eyes. It can also be twisted and bent to serve people's vested interests.

Like other communities, there exists a legal community which includes advocates, judges and all other court officials. At that time I was not aware that a court thinks twice before giving a verdict against a lawyer. The blind goddess of justice is not the only one to hold the scales in her hands. The judges also hold the scales in their minds where they weigh the pros and cons of each case. It is always the heavier side that wins.

So, the case moved to the High Court. The real issue was completely lost. My landlord kept reiterating over and over again that I had insulted the court and I should be punished for contempt of court.

At each hearing, the judge said, 'Vacate the house at your earliest otherwise I can send you to jail directly from here.'

On each date of the court hearing, I would sit in the corridor of the court waiting for my call. A strange terror filled my being. I was guilty without a crime.

Sitting in the corridor, I would watch the lawyers going up and down the stairs with their black robes swaying in the air. It made me feel as if I was surrounded by flying vultures who were fluttering their dirty, black wings in slow motion as they looked around for dead bodies.

Ten months passed in this fashion. The ominous month of November arrived. November 1984! My landlord was now roaring like a lion. In fact, all landlords with long-term Sikh tenants were roaring like lions at that time.

The judge had declared during the last hearing that the verdict would be given on November 30.

Arpana and I had been working in the relief camps following the anti-Sikh massacre. We worked from the crack of dawn to midnight every day.

The unfathomable suffering of the shattered, homeless people in the camps made us realize that our troubles were nothing compared to their tragedy.

It is less terrifying to see death than to see those who sit inert and surrounded by the shadows of their dear ones killed in the violence, their eyes bereft of hope or the will to live. They looked like heaps of burnt-out wood, ashes swirling around them.

Life appeared to be an absurd phenomenon in those days. Why should we strive so hard to stay alive? If death is the ultimate truth with silence and nothingness beyond, what else remains? And why should one work so hard to preserve it?

Our own struggle had lost all its meaning in the face of the enormous horror of November, 1984.

But the date of the hearing was, after all, unavoidable. It was imperative that I presented myself in court.

At the hearing, my landlord said, 'She is a prominent Sardarni. Her presence makes my house open to attack. Someone may set it on fire. I stay downstairs. There is danger to my children's lives.'

According to official government announcements, complete peace and normalcy had been restored to Delhi and the rest of the country by November 30. The genocide had stopped. Only the work of rehabilitation remained. Otherwise all was quiet.

But the court chose to take note of the threat of arson to my landlord's house. The two judges listened to it impassively. Was this the secularism we were so proud of? The carcass of that hollow secularism had already been burnt in the streets, its ashes blown in all directions. Secularism had now been fully exposed in the presence of an 'impartial' judiciary.

'Hmm. Vacate the house in six months otherwise...' And the earlier threat was repeated again.

I learnt later that one of the two judges joined a human rights organization after retirement. Where were the human rights when he had accepted in a crowded court that the presence of a Sikh woman tenant exposed the house of the landlord to the danger of arson and a threat to the lives of his children, the children who were studying in some school in Dehradun and stayed in a hostel?

My friends advised me to engage a top lawyer and make an appeal to the Supreme Court.

My lawyer took me to a well-known Supreme Court attorney. He charged five thousand rupees as his initial fee and listened to the whole story. I told him, 'Please take it into consideration that I am pitted against a lawyer. He is a member of your community and the judges also seem to favour him.'

'What difference does it make? It won't be possible for a case based on false grounds to hold for long. I will shake its foundations. You had not signed the agreement under any court orders. You had voluntarily agreed to enter it out of consideration for your landlord's future needs. He is now a Member of Parliament and has a government bungalow in addition to his own house. His children are still in the hostel. So why should you vacate the house? I'll fight the case,' he assured me.

Four days later, he summoned my lawyer and me to

read the petition he had prepared. He charged another five thousand rupees for preparing the petition, and informed me that for every appearance in court, he would charge his usual fee. I agreed. He instructed my lawyer to file it in the Supreme Court, adding, 'It will take at least six months before a hearing will take place. It may even be six years. It will be ten or fifteen years before the case is settled.'

A load seemed to have lifted from my chest. I felt light as air.

It was a peculiar scene at the Supreme Court. A few lawyers seemed to possess something like a licence which gave them exclusive rights to file a case.

Hundreds of documents were prepared. Almost a dozen copies were made of the whole bundle. The lawyer's fee was paid and the case was filed.

The courts were to close for Christmas on December 25. However, under the influence of some magic wand that my landlord seemed to have waved, the date for the hearing of my case was fixed for December 24, within ten days of filing it.

My lawyer and I were sitting in the court. Our case was announced. The Supreme Court lawyer walked in with measured steps.

He was still walking towards the place where his assistant was sitting with books and files when one of the two judges looked at him and said with a mocking smile, 'So, you have come to fight a case against a colleague!'

The senior advocate answered promptly, 'My Lord, I did not realize that this case was against a fellow lawyer. I beg to withdraw it.' He turned on his heel and walked out of the room.

I was flabbergasted. Was it a court case or a joke? Was this our 'democracy'? Was this what our judicial system was about? They were trifling with the law! They were mocking the rights of a hapless woman!

And the lawyers? They were worse than prostitutes for they at least do not go back on their word after taking money. Were they the keepers of law or criminals?

The Supreme Court lawyer had already charged me ten thousand rupees for his services. He had personally dictated the whole petition and given it to us. And now he was stating that he did not know who his opponent was!

Even a child would know that he was telling lies. The judges understood that, too. But they were the ones who had induced him to indulge in lies by taunting him for fighting a case against a member of his own community.

It was a Greek tragedy! Or a Charlie Chaplin comedy which leaves the viewer with a lump in his throat.

Anyhow, one of the judges said to me, 'Please vacate the house in six months. We agree with the verdict of the High Court.'

I stood up. I was standing alone in a room that was spinning like a top. Trying hard to control my voice I answered, 'No, your Honour, I shall vacate the house in a week's time.'

All right. A week was fine. What objection could the court have to that! My statement was recorded and the case was over.

The struggle and running around was over. The fight to protect my rights was over.

In that fight my opponent was the king riding on an armoured elephant on the battlefield whereas I was a foot soldier who did not possess even the basic weapon of defence. I only had the weapon of logic which loses its meaning in the hands of an insignificant person like me. Whereas totally illogical arguments and unsubstantiated statements assume the nature of poisoned arrows in the hands of influential people and aggressive lawyers.

Where would I find a house in such a short time?

I spent the next few days scanning the newspapers for 'To Let' advertisements. I would draw circles in red ink around them and start from home at six o'clock in the morning.

People would show me the houses quite enthusiastically but their faces went blank at the sound of the name 'Cour'. I could sense a nameless antipathy and scorn. They would tell me, 'We'll let you know tomorrow.' That was the last I would hear from them.

It was the same story with the real estate agents. They would mention several houses when I approached them but the moment they realized I was a Sikh woman they would change tracks and tell me that they would contact me after speaking to the house owners.

Seven days just flew by like frightened birds.

I started dumping my belongings in the garages of my friends. I sent two truckloads of furniture to the house of my cleaning woman, Sunehri, who lived in a village in Mehrauli. I was happy to get rid of a mountain of possessions and Sunehri was overjoyed at the windfall. She twittered like a bird, telling me exuberantly, 'I'll have to get one more room added to my house, Bibiji. I'll need to borrow ten thousand rupees from you.'

On December 30, I found myself in Nizamuddin, totally exhausted and still homeless. One last place remained. First I thought it would be futile to try it and instead of wasting my time, I should go home. For the next twenty-four hours the house in Neeti Bagh was still my 'home'. But then I went into a chemist shop and dialled the number given with the advertisement. I was utterly dejected. It was the last house on my list, my last hopeless hope.

My call was answered by someone who asked politely, 'Where are you calling from?'

'I am calling from a chemist shop in Nizamuddin,' I said.

'Please come straight to Mathura Road from there. At the end of New Friends Colony is Surya Sofitel Hotel. Zakir Tower is right opposite the hotel. I'll meet you at the gate of Zakir Tower ten minutes from now.'

Arriving at the site, I saw a gentleman waiting by his scooter at the gate. He had a kind, gentle face with a high forehead and bright eyes. He asked politely, 'Did you have difficulty in finding the place?'

He showed me a flat on the third floor. Most of the flats in the building were still unoccupied.

Then he asked me, 'Have you heard of Qurratulain Hyder?'

'Of course I have, and I have also read her works,' I answered.

'She lives in the flat below,' he informed me.

After that he asked some formal questions relating to the size of the family and my profession.

I told him I wrote stories and my daughter Arpana was a painter. He smiled in delight and said, 'Oh! My wife has been to her exhibition at Art Heritage. She was all praise for her work. I am sorry I could not go to it. Anyway, we'll see her paintings once you move in here.'

'How about the rent?' I asked.

He laughed gently and answered, 'Qurratulain Hyder is paying four thousand a month. What is your offer?'

'Three thousand?' I asked with trepidation. He answered with a disarming smile, 'One should offer a house to a writer and a painter free of charge. It is a lucky house where such creative people live. But I have taken loans for this house which have to be repaid with interest in monthly instalments. Do you think thirty-three hundred a month would be too high for you?' He looked at me apologetically.

Thirty-three hundred was fine by me.

'I'll get the lights, fans and the faucets fitted in five to seven days after which you can move in,' he said.

'Five to seven days? But I have promised the court that I'd vacate my present residence by tomorrow! Also, I forgot to tell you that my landlord is evicting me through the help of the court. A tenant's credibility is suspect in such circumstances. Please think about it before letting your flat to me.'

He smiled reassuringly and said, 'How can I go to court, and that too against an artist and a writer? Rest assured, I'll never do that.'

His words were like a soothing balm on the wounds that had been festering for the last one year.

If one reality of life consists of deceit, treachery, persecution and injustice, there is another, a small, innocent one which offers trust and which values human beings.

'Do you have to move out tomorrow?' he asked, then added, 'In that case, here are the keys…' and he placed a bunch of keys in my hand.

Agreement? Advance rent? Cheque?

'Finish with shifting first. We'll see to the formalities afterwards,' he said.

The bunch of house keys was throbbing like a living thing in the palm of my hand. It seemed to be breathing like a small bird.

That wonderful man was Dr Refaqat Ali Khan who was the head of the department of history at Jamia Millia Islamia University. His wife Masooma taught English literature at Miranda House.

The friendly association that started that day has now reached a stage where we consider each others' joys and sorrows as our own. Refaqat and Masooma are now among my closest friends.

44

I go back to the days when I had returned to my parent's house from my husband's for the last time.

It was the eighth time that I had come back to their house. But this time, when I stepped across my husband's threshold, the knowledge flashed across my consciousness like lightning that it was for the last time. Never again was I to re-enter that house.

Beeji's condition had deteriorated and she had to be admitted to a hospital where she expired.

As I recovered slowly from the shock of her death, I could feel my inner strength growing. My final decision not to go back to my husband had led to a revival of all my dreams and aspirations which had been so cruelly slaughtered over the years. It was as if my dead talents were waking up in a flurry of resurrection.

I was running Daarji's household now. As a result I was eating to my heart's content, drinking milk and eating fruit. My health improved and the pallor on my face gradually gave way to roses blooming in my cheeks. The dark circles around my eyes faded away.

It was like being born again. Perhaps for the fourth time.

My first birth took place in my grandmother's house in Peer Makki lane. I was born a second time in the arms of Baldev who had remoulded me both physically and spiritually. The third occasion was when I was married for everybody said that marriage is a rebirth for a girl. She has to leave behind everything of her past existence and move on to a new house with new people and new responsibilities. The fourth time I was born was when I had resolved never to go back to my husband's house again.

For the first time I started taking my little girls on evening walks, playing games with them and enjoying the honeyed sweetness of their childhood.

For the first time I felt that the three of us were complete in ourselves. We did not need anyone else. This realization gave me much inner strength. Strength and power. I had never felt so self-confident before. At about that time I became aware that a colleague at the directorate of education liked me. Had he been a senior officer, there could have been the risk of a compromising situation. But since I had no direct dealing with him, I started talking to him. Gradually I also started liking him, but only as a friend, nothing more.

How strange it feels when I think of it now. Meeting Oma was extraordinary. Oma, meaning Om Prakash.

What was even stranger was the manner in which our chance meeting turned into acquaintance, which developed into love.

Then I also think it could be that every human experience appears unique to the subject. Unprecedented, unparalleled, though in reality it is quite ordinary.

Pain and pleasure, grief and happiness, are as natural as the rain and the air. They happen to everybody. And the interesting thing is that they are happening to so many people simultaneously all over the world. Isn't it amazing that similar feelings are being experienced by people undergoing different sequences of events at different places? And still each person facing his individual destiny thinks that whatever is happening to him has neither happened before nor is it likely to happen in future, to anyone else in the world. It is extraordinary, isn't it?

Oma was a friend of this colleague. We met for the first time in the house of an uncle of his, a man called Pal.

Soon after this meeting, I suddenly became aware that Oma found me very attractive.

However, for several months I did not respond to his interest. Eighteen or twenty months went by. By then I had moved into the working women's hostel.

In 1965 I was in my thirty-first year and Oma was forty-six but he looked older. That could be on account of his height and build, or his awkward gait or his head that resembled George Bernard Shaw's. I used to feel extremely young in his presence.

I was also aware that he did not share my artistic interests and tastes. He looked like a baniya. Fond as he was of eating, he was fat, and making money was the sole purpose of his life. Occasionally, for a change, he liked to fall in love.

During those days he was having an affair with his typist. She was a short girl who looked poor. He bought her clothes every month and regularly treated her to a good meal and a movie. Ordinary typists were paid about two hundred rupees a month in those days but Oma gave her a salary of four hundred a month.

When he started showing an interest in me, I felt that he was trying to replace this girl with me. It was as if he was comparing the two of us and I was disinclined to compete with his typist.

Some months later, the girl got married and left. Oma gave her a sewing machine as a wedding present. One day when a group of us were sitting and chatting, he announced, 'I serve all those whose arm I take, till the very end. For example, see, she was leaving to get married but I gave her a sewing machine.' I was filled with revulsion.

He started asking me to meet him but I refused saying I was not free. He would say, 'It does not matter. But you'll be going to the school in the morning, won't you? I'll walk with you from the bus stop to the school. That is all.'

One day he said, 'Why don't you get your books translated

into Hindi and English?' I had never thought of that. Oma offered to help me get my work translated.

In retrospect I feel that it was something base in me which made me like his suggestion. His friends used to say that his typist had fallen in his trap because instead of a salary of two hundred a month, he was paying her four hundred. And there I was, ready to fall prey to the proferred 'bait' of getting my books published in Hindi and English.

At that time, however, what he said struck me as the truth and I believed he loved me and for that reason wished to promote my art and talent as a writer. He told me that the power of my writing should not remain confined to Punjabi readers alone. Others should also read my stories.

As soon as he realized that I was beginning to be disarmed, he started visiting me almost every day, in the afternoon or evening, on the pretext of discussing the translations. He would introduce me to different publishers. He also got my works translated by different people.

In this manner, inch by inch, he drew me close to him.

Oma worked hard in other ways, too. For example, he started reading books in Punjabi, as well as English. He would discuss them with me when he met me.

In those days, he was publishing guidebooks in Jalandhar, meaning cheap and easy-to-read keys to the textbooks prescribed in the school curriculum. I felt it was treachery to publish such books. They were like instant coffee: questions and answers served on a platter, negating any real mental effort on the part of the students.

Every time I protested, he would argue, 'I publish them because they sell. Teachers and headmasters themselves ask students to buy them. It is another matter that I conceal a hundred-rupee note in the copy that I offer a principal. Ninety per cent people keep it and that serves my purpose.

When they recommend the guides to their students who, in their turn, buy them, I pay due commission to the teachers as well. Neither the giver nor the taker defaults! And if a rare person takes offence on seeing the money, I take it back with an apology and an explanation saying that I had stopped at a dhaba to eat. The owner of the dhaba did not have change and returned this note which I must have absent-mindedly kept in this book. At such places I have to deal directly with the students.'

He was aware that I disapproved of his work. As a result he started printing quality books along with the guides. He set up a new firm for such books in which his son, who was still studying, became a partner.

Today, whenever I hear someone talking of his publishing house, or a book published by it gets a good review, I still experience a small thrill of pride. I feel I too, have contributed to it in some way.

Suddenly, his younger brother died of cancer.

Oma used to say that he had brought up his brother like his own son. He had got him married. His brother was an artist and he was working somewhere in Assam. Some months earlier, he had written to Oma that he was suffering from persistent stomach ache. Oma advised him to come to Delhi for treatment.

Medical investigations were conducted at Willingdon Hospital. The doctors sent him home with medicines.

Within a month, when his condition took a turn for the worse, he was readmitted to the same hospital. By then cancer had spread all over his abdomen. He expired on the sixth day.

For the first time, I saw Oma break down. The big, burly man was completely devastated. He sat in Pal's house and cried bitterly.

The next day, I was sitting by him in Pal's house trying

to console him when a phone call came that his late brother's wife had sprinkled kerosene on her clothes and set herself on fire in the bathroom of her parents' house.

The news was so horrifying that Oma lurched forward and was about to fall down when I sprang and held him in my arms.

That was the first time I had touched him.

His sister-in-law had suffered grievous burn injuries but she was still alive. They had taken her to Willingdon Hospital.

We hurried down the stairs to go to the hospital, but when we got into the car he instructed the driver, 'Take us to the fruit-juice shop first.'

I was so shaken by what had happened that the idea of drinking juice at that moment struck me as odd, not only odd but also terrifying. I feel bewildered when I think of the whole incident even today.

But that is the way Oma was. Extremely practical.

He used to say, 'It is all because of my birth sign, Libra. Libra means measuring scales. The person born under this sign thinks coolly before taking any action.'

I was the exact opposite. I was the wayward, unbridled one. I was the gypsy river, the wanderer.

And so, one and a half years went by.

~

After one and a half years...

November 1966.

A book fair was going to be held at Bombay. Cultural programmes in a particular language were being organized each evening to which two or three writers were invited. Nanak Singhji and I were invited for the Punjabi evening. It was for the first time perhaps, that the need for writers was felt in a Punjabi cultural programme. A Punjabi cultural programme otherwise consists of gidda, bhangra, boliyan, tappe and mimicry.

Oma's publishing house was to have a stall at the book fair and he himself was going to participate in the publishers' seminar which was a part of the fair. He suggested going to Bombay together.

I really did not want to go alone with Oma to a strange city so far away. At that time, he was like a man possessed. Being alone with him could have led to anything—arguments, fights, a break-up. I was scared of facing the situation.

I did not want to get into a relationship with Oma on the one hand but I did not wish to lose him on the other.

I spoke to Gautam, a friend of ours. He said reassuringly, 'You should not worry. I am also coming. We'll all stay together.'

And so I went to Bombay with Oma and Gautam. On display at Oma's stall was the book that I had recently translated—*Return of the Red Rose* by Khwaja Ahmad Abbas. It was a work that was an immense source of satisfaction and pride for me. It was not a mere transliteration. It was an exercise in absorbing, breaking down and remoulding the whole work.

Oma, Gautam and I went sightseeing and chatted by the seaside for hours in our free time.

At the site where the skyscrapers of Nariman Point stand today was a slightly raised dirt road that ran along the seaside for a short distance. We happened to be sitting there one day—Oma, Gautam and I, and two of Oma's other friends. The noise of the sea and the waves breaking against and retreating from the sand was all around us. We were sitting just a short distance from the waves. They did not touch us but the spray that rose from them was carried on the breeze and caressed our cheeks.

We started talking about the *Return of the Red Rose* which led to a discussion about Indira Gandhi. I said, 'One needs money all the time but I have not translated this book for money alone. I have done it with immense devotion and faith. I have faith in the writing of Abbas and I am fascinated by every beautiful and intelligent woman who has the art of achieving what she wants.'

'But generally women who struggle to achieve a position, fame or riches end up losing their femininity and grace which are essential to them as women. They become masculine. But this woman...' Oma stopped in mid-sentence, then continued, 'This woman has preserved her grace in full measure. As a matter of fact, the older she gets, the more beautiful she grows. Don't you think so?'

Gautam chipped in, 'Have you noticed Indira Gandhi's hands? I can fall in love with her hands any day.'

'Everybody is ready to fall in love with a woman who reaches that place,' I observed.

'Well, we are ready to fall in love with you too, madam,' Gautam said with a smile.

'I am not joking,' I said, 'Normally a woman is acutely sensitive to her age and that dominates and conditions her entire life and thinking. But age has no meaning for a famous woman. Any man between the ages of sixteen and sixty would be willing to fall in love with Indira Gandhi.'

'He maybe willing, but he can't love her.'

'Why? Why can't he love her?'

'Because where would he get the involvement, the obsession and the blind passion which are the prerequisites of love. He would always be conscious of being with a woman superior to him.'

'In my opinion, a perfectly normal man may become impotent in such circumstances,' one of Oma's friends said with a smile.

'Does it mean that a man can only love a woman inferior to him? Can't he love a woman who is better than him?' I was getting a little angry.

'No, he can't. I have seen so many marriages crumbling because the woman was intellectually superior to the man, or she was in a better job, or her parents were more prosperous than her in-laws. Moreover, a woman earning more than her husband also unsettles the balance in a marriage.'

Oma had been listening quietly for sometime. He spoke up, 'But it is also possible that a man loves a woman superior to himself with a view to enhancing himself and to reach greater heights of personal fulfilment.' As he looked at me after saying this, his eyes were eloquent with a kind of worship, a kind of devotion. Something tugged at my heartstrings. For the first time, perhaps. Gautam looked intently first at Oma, then at me and sighed.

The Punjabi evening was presided over by the renowned actor Balraj Sahni. Later he took us—Nanak Singhji and me—home for dinner. A few Bombay-based writers who had come to attend the function were also there.

The friendship with Balraj Sahni which started that evening lasted for years. In fact, it lasted till the end of his life.

It was a quarter to two at night when I came back. Oma was standing outside the hotel, waiting for me. He looked worried. He held my arm without saying anything. The hand clutching my arm was trembling.

The sea lay across the road from the hotel. It was girdled by a waist-high embankment which looked like the hem of a skirt, curving along the sea for a great distance. We went and sat on the parapet, listening to the sound of the sea. It was an erotic sound, full of the madness of passion.

The next evening we went to a restaurant for dinner. I can't remember the name, but I had never been to such a large and dazzling place before. I was hesitant but there were three of them—Oma, Gautam and his elder brother—so I eventually agreed and went along.

The three of them must have thought that I would be impressed by the dazzle and glitter. I thought I would play along with them in the beginning.

Along with that idea came the realization that I was different from the three of them—different and because of being different, an outsider. I was with them and still distant.

Drinks were ordered (Bombay had not fallen in the clutches of Morarji Desai till then). For me there was lemonade.

The orchestra was playing soft music. Initially I thought it was a sad tune but by the time I got used to the place and collected my wits about me I realized it was not. Instead, it was the music of slow intoxication—of desire when the entire night was ahead of you without the fear of your beloved falling asleep or leaving. It was like the slow, upward journey of lips starting at your feet.

After a while the lights in the place were dimmed. A bright spotlight was focused on the orchestra and the floor near it. A girl came out and began to dance. She wore a revealing black costume studded with sequins which fluttered like the feathers of a frightened bird with her movements.

Then she started shedding her clothes one by one.

The faces all around me were also being stripped slowly. You could see the masks of politeness, culture and refinement slipping off those faces. From underneath emerged hungry faces, full of naked lust.

I felt like puking. I held Oma's hand entreating, 'Please, I can't stand it.'

I don't know whether my face had turned pale or changed colour but the men grew nervous looking at me. Hurriedly, they asked for the bill. Oma took me out of the restaurant.

Behind the hotel there were dark, narrow alleys. Only a few doorways were lit.

Oma said, 'These are Chinese restaurants. Shall we have Chinese food?'

Reassured by the small size of the restaurants, I said, 'All right.'

Inside were dim lights, low tables and small chairs. In spite of the air-conditioning the air inside the room was permeated with the pungent aromas of food.

At that time I did not even know the names of the dishes. Oma and Gautam ordered the food.

An awkward silence hung over the table after the order was taken.

'I am sorry I have spoiled your evening,' I said, breaking the silence. I really felt sorry for the three of them, and guilty for having behaved the way I had.

'No, no, how could our evening be spoiled as long as you are with us,' Gautam said, trying to sound gallant.

'Absolutely,' Oma smiled.

'It was because I have never seen anything like this before. As a matter of fact it is the fault of my middle-class background,' I tried to explain.

'But all these restaurants run on the middle class. The rich go to fancy clubs and suites in five star hotels,' Gautam said gravely in his typical, singsong style with dashes and commas after every few words.

'After all, how does the middle class live? Small houses, bare walls, corners bereft of beauty. It is restaurants like these that offer them an escape from the boredom and monotony of their lives,' Gautam's brother said, flicking ash from his cigarette into the ashtray.

'And revolutions all over the world have started in the middle class. According to Marx, when the wheel of history turns, the top, or the capitalist class grabs all the wealth of society, the middle class goes on disappearing and the exploited lower class then rises in revolt. But someone should ask who shows them the way? Who tells them that they are downtrodden and therefore, it is inevitable that they should be angry? The man who gives them direction, who offers this philosophy, who thinks and feels and prepares the ground for revolution is always born in the middle class.

'In the same middle class are born the creative ones who produce the most beautiful literature and the greatest art. Brilliant minds. Inventors. Pathfinders.'

'Long live the middle class!' Oma said, laughing.

By then I was enjoying the food. The restaurant looked pleasant and it was turning into a glorious evening.

॰॰

The sun was very pleasant on the day we were sitting and gossiping on the sands of Versova Beach. There was Gautam, Oma, a friend of his from Bombay and myself.

Gautam said, 'Bauji, remember our last visit to Bombay?'

From Oma's embarrassed smile, I guessed there was a story behind it. I begged them to come out with it. Eventually, they confessed that they had visited the brothels during their last visit to the city.

Oma's friend from Bombay said, 'Hookers are the same everywhere. The same profession—and yet, the brothels in each city have a special flavour. They have their own culture, their own style. Prostitutes from each place have their own way of walking and talking, their own expressions. Like Heera Mandi in Lahore could not exist anywhere else in the world. It's an amazing place. Singers there have perfect knowledge of music and the dancers are really accomplished. They hone their art to perfection through years of practice and know how to perform with finesse and beauty. It is not the body that matters, it is the soul, and the art that goes with it. Some of the finest singers even today have their roots in the brothels of Heera Mandi.

'But Bombay whores are in a class by themselves. They are fast, like taxis. Girls from all parts of India congregate here. You get all kinds of stuff here. But everything is done in a hurry. It is tasteless, bland, like masoor dal short on salt and devoid of chillies!'

'Why don't you show me a few brothels?' I asked sieving the sand through my fingers.

'You want to see the brothels? But women cannot go there.'

'Why can't they?'

'Just like that. It is not done.'

The expression 'cannot be done' always makes me want to dig my heels in. It brings out an absurd side in me.

I said, 'If anybody questions you, you can say she too wants to do this work and is looking around for a nice brothel.'

Oma laughed and said, 'And we are wasting our time!'

'You? You can be a pimp...'

Gautam looked incredulously at my face. The friend from Bombay, embarrassed, started counting the waves in the sea. Oma said, 'After all that, what if you are not allowed to leave the place?'

'Okay, then do this. You should say, we have found this one woman, but we are looking for two more.'

'What makes you think they won't look at your face? You have to deal with the pimps before getting into a brothel and they have eyes as sharp as surgical knives.'

'Don't you worry about that. I shall paint my cheeks with bright lipstick and put on another layer of red on my lips.

And I'll swing my hips and walk like this!' I walked on the sand mimicking the vamps I had seen in the movies.

'All right, let us go.' By now all of them had become partners in the game.

'But where shall we get the addresses of the brothels?' I asked anxiously.

'Don't worry about that. Every taxi driver here is a mobile directory of the brothels—Encyclopaedia Bombayana. We'll hire a taxi. We'll tell the driver at each place that we didn't like anyone there. He should take us some place else. We can spend at least eight days exploring the area.'

We spent that night going round the brothels of Bombay.

Dark staircases and rooms with dim lights. Spacious bungalows with glittering lights. Narrow, dark alleys. Roads lit up with neon lights. Emaciated faces crumpled like discarded paper. Faces looking like trash thrown on garbage heaps. Melancholy faces devoid of colour. Full, smiling, glowing faces. Faces accomplished in singing and reciting shairi. Faces unfamiliar with Hindi or English. Alien faces dumb with ignorance and looking like discoloured walls with plaster peeling off them. Faces from Ajanta and Ellora. Faces like the calendar version of Sita and Radha. Countless, numberless faces.

We returned to the hotel in the morning. My heart was heavy with untold melancholy. I burst into uncontrollable sobs as my head touched the pillow.

Walking along the seafront the next evening, Oma held my hand, and caressed it tenderly. 'I have seen whorehouses before, not only in India but in Europe and America. Also in Japan, Singapore and Hong Kong. But going around them with you was different. It made me so sad. It was like wandering around old mausoleums. I was disturbed all through the day. Why was it so? I just don't understand.'

Maybe that was the time and the place when I first took Oma's feelings for me seriously. That is when I felt that something emanating from his soul had come and mingled with my blood. There, near the sea, in the last fading light of the day, in the melting shadows of the evening.

I could feel drops of blood swirling, expanding and shrinking by turns as they raced through my whole body.

The awareness of my own body came back to me like a prodigal child returning home after years of absence.

I was listening to the sound of the ocean, holding my body's seashell against my ear.

45

I could write a whole book on the part of my life that I lived with Oma.

It was a life which included the balmy sun of love, the freezing frost of loneliness, violent, running arguments, drunken happiness and an indolent tranquillity, all in one. I seemed to have crossed seventy years in those seven years. Seven hundred years. The seven rivers. Seven births.

The intensity of my feeling was like potent wine that sears your insides. Everything, each moment, shone sharp and bright in all its clarity like small, pointed daggers.

But isn't that the way each love story is? Each story about a relationship which is marked by distrust, which is not normal and in which one is not sure about what is going to happen the next moment?

Each day of that seven-year relationship has a story that stretches over centuries.

But in this endless city of sand a few fragments glimmer in the bright light of the sun. They are like the stars that lie scattered after escaping from the knotted edge of one's pallu.

We all know that each star, irrespective of whether it is in the sky or lying broken in the dust, is a world in itself. It has its own complete cosmos.

The loneliness was terrifying that evening.

Isn't it strange that loneliness does not pinch you so hard when you live alone but when the person you love passionately and with complete devotion is not with you, it feels like walking barefoot on the edge of a sword?

Flustered by the feeling of loneliness, I locked up the house and came out.

I can't really call it a 'house' for it was a lonely hostel room. There was no one there to see me smiling or crying. No one to feed me when I was hungry, nor anyone to snatch food from my hand when I ate.

Coming out, I stood forlorn and hesitant on the edge of the road for a long while.

Where should I go?

I started walking towards India Gate. The moment I crossed Baroda House I felt as if I had left the city behind. Travelling on the road in a bus you do not feel anything but when you walk through those lawns, you feel as if the city has disappeared.

Skirting the wide boundary of the National Sports Club, I walked up to the zoo. It was closed. I followed the boundary wall till I was on the road curving in from the Sunder Nagar side. I could hear the noises of the zoo and inhale the pungent smell of the animals' bodies.

Walking on, I arrived at Nizamuddin but did not go up to the dargah. I was on the other side. Reaching the mausoleum, I sat down on the grass.

The evening shadows were getting deeper gradually. Night seemed to have descended like little birds folding their wings and settling on the top branches of the trees. The dome of the monument was half-engulfed in darkness. I was so melancholy that I felt like sneaking into the mausoleum and lying down close to a grave.

Just then Bhajji (who is now recognized as Yogi Bhajan in America) and his wife Inderjit happened to pass by. Perhaps on their way from the market, they were taking a shortcut through the lawns to avoid the traffic on the road. I had not noticed them. Night had fallen and I was oblivious to my surroundings.

Stopping by me, Bhajji said, 'Jeet?'

Startled, I looked up. He was towering over me like a date palm. His wife stood next to him.

They forced me to come to their house in C Block.

Quite late in the night they put me on a bus. That must have been the last bus on that route.

I got off the bus at Curzon Road. The bus stop was almost opposite the hostel. I started walking towards the hostel gate but stopped short in my tracks.

In a lonely pool of street light, Oma was sitting on his suitcase and leaning against the lamppost, fast asleep.

That is how I see him when I remember him today. Waiting for me by the roadside, leaning against the lamppost, asleep.

He had come from Jalandhar by the night train. He had arrived around nine o'clock. The hostel watchman must have informed him that my room was locked and I was not there. Sitting out on the road and waiting for me he had fallen asleep.

Thinking of him now I feel that he was luckier than I. At least he was sure that the door which was locked would open shortly. I would come back before the night ended. But I had no idea whether the door outside which I stood silently, the door across which were his home, his family, his business and his whole world, would open or not.

༄

Another evening.

By that time I had moved to a flat in the newly constructed UNCTAD building opposite the working women's hostel.

Oma had hardly spent two days in Delhi when his son Surinder arrived from Jalandhar.

Oma did not have a place to stay in Delhi in those days. Both he and Surinder used to stay with me in my flat in the UNCTAD building.

As it was, they used to visit Delhi by turns. Surinder had never come to Delhi when Oma was there. On this occasion Oma had returned to Delhi after visiting Calcutta, Bihar and Orissa in connection with his business. And Surinder had landed up from Jalandhar.

I was meeting Oma after about three weeks and we had spent only two days together. We were still unsatiated. When Oma was not with me, loneliness seeped into my being like slow icicles which grew into a huge rock of ice, a glacier which needed time to thaw and melt.

Surinder said he had come because cement was not available in Jalandhar for the courtyard which his mother was getting paved with bricks and mortar. So she had sent a message that Oma should be sent to Jalandhar as soon as possible.

Flustered, Oma started preparing to leave.

I said, 'No, you are not going today.'

'Don't be crazy. Surinder is here now. What use is it my staying here now?' he answered.

'What do you mean by "use"? Is it that you stay here just to sleep with me? You are such a baniya!' I was getting angry.

'Speak softly. Surinder will hear us.'

There were only two rooms in the house. Surinder was changing his clothes in the adjacent room.

'Let him hear. I don't care. Am I his chattel? Or yours? This is my house. I'll speak as I like here.'

Oma began to get irritated. I got angrier at his irritation, and more obstinate. Why should he go? Just because his wife was summoning him? Because cement was not available? What did I care about cement when life itself was not available to me. His quick decision to go hit me like an affront. I was being humbled before the woman who lived in Jalandhar.

Oma used to tell me that he did not relate to her at all, that he had nothing to do with her. He had broken my resistance over eighteen months by saying repeatedly that he was all alone in the world, that he never had any communication with the woman he was forced to marry, that he was only following the rituals of producing and bringing up children. Those rituals had been completed and he was a free man.

He used to tell me, 'Once you come to my arms and give me your love, I'll spend my whole life with you. I'll divorce that woman.'

The house in Jalandhar was the one with which he planned to bribe his wife in exchange for his freedom. And now he was running in the direction of that woman after humiliating me. I was determined not to let him go.

Surinder came into the room and we fell silent but I felt as if my feet were placed on burning coals.

Oma was in the habit of saying, 'Okay, we'll see' in order to defer action at a difficult moment and it sounded as if some solution or the other would really be found. That is what he said now. The three of us got into a taxi and started towards Connaught Place.

Oma had to attend to a few chores in Connaught Place. When he had finished, we had tea.

Surinder looked at his watch and said, 'You don't have train reservations. Why don't you have your dinner now? You have to reach the station on time. The train leaves at eight-forty.'

'He is not going today,' I said firmly but my heart was pounding. It was the decisive moment.

Either that woman or I...

'Of course he'll go today. Definitely. Mataji has sent for him.' Surinder had never spoken to me so brusquely before.

I thought he was challenging me. I got terribly agitated and felt my temper rising. And when Oma actually started towards the railway station, I was convinced that was our last evening together. It was the last meeting.

Why should I live with the humiliation of defeat like this? I simply couldn't accept it. To hell with him.

Till the last moment I expected that he would turn around and tell Surinder, 'No, I can't upset Jeet like this. I'll go tomorrow morning.'

But he said no such thing and boarded the train.

The train started and I went into a searing rage which was like boiling hot bitumen. I don't remember what I told Surinder. He must have been frightened by my fury.

Coming back, we lay down in our separate rooms as if we were lying in our graves. I could hear the blood pounding in my veins.

The next morning I made a paneer parantha for Surinder's breakfast and placed it before him without a word. He didn't eat it and left. I let him go.

That morning I just could not do anything. I was strangely exhausted. A pall of dust, silent and full of pain, seemed to be stretched over my heart.

I was lying listlessly on the bed when I heard a knock on the door. I felt as if someone from the other end of life, from a world beyond ours, was slowly and persistently hammering at the half slumber pervading my being.

I opened the door. Oma was standing outside.

Stepping inside, the longing with which he held me in his

arms reduced an endlessly vast desert into a mere sand dune between us. And then that dune too started diminishing in size.

Some relationships are so terribly intense that one wrong step—which may not even be wrong because no one can say for sure what is wrong and what is right—taken backward seems to create an entire wilderness of sand between two individuals. All you can do is to die after wandering through the sands, nothing else is possible. But the same step moving close to you—and the vast desert is reduced to just a fistful of sand. And the particles of sand trickle down slowly in the pale, magical starlight, weaving spells.

I stood leaning close to him listening to his heart beating, his heartbeats blazing a tattoo into my being.

It seemed that the boundless pleasure of that moment, expanding into a flood to quench a lifelong thirst, was sufficient for one lifetime.

But what does 'sufficient' mean? Has anything ever been sufficient? That moment goes by and the hunger, and the thirst and the fear and the loneliness and all the naked agony come back to you.

I asked Oma, 'You left only last night. How have you returned from Jalandhar so early in the morning?'

'I did not go to Jalandhar,' he answered, 'I got off the train at the next station which is Sabzi Mandi, and came back. Then I thought of Surinder—what would he think! So I went to Pal's house. I have been sitting here, in the front lawn, since dawn and waiting for Surinder to leave. Now that he has gone out...You were so depressed last night. I could not have gone leaving you in that state.'

It was an extraordinary state to be in. A strange feeling like contentment came over me though it was a very lean period in my life.

It was the period when I was the sole breadwinner. To supplement my monthly salary of six hundred and fifty rupees, I used to write articles and did translation work late into the night. I suffered a real setback when the USIS (United States Information Service), in order to cut down expenses because of the Vietnam war, reduced the volume of the writing and translation work they used to give me. I had to take care of the rent, food, the children's school fees, clothes, books and bus fare. I just could not stretch my resources to last through the whole month.

One day Oma said to me, 'We also publish translations. Why don't you take up some of them?'

'What kind of translation?' I asked.

'We have to get translations of the USIS books. We are going to publish them. However, we won't be able to pay you twenty rupees per thousand words as they did when you were working directly for them. We have to grease the palms of their Indian officers to get work from them. We have to provide for that extra expense from the translations themselves.'

'How much will you pay?'

'Fifteen rupees for a thousand words.'

'That is fine,' I said. That was how I started getting the USIS work through Oma.

That was the time when the father of my daughters threatened to have them kidnapped and I had them admitted to Auckland House School in Shimla, where they lived in the hostel. It added tremendously to my expenses. Sometimes I starved for days. In those conditions, I launched the *Rupee Trade* magazine. Each magazine runs at a loss in the beginning and mine was no exception.

Only God knew how I survived. I lit the stove only when Oma or Surinder came to stay with me. When they were not around I lived on a bottle of milk and half a loaf of bread. That was all I ate each day.

What was it that made me share everything with Oma? But I refused to share my poverty with him. Not only with Oma but also with Daarji or anyone else.

My friend Toshi was the only one who got to know about it. That too, partially.

I would sometimes think of a passage from Rajinder Singh Bedi's *Ek Chador Maili Si*. Rano's neighbour and friend tells her, 'A man can never feel his responsibility towards a woman, he can never love her fully, unless and until he spends on her.' I think that is the reason why Oma never felt his responsibility towards me. If I was adamant about standing on my feet financially and would not accept any help from him, then why did I get flustered when I fell ill and was alone? Why did I call out for him? And what right did I have to get upset with loneliness?

And yet, I just could not cut the Gordian knot inside me. I could not bring myself to ask Oma for money. I had to live life on my own terms and maintain my dignity and self-respect. I had to earn my own livelihood.

In seven years I had accepted only one saree from Oma; to wear at Surinder's wedding. It was his son's wedding and I couldn't possibly hurt him by refusing it.

Another saree was given to me by his wife. It was from among the sarees sent as gifts for the relatives by Surinder's in-laws. Surinder must have asked his mother to give me one.

I never wore those two sarees again. I folded and stored them away, for which occasion, I do not know.

I had never given too much thought to clothes. When I was living with my husband, I had possessed two sarees which I had bought for eleven rupees each from Cheap Silk Store in Karol Bagh. In addition, I had three pairs of salwar-kameez. To spend more on covering yourself seemed almost sinful to me.

I also had an old black coat to wear in winter. This coat had been sent to my friend Gargi by her sister in America or London but it turned out to be small for her and she had sold it to me for eighty rupees. Full eighty rupees, which meant my salary for about thirteen days—because at that time my salary was two hundred rupees a month out of which one had to spend ten paise on a revenue stamp. I had thought hard before spending that money on myself.

And food? What was food to me? I had been through days when I used to buy rotis worth two annas. Dal came free with them. I would carry this meal to the inner room of my house where I ate it sitting quietly in a corner. It was sheer heaven if you got a piece of raw onion or a slice of radish to go with it. I would feel like a queen without a crown or a throne on that repast!

I had seen such days in my husband's house.

But now I was in control of myself. I could eat what I wanted and refuse what I didn't. I was free to come and go, walk and wander, sleep and wake at will. The Queen Empress!

Every time I received a bulk payment for translation, I sent the children's school fees for the whole semester and got new clothes for them. I would also buy pots and pans, quilts, sheets and towels for my small house when I could. And books. In fact, books were my first priority.

But whenever I did manage to save up something in spite of such expenses, Oma and I would go on a trip outside Delhi. We had an agreement that on such trips we would share the expenses equally.

Even today whenever we have money—Arpana and I—we consider it a sin to put it in the bank. We should be loyal to money—we should not consign it to a cold, dark corner of some bank and turn our backs on it. We should show respect to it by spending it. One of our favourite ways of spending money is to travel. However, like Ghalib, we always return to Delhi.

I went all over India with Oma but of course we did not go around the country like tourists. Wherever we went Oma would contact booksellers and librarians to promote the books he published. And I met the local directors of industries, managing directors of export corporations, directors of information and export promotion councils in connection with my magazine, *Rupee Trade*.

So we spent the day taking care of our respective livelihoods, and in the evening we visited places of interest and had fun.

I used to marvel at the way my life was running at that time. I wondered why it could not always be that way.

But how long could Oma stay away from Jalandhar like that? For how long could he run away from his wife and family and remain hiding in my arms hundreds of miles away?

Whenever I would think that we had to run so far for the sake of a little peace and joy and such brief togetherness, I would feel a strange and bitter resentment.

The thought that those were stolen moments, stolen from real life, unreal, illusory, like dreams, filled me with a sensation of sand in my mouth.

I would reassure myself saying, 'So what if they are just dreams. At least they are mine.'

And what is life without dreams!

Some of our weekends were spent in places not too far from Delhi. We left on a Saturday afternoon and came back on Sunday evening.

One Saturday we had gone to Sariska. We had started from Delhi in the morning and reached Sariska by lunch time.

It was a wildlife sanctuary, a reserved forest where tigers, leopards, antelopes, blue bulls, wild boar and winged creatures moved around safely, free from the fear of human tyranny. Otherwise, according to the laws of the jungle, all large animals try to eat small animals and the small animals try to protect themselves. The life of that sanctuary also followed the rules of nature.

Oma used to get famished by meal times. He made no distinction between a dhaba and a restaurant when he was hungry. He would buy a plate of rotis and dal from a dhaba and eat it off the bonnet of his car.

As soon as we reached the resthouse he called the chowkidar. 'Is there anything to eat?' he asked

'No, Sir. We do not keep any meals ready here. If you just tell me what you'd like to eat, I'll cook it in a jiffy,' the man replied.

After a brief discussion, we decided on chicken curry and roti. The chowkidar said it would take him an hour to prepare.

As the chowkidar got busy preparing the meal, we decided to explore the woods. We asked the resthouse in-charge the way to the sanctuary.

'It is from the back of the resthouse. But you can't go in the car. You'll have to go by jeep,' he replied.

'Where does one get a jeep?'

'We have our own jeep. You can hire that. The game warden will go with you.'

'When can we go?'

'At night. If you want to see the tigers and the leopards, you'll have to go at midnight.'

'But we want to see the forest and also the antelope,' I said.

'In that case,' he said, 'have your lunch now. In the meanwhile I'll arrange for the jeep.'

After lunch we took the jeep and went deep into the jungle. It was a desolate wilderness, overgrown with dense trees and scattered shrubs at different places. A dirt road lay in the middle from which narrow pathways branched out in different directions. You could see herds of antelope grazing here and there in the distance. At the noise of the jeep, they would lift their heads in our direction and gaze at us intently with their round, clear, crystalline eyes. They reminded me of small children who stop playing to watch with fascination an aeroplane flying overhead.

Flocks of water fowl and herons flew overhead, looking as if they were floating in the melting blue of the sky. 'Is there a lake nearby?' we asked the game warden.

'Not so close, but there is a lake some distance away at Silised.'

'Let us go to Silised,' I suggested.

'Next time,' Oma replied.

As we drove around I noticed an old crumbling building in the forest. Surrounded by the desolation of that wilderness, it was like a ruin, alone, abandoned.

'What is that?' I asked. I felt suddenly afraid.

Isn't it strange that we are often scared of objects which are lifeless in themselves. People are scared of corpses and tremble with fear while passing by cremation grounds.

'It is a temple, centuries-old and now in ruins. Nobody visits it,' the game warden informed me.

'But people do go to ancient temples. Why doesn't anyone come to this one?' I persisted.

'According to the legend, some king fell in love with a Banjara girl whose clan had set up their camp here. He married her. Those Banjaras happened to be nomadic shepherds who had to move away from the place. They went away, leaving the girl behind. The king built a palace right there for his wife but she was lonely in this wilderness and did not like it at all. The king had this temple constructed for her. It is believed that her ghost haunts this temple and these ruins are under the curse of her sighs.'

I declared that I was determined to go up to those ruins and see them for myself.

I could see a dark line forming on Oma's face. Whenever he disagreed with something I said, he would frown in this manner.

The game warden also urged me to desist from going into the temple. He said, 'It is not wise to go up there. No one has ever climbed those stairs. Snakes crawl all over those walls.'

But I got out of the jeep and started walking in the direction of the ruins. I seemed to be drawn by an invisible magic string.

There was a raised platform in front of the stairs. Under the impact of long exposure to the sun, the rain, countless summers and winters, its bricks and stones had become so smooth that you could slip on them. Blades of grass and dry twigs peeped from the joints between the stones and the stones themselves were covered with moss.

Beyond the ruins was a pond which probably served as a water hole for tigers and leopards at night in the shadow of that ancient, dead temple. And the primordial smell of their breath mixed with the flowing of the blood in their veins probably moved up those stairs along with the wafting breezes.

I started climbing up the stairs. They were narrow, like the wedges in the inner wall of a well with just enough space for a toe hold. The place itself was like a deep well turned upside down whose depth ended at the top. God knows whether it ever ended or not.

The stairs were so steep it was like climbing up a mountain slope. A strange terror seemed to be rustling down the steps in my direction.

Oma was standing down there. Watching me from a distance but beyond my feelings of fear and terror.

He was looking at me but he was indifferent to the terror vibrating through my veins like the beating of kettledrums.

Step by step on those stairs, I was moving away from him.

Moving up I had a feeling of standing at the edge of a murky vacuum. It was like the moment before you jump into a dark, abandoned well. It was the split second before you stretched out your arms, lifted your body and jumped down. A fraction of a second.

The walls on both sides of the staircase seemed to be shrinking as I went up. And they really seemed to be crawling with snakes. I looked closely at them and discovered that they were roots of trees. But where were the trees? Was I in the underworld?

In the past sometime, those walls must have supported henna-stained hands as that Banjara girl climbed up the stairs. Enclosed in those walls, she who was used to wandering through vast distances like a doe, must have felt suffocated. She probably went to the roof seeking fresh air, open skies and God. Climbing those very stairs. And then coming back crazed and surrounded by loneliness, disappointment and defeat.

Those walls seemed to carry the imprints of the palms of her hands. And those palms had wounds. And blood was still dripping from them.

Were all those the imprints of that girl's hands? Countless, wounded palms engraved on the walls.

Suddenly I found myself on a step, the step after which had crumbled and fallen. The next step was extremely steep—

almost at the same height as my head. I could only touch it. Climbing it was out of the question.

And suddenly, I was thrown back from there. It was like being pushed back violently by some hand.

I don't know after how long...but I was in Oma's arms. I was trembling and crying bitterly.

An anguish, centuries-old, came lamenting through the stairs, embraced me and descended to settle in my heart.

46

It was a bitterly chilly evening in December. I was walking from my home in the UNCTAD building, towards Pal's house.

It was not yet half-past seven in the evening. Curzon Road, which is now known as Kasturba Gandhi Marg, was strangely deserted and quiet.

When I passed under a lamppost, the road seemed to be awake. A spray of light lay scattered under that lamppost—a spray the colour of ash. The road stretched on both sides, and the sidewalks looked as if they had just been washed and cleaned like a kitchen floor. Painted with moonlight. Pure. I could see the traffic on the road but once I moved ahead of the lamppost, everything looked irrationally somnolent again. Dull, half-asleep, desolate.

At each street turning were white boards that carried the names of the roads in English and Hindi. When I passed under a tree between two lampposts, ominous shadows seemed to be huddling under it.

Oma's train was due to arrive at nine at night and he would make it to Pal's house at nine-thirty at the earliest. The time in between seemed to stretch on endlessly. I thought I could pass it by walking to Pal's house.

In the opposite direction lay the spacious lawns of India Gate. I wondered what it would be like to walk through them at night. But on one occasion last winter Oma and I had been walking there, shivering in the cold air. Oma was holding my hand and perhaps I was leaning against his arm as I walked. Suddenly two men emerged from behind a tree. They blocked our way. One of them said, 'What are you doing here?'

'What do you think we are doing? We are strolling here,' Oma said, annoyed, and took my arm.

'Strolling, indeed...' he mimicked and guffawed. The other man stood arms akimbo, and glared at us.

'How is she related to you?' he demanded.

'It is none of your business.'

'Come to the police station. You'll soon learn what our business is.'

I was furious. 'Who are you?' I thundered.

'We are from the police,' they answered.

'Nonsense,' I shouted, 'what is the proof that you are from the police?'

One of them outshouted me, 'Come to the police station. You'll get the proof there.'

'Okay, let us go to the police station. Will you walk or shall we go in a taxi?' I asked.

However, Oma had got flustered at the mention of the police station. He asked them, 'What do you want?'

'Your watch and wallet,' said one of the men.

I was astonished to see Oma taking out his wallet and placing it in the hand of the man.

The latter put it in his pocket, stretched out his hand and demanded the watch.

And Oma took off his watch.

I was so ashamed that even today I get the sensation

of ants crawling on my legs at the memory. Why did Oma make that compromise? As if we were doing something to be ashamed of!

They left after taking the watch and the wallet but not before they told us threateningly, 'Go home now otherwise someone else will get after you.'

Was this Delhi? The capital city? The whole country was administered from here. Could two bad characters waylay and rob innocent persons just a mile away from Parliament House? And that too, after making their victims feel guilty?

But I was angriest with Oma for not resisting that blackmail with courage. Such a big, tall man. Couldn't he have punched them and put them in their place?

'Don't be crazy,' he said, 'You chase away the goondas by punching them only in the movies. Supposing they had knives?'

'But I was with you. After all, there were two of us!' I persisted.

'What if they really were from the police and they actually took us to the police station?'

'So what? Were we committing a crime? Is it a crime to stroll on these lawns?'

'You don't understand. If they said that we really were... doing something, what proof do we have that we were only taking a walk?'

'But what exactly can you do in these open lawns? Were we sleeping here?' I was livid with anger. It was rage over helplessness, a revolt against a grave mistake, against cowardice.

'Do you know that even kissing in a public place is an offence. Supposing they said that...' Oma was trying to reason with me.

But I was adamant, 'When we were not doing anything, how could they...'

warm sun on a winter day. And then cuddling up to Oma to sleep at night. And why sleep at all, for staying awake was equally good. I would listen to Oma's sleepy voice and absorb the warmth of his body and the bed into my own, like a sponge. I stayed awake to watch the slow-moving moments and thought with a full heart, 'This is happiness. This is happiness trickling through my fingers, each passing moment.'

If anybody has ever seen happiness, it is me. Solid, warm, breathing happiness. This is happiness, this. *Yeh sukh hai, yehi sukh hai.*

Walking along Curzon Road, these words were reverberating in my mind like strains from a forgotten melody heard long ago. The air itself repeated them in affirmation.

Yeh sukh hai...like the fire lit by the reeds in the fields whose flames go up and tremble down by turns.

Words stumbling like drunken men, rising up to the endless expanse of the sky and then falling back to the recesses of my heart like a flock of pigeons descending on the roof of a house.

Where was that happiness that day?

That day I was wandering between two pools of darkness in search of those words. From one lamppost to the next. From one basin of light to the other.

It had rained in the evening. The rain had stopped at a quarter past seven. The remaining light of the day had suddenly blended in the darkness of the night like wet ashes.

The last, brown twilight of the rain-washed but cloudy sky looked like a squirrel sleeping in translucent darkness—brown, furry and soft.

I had started from home after the rain stopped. At any rate, I could not have covered the distance between seven-thirty and nine-thirty sitting at home.

I could not understand why Oma had not telephoned me.

He had called up Pal to say he was coming from Jalandhar by the night train. And Pal had telephoned me to say, 'He'll be here by nine-thirty. Please come over to my place. We'll have dinner together.'

'But suppose he comes straight to my house?'

'No, he won't do that. He is coming here.'

'Did he say he'd come to you directly?'

'Allow him to come directly to my place sometimes,' Pal was laughing. He was trying to evade the issue.

'Of course,' I said, 'but I wonder...'

'You can come and wonder at my house this evening.' He was still laughing.

'Did he ask you to invite me or are you inviting me on your own?' I asked.

'Why? Can't I invite you to my house? After all I am your brother-in-law of sorts...'

'Okay, I'll come on your invitation. But please tell me whether...'

'Yes of course. His Majesty has passed a decree. And what I'm telling you has been decreed by him, that we'll have dinner together tonight, at my house.'

'All right. I'll be there,' I had said.

My whole day was spent with strange misgivings and apprehensions. It was like feeling thirsty but unable to drink water, like being totally exhausted but unable to sleep. The feeling was somewhat akin to the frustration with which you search the whole house after misplacing your spectacles or pen.

It seemed as if somebody was scratching the inside of my chest with his nails. I was bewildered. I wondered what the matter was.

I reached Pal's house. He was working on his ledgers with his accountant. When I arrived, he closed the files and dismissed the accountant.

'What is the matter?' Pal asked me, 'Why are you so morose? You know that His Highness is arriving today.'

'Why should I be morose!' I protested.

'What would you like to drink?'

'Nothing.'

'Have a cup of coffee at least. That'll give me an excuse to have one myself.'

'Why do you need an excuse to have coffee?' I tried to smile.

'Where do I get coffee? Especially at this hour, the dangerous hour which one has to somehow kill with whisky!'

'All right then. You can have this luxury at my expense today!'

'Thank you.' He got up and went across the courtyard to the kitchen to instruct his servant to make two cups of coffee.

While the coffee was being made, he played the latest music he had taped. It was a set of ghazals sung by Noorjahan.

Coffee arrived. We drank it quietly. The room was full of Noorjahan's voice, otherwise the air in the room would have become heavy. Heavy, and full of smoke.

Every now and then I would sneak a glance at my watch. Time had almost come to a standstill. It seemed like a century before the doorbell rang.

My heart was thudding as the servant went to open the door. The suspense that stretched between one breath of mine and the next was about to snap like a rubber band when I heard Oma's voice saying, 'Is everything all right? Is Sahib at home?' With that Oma entered the house.

Whenever I went to receive Oma at the railway station, I would run from a distance to meet him, and he would take me in his arms in a half embrace. And when he came directly to my house, I had to stretch my arm behind his back to shut the door, and right there, at the threshold that embrace would go on and on.

But what kind of meeting was this? There was a turbulent, three-foot wide river in the middle. I was no Sohni and Oma no Mahiwal; and I did not have an earthen pitcher with which to cross that river. I knew that it would not be possible to swim across those turbulent waters.

Oma inquired after my health. We talked about the weather. He went to the bathroom to wash his hands and face. Pal called out from outside the bathroom door, 'Why don't you finish with your bath, too.'

'I'll have to change into a kurta-pyjama then,' Oma answered.

'No, no. He'll bathe at home,' I said quickly.

'I think you should take a leisurely bath and relax over a couple of drinks before dinner,' Pal continued talking to Oma.

Oh God, I thought, if he did all that at leisure, when would we go home?

'But we have to go...' I said in a small voice.

'You have come just now, why are you already talking about leaving? *Abhi abhi to aaye ho...*' Pal burst into song.

I suddenly had the feeling that the whole thing was a well-rehearsed drama.

There was a conspiracy in which I had no part. It was a conspiracy against me, a conspiracy to murder me.

That was the moment when I began to get angry. Alongside the bitterness was a sense of helplessness.

Pal was laughing, so was Oma. Their whisky glasses were full.

Whenever Oma's friends got together, alcohol was not served to me. They all knew that I did not like its taste. Much later I had cultivated a slight taste for champagne for the sake of avoiding the taunts at parties but this incident took place before my champagne days, in what seems like the Stone Age.

However, I always took the first sip from Oma's glass.

That evening too, I took the first sip though it was just a ritual that had lost its sparkle.

'How is Gautam doing?' Oma was asking Pal.

'Kicking.'

'Has he found a new author?'

'Not that I know of.'

'And how is your Mumtaz Mahal?'

Mumtaz Mahal was the nickname invented for Pal's wife by their friends.

'She is ruling the roost in London.'

'And Rano?'

'Rano weighs the same,' Pal laughed.

Everything sounded so childish and daft—their meaningless conversation, glasses of whisky, soft music on the tape, the kebabs on their plates. I felt nauseated and had a strong impulse to run away from them.

But where would I go? Was there any peace outside those walls? Wasn't life outside equally daft and childish? Weren't the streets desolate? People unhappy? Wasn't there loneliness? Suffocation?

There was no way out. Flustered, I drained off half of Oma's glass. The room seemed to melt and tremble around me, like a boat floating on water. Oma was looking at me with astonishment. Pal had averted his gaze.

A bitter fire seemed to sear down to my insides. Some liquid seemed to have filled my head—not water, but something like liquid wax.

What a foolish thing I had done! I had hoped that it would take the edge out of the sharp pain I was experiencing. On the contrary, my unhappiness grew sharper, glinting like a dagger's edge in the sun.

I made an effort to cross the desert lying between Oma and myself—a desert where sand glittered with wild and

'What is the proof that we were not doing anything?' he repeated.

I fell silent, then started crying. Oma tried to comfort me by saying, 'In such situations the wise thing to do is...'

'Wise! My foot!' I cut him short.

'And what if they asked for our names and addresses in the police station?' he asked.

'So what? Don't we have names and addresses?' I countered.

'No, no, I can't afford to record my name and address in a police station. I think we got away lightly by parting with those things. There were only two hundred and fifty rupees in the purse and the watch cost a hundred and fifty.'

So, that was it. It was not acceptable to Oma that his name and mine should ever be written together at any place.

I turned round and walked swiftly to my hostel. He kept calling out from behind.

As I walked on towards Pal's house, that incident kept coming back to my mind. I wished I could spend two hours walking on the lawns of India Gate but I could not do so. Instead, I was walking on the road; alone, friendless.

༄

Oma did not like the winter at all. He used to shrink a little in the cold. Such a tall, well-built man walking with his head bent down looked like a grizzly bear walking in the snows! I felt such love to see him like that.

On the contrary, I adored the cold weather. I spent ten months of the year waiting for two months of winter. I loved strolling out on the open lawns and roads in the freezing cold of winter evenings and sitting bundled up in a blanket to sip hot tea and read books by the crackling woodfire. What could be more enjoyable than sitting and munching carrots in the murderous cruelty. I took his hand and said, 'Come, let us go home.'

'Why don't you sleep here tonight?' Pal asked Oma.

'I'll do that,' Oma said, adding, 'I have to catch the first flight to Bombay in the morning.'

Earlier the ceiling of the room looked as if it was melting but when it fell on my head, it felt solid and heavy.

'Bombay?' I asked in confusion.

'Yes, there is a conference of the Federation in Bombay.'

'I'll go with you,' I said obstinately.

The air between Oma and me was thick with purple, red and black spots, spots which were the colour of blood, the colour of black ink.

'What would you do there? The conference is for four days,' Oma asked. I could detect the first fissure in his composure.

'I'd do nothing,' I answered, 'I'll spend the days going around the streets and spend the evenings and nights with you.'

I don't know when Pal had left. Oma and I were alone in the room.

That murderous moment could have been averted had he been alone in the room with me right after coming from the station. But that time had gone by. Now it was too late.

A river of fire was now flowing through the blazing desert stretched between Oma and me.

By now I was doggedly importunate. My voice must have risen sharply. Oma shook my arm three or four times and said, 'Have some consideration for Pal's house. What will the neighbours say!'

But I was registering nothing.

He held me by the arm and took me out. I thought we were going home.

But we were going in exactly the opposite direction, towards the Gole Dak Khana.

'Where are we going?' I said in a voice full of bitter resentment and entreaty at the same time. 'Let us go home.'

'No. I can't go anywhere in this state of mind,' he countered.

'Can you walk the streets in this state of mind?'

'I can't. But is there a way out?'

'I am your only problem, am I not? Aren't you looking for a way to get rid of me?' I was trying to cover up the tears in my voice by getting angrier and angrier.

It was incredible. At a moment when I should have just said, 'Take me in your arms,' I was getting embroiled in a fight.

No, but why should I say that? That should have happened spontaneously, without thinking. And then all the deserts would have shrunk within themselves, and disappeared. The blazing fire would have gone out automatically.

If the right things happened at the right times, life would not be called life.

And we were walking in the direction exactly opposite to where those deserts could have vanished. Not towards home but towards Gole Dak Khana.

'I don't know exactly what you want. I had taken such trouble to manage a night in Delhi. I haven't even gone home because Surinder is there since yesterday, and...'

'Why didn't you come home directly?' I asked. A mention of his troubles always made me soften. On that occasion too, my voice started losing its edge.

'I thought maybe Surinder would come to you to enquire if I was coming. Back home in Jalandhar, my wife is already asking questions.'

By then I was sobbing away to glory. I had never cried on

the streets like that. It must have been the alcohol. Perhaps whisky does not allow you to conceal your pain.

It was naked pain. Naked, unveiled anguish, and that is why it was so ugly.

Even now it appears extremely ugly and repugnant when I think of it.

The road going in the direction of Gole Dak Khana was deserted. A cold, chilly wind was blowing. However, I can think of how cold it was only today. At that time I did not feel the cold at all.

'I don't understand it,' Oma said irritably, 'Aren't you ashamed of making a spectacle of yourself out here?'

It was like a slap in the face. I stopped crying. 'Ashamed? I really feel no shame. If I did, I would not have followed you like a lamb all these years! So many years...! Why would I leave myself at your mercy if I had a sense of shame?' My anger came flooding back with full force. I continued, 'What a thing to do. You disappear for so many days at a time. And now when you finally decide to come, you phone up Pal to "summon" me! Planning to spend the night at his house! As if I am a nonentity, someone totally insignificant! Am I a chair or a table which you can use as and when you like and take with you wherever you like?

'All the important decisions are in your hands because they affect your life. Now what can I do if I too am tied to that great and important life of yours! Because I am tied to it, I have to be dragged along with it!

'The important thing is that it is *your* life and there are important people in it—your wife, your daughter, your son! The Prince of Wales! As long as he needed a place to stay in Delhi, he came and stayed with me. Because I have to please you, I took care of him, too. But when you realized that he was, maybe, falling in love with me, you promptly arranged for a house for the Prince Charming!

'Because your son is in Delhi today, you have no guts to stay with me. And you have the nerve to drag me down to Pal's serai with you! What do you take me to be? A kothewali from G.B. Road?'

'Shut up.'

'I won't. You have to take a decision today.'

'You are out of your mind. You have these fits every two or three weeks. "Take a decision" indeed. Why don't you take a decision for a change? I am willing to accept whatever you decide!'

'Why do you presume that I would decide that we should part? Isn't that the decision you are counting on?'

'I am willing to accept any decision you take,' Oma repeated irritably.

'And what if I decide that I shall live with you, in your house?'

'Come, live with me! In my house! She would herself chase you out with a rolling pin.'

'And won't you protect me?'

'I don't know what I would do. And why should I tell you even if I do? You do whatever you wish to do first. I'll follow that by what I have to do.' His words and his voice had a blank, neutral tone. It was a naked challenge!

I could control myself no longer. Holding his shirt tightly, I said, 'I'll go and live with you, that is all. But first I'll go to Bombay tomorrow morning.'

'Let go of my shirt,' he said angrily trying to push my hands away.

I held on to his shirt even more tightly. I was crazed with anger. A primitive, wild, boiling rage.

He jerked my hand with force. Two buttons came off his shirt.

Hurriedly, he started walking towards the crossing. He

stopped a taxi. He opened the door and got into it. The door of the taxi closed with a bang.

I was so confused at that moment that it did not occur to me that he was leaving—that is, leaving me alone. I kept thinking that he would bring the taxi to me and ask me to get in.

I did not follow him when he was walking towards the crossing. My legs had gone numb and my torso seemed to be standing attached to two wooden staffs. Assuming all the time that he was bringing the taxi to me.

The taxi drove away and I panicked. Nervous, I looked around. I was standing alone and shivering in the silent, freezing, dark night. It had rained in the evening so it was unusually cold. The streets around me were all deserted.

It must have been past midnight by then. I spent the rest of the night treading the roads, wandering around them.

Today it seems as if all that happened in some other era and it was another woman who wandered around alone in the streets on a murky, freezing, winter night.

I went to Pal's house. He opened the door slightly but held it with both his hands from inside. Through the chink in the door, he told me, 'He hasn't come here. He must have gone to his house in Jangpura.'

'Tell him I am waiting downstairs on the landing when he comes,' I said defeatedly.

'I'll tell him if he comes.' Pal's assurance smacked of a lie but there was nothing I could do.

I learnt much later that Oma was actually present in the house. He was drinking, and Pal had been trying to comfort him.

Exhausted, I climbed down the stairs of Pal's house. I sat

for a moment on the first step and listened to the rustling sound in my brain. It was like listening to a corpse turning over in its grave.

I came home feeling absolutely drained. The house was frighteningly empty. My first thought was of a cup of tea. I lit the stove and placed the kettle on it but found the whole exercise futile. I turned off the stove.

I walked to Jangpura.

The barsati where Surinder lived was completely dark. If Oma had come there, the lights would have been on. I had no idea how much time had elapsed between his leaving in the taxi and my coming to stand in front of his house, gazing longingly at the darkened window of his barsati room. What should I do now? How to find out whether he was in or not?

It was futile to attempt to reach the barsati. The people living downstairs used to lock the gate at night. Also, the occupants of the first floor, who owned the entire house, bolted the door of the staircase from inside.

You had to cross the gate first and then the door of the staircase in order to get to the barsati.

At that hour it was impossible to cross those two doors. Oma would have never forgiven me if he had to suffer any kind of disgrace in front of his neighbours.

There was a petrol pump a short distance away from where Oma used to buy petrol. A public telephone was attached to its outer wall. But how about money? I took out my purse and found two coins in it. The man on night duty at the petrol pump stared at me.

I dialled the number of Oma's house. Surinder picked up the phone.

'Surinder? This is Jeet. Has Bauji arrived?'

'No he hasn't. But you...at this hour?'

Surinder seemed to have woken up flustered from his sleep

and was probably astonished to see the time. 'It is nothing important. He had to go to Bombay. I thought maybe he'd take a break in Delhi.'

'Well, no. He has not come here.'

'Okay. Please go back to sleep. I'll call up in the morning. I'm sorry.'

The next number I dialled was Pal's. 'Has he come?'

'No he hasn't.'

I hung up and looked at the attendant with some surprise, wondering why he was standing there. I seemed to have forgotten why I was standing there, too.

We were watching each other with surprise. It must have been just a fraction of a second but at that time it seemed as if we had been looking at each other for a century and trying to figure out what it meant.

I looked at my watch in the dim street light. The time was a quarter past three. I thought that he was bound to come before five o'clock if he had to catch a flight at six o'clock. And if he was sleeping inside he would have to come down to go to the airport by five o'clock.

I saw a pile of bricks lying in front of the house and sat down on them. Only I know how I spent the time from a quarter past three to a quarter past five, then half past five. Maybe even He, who has created the cosmos over millions of years, and made human beings so that a river of pain continues to flow from one end to the other, does not know.

At half past five, when I hired a taxi to go home, the stars had begun to lose their brilliance.

Walking unsteadily, I came home. A storm was raging deep inside my heart. I could feel the swirling dust. Blind and deaf storms were rising heavenwards from my being.

The sky was covered with a layer of dull pink. The colour blue had faded. It reminded me of the fish which die in an aquarium and rise to float on the surface of the water. The colour of the upturned bellies of the dead fish gradually changes from white to the pale, dull colour of dust.

I felt a large number of dead fish were floating on the surface of the water inside my chest. Moment by moment the colour of their bellies was changing to the colour of dust.

A lone tent was fluttering in the swirling dust of the storm like a pigeon stuffed in the mouth of a cat with its feathers desperately fluttering in its last agony.

Today I am astonished to look back at those horrendous days. How I was dominated by these two states at the same time! The state of the floating dead fish and the state of the fluttering tent going to pieces in the swirling sands.

I collapsed on my bed. I lost all awareness of time and of my surroundings.

It was the desolation of a cremation ground. The bed was like a boat without its oars. The room, like a dark grave.

And I was like a boat lying overturned on the sands after drowning all its passengers.

Suddenly I thought of going to Bombay.

I got up quickly and called up Indian Airlines. They informed me that the morning flights had all left and there was only one flight at eight in the night on which eighty-one passengers were already waitlisted.

I contacted everybody I knew in the Ministry of Tourism and Civil Aviation and managed to get a confirmed seat on the eight o'clock flight, arranged for money and went to buy my ticket.

I was seized by a strange restlessness and urgency. It seemed that not reaching Bombay that day would be tantamount to doomsday.

My hands trembled as I arranged a few clothes in a bag. My legs were shaking.

In the evening a thought struck me. Where would I search for him? The biggest printing-press owner of Bombay, who was also the vice-president of the Federation of Publishers, was an acquaintance of mine. I phoned him and told him as much as I could. I requested him not to mention me to Oma but to come to the airport to pick me up and drop me at the hotel where Oma was staying.

∽

Bombay.

The press owner had come to the airport. I felt reassured to see him as though there was no danger any more. The doomsday had been averted. I felt that I had been saved from a terrible disaster. I was about to reach my destination. My 'home' was close by.

He took me to Ballard Estate in his car. Stopping in front of a hotel, he said, 'Just wait in the car for a moment. Let me go and check.'

'There is no need to check anything,' I said, 'You can drop me here and go back. You have already been delayed so much.'

But he did not listen to me. When he got out of the car and went into the hotel, I suddenly felt sure something was wrong somewhere.

He came back after two minutes, walking slowly. He got into the car and started it.

'What happened?' I asked anxiously.

'He checked out an hour ago,' he said, looking at the steering wheel. He avoided looking at me.

I was shocked. It seemed as if the car had crashed against a huge black mountain.

'How come? At this time? At night? What do you mean, he has checked out?' I asked.

'I don't know,' he answered.

'Did you tell him about me?' I asked again.

'Yes, I did,' he answered guiltily.

It was clear that he had betrayed me.

Superfluous woman, who is not even his wife, chasing him like this! Let me teach her a lesson! Let her go around in circles! Who is she to first fight with him and then come chasing after him?

He turned to me and said, 'Come, I'll arrange for your stay in a nice hotel. We can look around for him tomorrow morning.'

'Please drop me at the YWCA on Madam Cama Road.'

He dropped me there and left quietly after saying, 'I'll call you up in the morning.'

I did not reply.

There was no room available at the YWCA. 'No room is going to be vacated before ten tomorrow morning,' I was informed.

'It is all right,' I said, 'as it is I am not going to sleep. I'll spend the night here in the lounge.'

At one-thirty in the night it suddenly occurred to me that Gautam too might be in Bombay if it was a meeting of the Federation. I knew that he always stayed at the Taj. I called up the Taj. The reception said, 'Yes, he is staying here. We'll just inquire and tell you.' After two minutes they said, 'He is not in.'

I knew that too, was a lie. I was sure Oma was with Gautam.

It was 2 a.m. and I was walking on the dark street in the direction of the Taj. At the rear of the hotel where a statue stands in perpetual darkness and where the victorias are parked, a number of people passing by whispered to me, '*Jaana mangta*? How much?'

But it was an apocalyptic night and I was lifted far above those things. I had no fear, nor any shame.

While rising from my grave on that doomsday morning, I had left fear and shame behind in the soil of the grave. I had shaken them off and with total indifference to myself, started moving fearlessly like the leaping light of a lamp.

I reached the Taj. The receptionist had already told me the room number. On the door of the room hung a card with 'Do Not Disturb' printed on it.

Still I turned the knob, rang the bell and knocked on the door. No response.

For a long time, I do not remember how long—maybe the rest of the night—I just stood outside that door. I left only after a waiter came up to me several times and asked, 'Can I help you, ma'm?'

The sea lay across the road from the Taj. You could see the bright lights of the ships floating in water in the distance. Narrow pathways formed by those lights lay trembling on the inky waters of the sea.

For a moment I wondered if I should go and sink silently in those waters.

And then I saw the innocent faces of Arpana and Candy near those narrow pathways of light. Huge, wide eyes in those innocent faces gazing intently at me.

I turned back and started towards the YWCA. As I passed by the carriages someone came close again and whispered something. This time I looked at the man carefully. A thought, like the straight cut made by a sharp-edged knife, flashed through my mind. 'At least this one needs me!'

I spent the next day searching for Oma. In the evening I learned that he had left for Bangalore.

'When?'

'Just a while ago. By the evening flight.'

I called up Indian Airlines. There was no other flight for Bangalore that night. The next flight was scheduled for six o'clock the next day. Next morning—before which stretched a whole night.

It is so strange to think of all that madness today! Chasing someone from city to city, searching for him! And he running ahead of me, worrying that I might catch up with him!

The ball was in my court. And I was destined to be faced with my last defeat.

It was amazing. People regard me as a practical businesswoman, a mere working woman. Was it really I who was running obsessed from city to city?

Had I been a wife, the whole world would have been in sympathy with me. 'Poor thing! Look at the way she is searching for her husband. She is wandering demented from city to city.'

But I was 'the other woman' who is a ridiculous entity; an illegitimate woman possessed by an illegitimate passion! The sanctity and dignity of love are lost in association with her. With reference to her, love becomes either an object of ridicule or hatred.

How strange it is, isn't it, that the same sentiment between a man and a woman is represented through the warp and weft of relationships in so many colours.

Reaching Bangalore the next day, I wondered where I should look for him.

Years ago I had visited Bangalore with Oma. We had stayed at a hotel which was still under construction. The floors smelt of wet, new cement and the doors of fresh polish. The mattresses on the beds had still not compressed and they looked funny. I still remember how loudly our beds had creaked every time we turned over in our sleep.

The man we had met in Bangalore on that trip owned

a very large bookshop. He was the brother of Sadanand in Bombay. He had invited us to dinner. Afterwards I had laughed so much about the way we were fed dal ka halwa and ras malai on the one hand and thin, dry papad-like phulkas on the other. Sadanand's brother had declared that one did not put on weight with such phulkas.

I went to the shop of Sadanand's brother. He was surprised to see me. He said, 'He would have sent a telephone message or a letter to me if he was coming here. He has not come here at all.' He offered me a chair in his office and made phone calls to half a dozen people but no one had any idea about Oma's presence in the city.

That was the end of my search.

I was running through a silent, black tunnel concentrating on the images of light, the sun and the air at the other end so that I should not get flustered and suffocated by the frightening darkness and the closed, musty, stale air of the tunnel.

Suddenly the whole tunnel collapsed. Tons of rubble fell down on me. And a scream came turning back on its heels from the tunnel.

I hired a taxi but did not know what to tell the driver. What should I tell him? Where should he take me?

'Is there a restaurant nearby where I could have tea?' I asked.

The taxi driver chatted with his companion on the way. They were talking about a Sai Baba who had come to Wild Flower outside Bangalore from Puttapurti. He was constructing a college there. People from Bangalore were thronging there for his darshan.

A defeated person is a weak person. A defeated person always wishes to find a corner where he can cry.

My naked wandering on that deserted road was full of a

sense of insecurity. What one needed in that vulnerable state was the support of a wall, and not a bare road.

Perhaps for that reason, I told the driver to take me to Wild Flower.

Innumerable people were sitting in an open maidan. A college building was under construction at the other end. People standing around a hand pump situated between the building and the maidan were taking turns drinking water. The construction workers were carrying canisters full of water from the same hand pump to the construction site. On the left side was a large, palatial house which had a gate at least twelve feet high.

A woman asked me something. Either I didn't understand it, or I didn't hear her properly so I answered, 'I have come to meet Sai Baba.'

She stared at me as though I were mad. 'But he comes out at half past four in the evening to give darshan.'

I sat down under a tree right there.

I had no desire, nor any quest, for anybody's darshan. I had lost count of time and felt no need to look at my watch. I sat immobile, like a stone.

The gates opened and Sai Baba came out. Beautiful saffron robes—a gorgeous deep saffron. He had wooden sandals on his feet and on his head, a mass of curly, black hair. His hands and feet were expressive like a Bharatnatyam dancer's. There was something gentle, pliant and smooth-flowing, like waves, about him. A serene, easygoing manner.

People rushed forward to touch his feet. He raised his hands in blessing, floated here and there among them without saying anything. For a moment he stopped and looked up at the building under construction and spoke to the mason for a while. He went back and the gates closed behind him.

I continued sitting at the same place.

The woman who had spoken to me earlier gave me a strange look and said, 'If you had to meet him, you should have moved forward to touch his feet or given a slip of paper to his secretary for an appointment. You have just been sitting here like a fool.'

I asked her, 'When will he come next?'

'Tomorrow, at ten in the morning,' she answered. 'Where do you stay at night? We have taken a room on rent in the market on the other side. We can help you find accommodation if you wish.'

But I had neither the strength nor the will to get up. I was feeling half-dead. Maybe that is what being dead meant—seeing everyone but not being a part of their life, to be surrounded by the world around you but remaining untouched by it.

Was that sorrow? No! Not at all.

Instead, it was the absence of both joy and sorrow. Absolute numbness.

A scream returning from a blind and deaf tunnel which had collapsed. Faint. Inert.

॰

I spent three nights and almost three days right there, under that tree, living on the water from that hand pump.

On the third day I came out and hired a taxi. I caught a flight from the airport and returned to Delhi.

I reached the hostel. I felt feverish as I lay on my bed. Fever is such a helpful thing at times. It waited till I could reach my bed.

It kept me constant company for twenty-two days. Maybe it realized I needed a companion.

Maybe it had come to know how lonely I was.

Epilogue

Some are born in gypsy families and others become gypsies through a conspiracy of circumstances. I belonged to this latter category. But eventually, I did find a permanent place to rest, a home for myself and Arpana and Candy, who is part of both of us, a home of bricks and mortar. This is how it happened.

Indira Gandhi had asked me to compile a directory of Indian women in April 1975, for a women's conference in Mexico. During that period, I met Mrs Gandhi several times, and one morning, she invited me for breakfast. She asked me what I did, and I told her about my writing and also about a school for girls from the slums that I used to run in a DDA flat in Saket, which Daarji had bought for Candy. Mrs Gandhi told me to visit a vocational school in Nizamuddin and see how they ran it. I became very interested in starting a similar school. Mrs Gandhi wrote to Jagmohan, who was the Vice-chairman of DDA at that time (1975), and asked him to allot me a plot of land in the Siri Fort area, which was then a jungle.

I was allotted a one and a half acre plot in 1977, but soon afterwards, Indira Gandhi lost the elections after the Emergency, and the government changed. The new government put the allotment on hold, and I gave up on the idea.

Ten years later, in 1987, the DDA offered to give back the plot. But I now opted for a much smaller plot, and so they allotted me a 1,100-square metre plot. I sold the flat in Saket, bought the plot, and started building on it. I did not have enough money to complete the construction, so I sold all the property Daarji had bought for my old age—the commercial flat in Nehru Place, and even Daarji's own house in East Patel Nagar—Daarji had moved in with Arpana and me in the rented flat we lived in when we were in Niti Bagh, and continued to live with us till he passed away in 1982.

Whenever we ran short of money, Arpana would sell one of her paintings. Just as some houses are built brick by brick, you could say that our house was built painting by painting!

Finally, the building of the Academy of Fine Arts and Literature was completed in 1994. Part of the building is a vocational school for slum children. There are also two galleries—one of them has Arpana's permanent collection of paintings, the other is for young artists which we rent out for a nominal amount, or free, if they cannot afford it. There is also a library full of books, with a reading room open to all, and two free museums—one for miniature paintings and the other for tribal and folk art.

We had not planned to live in it ourselves, but it was difficult to commute each day from East of Kailash, so we carved out two rooms for Arpana and myself, in a portion of the conference hall where gatherings of writers and artists take place, and that is where we live to this day.

www.ingramcontent.com/pod-product-compliance
Lightning Source LLC
Chambersburg PA
CBHW051108230426
43667CB00014B/2488